Echoes of a
Queer Messianic

SUNY SERIES
LITERATURE...IN THEORY

SERIES EDITORS

David E. Johnson (Comparative Literature, University at Buffalo)
Scott Michaelsen (English, Michigan State University)

SERIES ADVISORY BOARD

Nahum D. Chandler, *African American Studies, University of California, Irvine*
Rebecca Comay, *Philosophy and Comparative Literature, University of Toronto*
Marc Crépon, *Philosophy, École Normale Supérieure, Paris*
Jonathan Culler, *Comparative Literature, Cornell University*
Johanna Drucker, *Design Media Arts and Information Studies, UCLA*
Christopher Fynsk, *Modern Thought, Aberdeen University*
Rodolphe Gasché, *Comparative Literature, University at Buffalo*
Martin Hägglund, *Comparative Literature, Yale University*
Carol Jacobs, *Comparative Literature and German, Yale University*
Peggy Kamuf, *French and Comparative Literature, University of Southern California*
David Marriott, *History of Consciousness, University of California, Santa Cruz*
Steven Miller, *English, University at Buffalo*
Alberto Moreiras, *Hispanic Studies, Texas A&M University*
Patrick O'Donnell, *English, Michigan State University*
Pablo Oyarzún, *Teoría del Arte, Universidad de Chile*
Scott Cutler Shershow, *English, University of California, Davis*

Echoes of a Queer Messianic

From *Frankenstein* to *Brokeback Mountain*

Richard O. Block

Cover: Cigoli, Ludovico (1559–1613). Sheet of studies for Narcissus and the nymph Echo, and Academic male figure. Pen and brown ink, brown wash, red chalk, on paper, 28.6 × 39.7 cm. INV905-verso. Photo: Thierry Le Mage.
Musée du Louvre, Paris, France.
© **RMN-Grand Palais / Art Resource, NY**

Published by State University of New York Press, Albany

© 2018 State University of New York

All rights reserved

No part of this book may be used or reproduced in any manner whatsoever without written permission. No part of this book may be stored in a retrieval system or transmitted in any form or by any means including electronic, electrostatic, magnetic tape, mechanical, photocopying, recording, or otherwise without the prior permission in writing of the publisher.

For information, contact State University of New York Press, Albany, NY
www.sunypress.edu

Library of Congress Cataloging-in-Publication Data

Names: Block, Richard O. author.
Title: Echoes of a queer messianic : from Frankenstein to Brokeback mountain / Richard O. Block.
Description: Albany : State University of New York Press, 2018. | Series: SUNY series, literature . . . in theory | Includes bibliographical references and index.
Identifiers: LCCN 2017027539 (print) | LCCN 2017040527 (ebook) | ISBN 9781438469560 (ebook) | ISBN 9781438469553 (hardcover   ) | ISBN 9781438469546 (pbk.   )
Subjects: LCSH: Homosexuality in literature. | Homosexuality and literature. | Monsters in literature.
Classification: LCC PN56.H57 (ebook) | LCC PN56.H57 B56 2017 (print) | DDC 809/.8920664—dc23
LC record available at https://lccn.loc.gov/2017027539

10 9 8 7 6 5 4 3 2 1

For Mary Ellen Shannon

Solely for the sake of the hopeless is hope given us.
—Walter Benjamin

Contents

ACKNOWLEDGMENTS xi

INTRODUCTION xiii

CHAPTER 1
A Man's Best Friend Is His Monster: Mary Shelley's *Frankenstein* 1

CHAPTER 2
Peter Schlemihl's Wondrous Story or the Genesis of a
Queer Jewish Outlaw 29

CHAPTER 3
Queer Prosthetics or Male Tribadism in Kleist's "On the
Puppet Theater" 55

CHAPTER 4
Queer Echoes Traversing Great Spaces: Roland Barthes's
A Lover's Discourse and Johann Wolfgang Goethe's
The Sorrows of Young Werther 77

CHAPTER 5
"I'm nothin'. I'm nowhere.": Echoes of a Queer Messianic in
Brokeback Mountain 101

NOTES 125

BIBLIOGRAPHY 143

INDEX 153

Acknowledgments

I would like to thank the Walter Simpson Center for the Humanities and the Althea B. Stroum Center for Jewish Studies, both at the University of Washington, for their help and support during the years. Individuals are many, so I simply list them: Leandro di Prinzio, Elizabeth Cnobloch, Michael DuPlessis, Karen Pinkus, Peter Fenves, Liliane Weissberg, Simon Richter, Robert Tobin, Kwame Holman, Japhet Johnstone, Lena Heilmann, Alice Bloch, Davide Stimilli, Duane Perolio, Chris Elam, Roy Vargason, Richard Pucko, Gayle Jessup White, Ann DeLancey, Ann Collier, Luciana Pignatelli, Roberto Orazi, Celia Baker, Robert Block, Kathy Dougherty, Edward Bloch, Ellen Rosenberg, Jay Wolke, Avril Greenberg, and Barbara von Mólnar.

Earlier versions of the following chapters appeared as follows:

"Queering the Jew who would be German." *Seminar: A Journal of Germanic Studies* 40, no. 2 (2004), 93–110. Portions reprinted with permission of University of Toronto Press. © U of Toronto P.
"Textual Narcissism: Undoing Queer Readings in Kleist's 'Über das Marionettentheater,'" in *The Self as Muse: Narcissism and Creativity in the German Imagination, 1750–1830*, ed. Alex Mathäs (Lewisburg: Bucknell UP, 2011), 171–194.
"'I'll Love You Forever, Wilhelm.' Queer Echoes in Roland Barthes' Reading of Goethe's 'Werther' and Nietzsche's Eternal Return of the Same." *Literatur für Leser* 10, no. 3 (2011), 147–165.
"'I'm nothin'. I'm nowhere': Echoes of Queer Messianism in *Brokeback Mountain*." *The New Centennial Review* 9, no. 1 (2009), 253–278. © Michigan State UP.

Introduction

"Death in Venice": Some Indices of the Messianic

As a dying Gustav Aschenbach settles a final time into his "sdraio" or chaise upon the mostly deserted beach of Venice, Tadzio appears to signal him. Aschenbach's last breaths, his final but feckless attempt to grasp the image of the beloved, all respond to the enigmatic but irresistible gesture that points beyond, to something on the other side of consciousness, even perhaps to a love redeemed, somewhere, someplace, somehow in the future. Given the importance of the following passage for this project, I quote it at some length. The purpose here is to read these final scenes as opening onto a possibility that is neither fully articulated nor foreclosed. At the same time, I am arguing that the plague and Aschenbach's passion are inextricably linked, even indistinguishable. And it is this convergence of disease and passion, as it points to something beyond the tragic fate of its victim, that is a central concern of this book. Working through the implications of this passage, which will take some time, will also serve as an example of how messianic echoes are pursued in the chapters to follow.

> Now, he paused again with his face turned seaward, and next began to move slowly leftwards along the narrow strip of sand the sea left bare. He paced there, divided by an expanse of water from the shore . . . a remote and isolated figure, (verbindungslos) with floating locks, out there in the sea and wind, against the misty inane. . . .With a sudden recollected impulse, he turned from the waist up, in an exquisite movement, one hand resting on his hip, and looked over his shoulder at the shore. [Aschenbach] . . . lifted his head, as it were, to answer Tadzio's gaze. . . . It seemed to him the pale and lovely summoner out

there smiled at him and beckoned; as though . . . he pointed outward . . . into an immensity of richest expectation. And, as so often before, [Aschenbach] rose to follow. (Mann 74–75)

Who is this Aschenbach, abject and alone, squandering his final breaths in a series of hapless gestures as he beholds the magnificence of a figure framed by the endless, boundless sea? The trajectory of Eros has not lead Aschenbach to the union of truth and love anticipated by Plato, but rather to a "pernicious intoxication" (Mann 73), a floundering toward an abyss that was never far away for the bourgeois artist now enraptured by an impossible and even scurrilous desire. To touch or address or even approach this magnificent, prepubescent embodiment of classical perfection would defile such beauty, blaspheme it. Preserving but never possessing that love has driven Aschenbach through the hidden and dirty passageways of Venice, as he tries to keep in and out of touch with Tadzio. Simultaneous with this game of hide-and-seek is Aschenbach's attempt to track rumors of a plague and its cover-up. The apparent origins of the plague are as mythical and sinister as Tadzio's appeal is erotic and irresistible:

> For the past several years Asiatic cholera had shown a strong tendency to spread. Its source was the hot, moist swamps of the delta of the Ganges, where it bred in the mephitic air of that primeval island-jungle, among whose bamboo thickets the tiger crouches, where life of every sort flourishes in rank abundance,

Figure I.1: "He paced there, divided by an expanse of water from the shore . . . out there in the sea and the wind, against the misty inane."

and only man avoids the spot. Thence, the pestilence had spread throughout Hindustan, raging with great violence; it brought terror to Astrakhan, terror even to Moscow. (Mann 63)

The confirmation of his greatest fears, the relentless march of a disease that emanates from where no person dare visit, could just as easily describe the morass that engulfs him, as he tries to explore without exposing himself to the voracious desire that keeps him in pursuit of his beloved. "He was not feeling well and had to struggle against spells of giddiness only half physical in their nature, accompanied by a swiftly mounting dread, a sense of futility and hopelessness—but whether this referred to himself or to the outer world he could not tell" (Mann 73). The hallucinatory effects of the plague thus derive from its origins and situate it outside the fertile grounds and classical skies of ancient Greece. Aschenbach has gone too far. Or his lust has taken him too far. The question now arises whether Aschenbach is in pursuit of the plague or is the plague in pursuit of Aschenbach? "And yet our solitary felt he had a sort of first claim on a share in the unwholesome secret; he took a fantastic satisfaction in putting leading questions to such persons as were interested to conceal it, and forcing them to explicit untruths by way of denial" (Mann 57). The secret in this instance is the plague, but the description equally resonates with exploration of closeted desires. "It [the plague] ought to be kept quiet,' he thought, aroused. 'It should not be talked about'" (Mann 53). In this instance the convergence of the plague with illicit desire is unmistakable. Lastly, note how the plague's renewed strength mirrors the heightening of Aschenbach's passion. His questionable source, a British travel agent, seems all too capable of embellishment well attuned to Aschenbach's fears and passions: "Yes, the disease seemed to flourish and wax strong, to redouble its generative powers . . . For the onslaught was of the extremest violence, and not infrequently of the 'dry' type, the most malignant form of the contagion" (Mann 63–64).

Aschenbach is not just exposed to this diseased passion but is in fact a carrier of it. The plague, fortified by its bond with illicit passion, carries as much of a malignant risk for the narrator as it does for Aschenbach. Submerged in a miasma of his own making, Aschenbach no longer curries the narrator's favor. On the contrary, the narrator evinces repulsion to the point of a virtual excommunication from the graces or sympathies of Western civilization. As Eros draws him closer and closer to the precipice ("So they too [the passions], they too lead him to the bottomless pit"; Mann 73), the narrator gradually withdraws, finally expressing absolute rejection of Aschenbach, when the latter finds himself enraptured by the plague that his forbidden passion self-generated:

> Too late! He thought at that moment. Too late! But was it too late? This step that he failed to take would very possibly have been all to the good, it might have had a lightening, gladdening effect, led perhaps to a wholesome disenchantment. But the fact now seemed to be that the aging lover no longer wished to be disenchanted, the intoxication was too precious to him. (Mann 47)

For Dorritt Cohn the passage signals a definitive turn by a narrator no longer willing to indulge Aschenbach's sordid descent in quest of physical beauty. Aschenbach's indisposition to "self-criticism" requires the narrator to abandon him (Mann 143–45). In other words, Aschenbach needs to be quarantined.

The final sentence of the novella seems to confirm the narrator's full reversal. "Before midnight, a shocked and respectful public would receive news of his decease" (Mann 75). In contrast to the unbridled outpouring of passion evinced by Aschenbach, the narrator and the world maintain their dignity with a properly restrained expression of sympathy. But is that really all there is? Does something else not unhinge the narrator? The first description offered above described Tadzio as isolated and without ties (verbindungslos), when he gestures to Aschenbach. On the one hand, his beauty is not defiled or compromised, at least in this moment, by any earthly consideration. On the other, does he perhaps gesture toward the possibility of a world without ties or restrictions, one whose entry is barred, i.e., the narrator with his/her ties to respectable society? Initially, it is barred to Aschenbach as well. Perhaps, there is no crossing that threshold. Aschenbach is thus tethered to the structures of respectable society that both produce and condemn his quest to capture the sensual in art. His final monologue, bemoaning the fate of the artist hopelessly condemned to pursue damnation, becomes then his recognition of the tentacles of respectable society and their reach in determining the acceptable limits of love. "His [final] monologue takes on the meaning of an anagnorisis, the expression of that lethal knowledge the hero of Greek tragedy reaches when he stands on the verge of death" (Cohn 144). Left unanswered is how such recognition informs his final gaze through love-sick eyes at the forbidden.

The narrator's pleasure in telling the story of a man fallen from grace has more than the casual hint of a pleasurable sadism, not far removed from the Schadenfreude of his friends back home when his late work is met with rejection.¹ Upon landing in Venice, Aschenbach is plagued by a group of Polish "ragazzi" on vacation; their source of greatest displeasure comes in the figure of an old and pathetic fop who appears suspiciously out of place among so many young men. "Aschenbach was moved to shudder as he watched the creature and his association with the rest of the group. Could they not see that he was old, that he had no right to wear the clothes they wore or pretend to be one of them?" (Mann 17). Indeed, there is much that is vulgar or "gemein" about the fop's eventual drunkenness, as he tries to find a way to ingratiate himself with the virile lads surrounding him. What most disturbs Aschenbach is the premonition that he will suffer a similar humiliation, that those dark forces of Eros will entrap him in an affair as ridiculous and crude. Little recasting of the citation above is required to turn the disdain on Aschenbach, particularly as he frantically pursues the plague, while his makeup and hair dye peel away and with them any veneer of respectability (Mann 69–70). In this instance, the fop staggers from side to side, but however ridiculous he may appear, the fop has the last laugh. "Give it (*dem Liebchen*) our love, will you, the p-pretty little dear" (Mann 17). The fop knows all about Aschenbach; he knows Aschenbach's story and what he will have been up to. And so the novella unfolds the history of the fop's double, Aschenbach, and his willingness to disgrace himself, to invent and infect himself with the plague so as to preserve but demonstrate an unconditional love for an impossible subject.

Moreover, the fop's bitchiness resonates with the exasperation of the narrator when he/she finally abandons Aschenbach: "Too Late! Too Late!" Aschenbach sighs, as once again he is swept away by Tadizo, or as the fop prefers, "the p-pretty little dear." Just as the fop knows that it is too late for Aschenbach (the two are brothers of a sort), the narrator questions Aschenbach's resignation: "But was it too late? [. . .] [T]he truth might have been that the aging man did not want to be cured, that his illusion was far too dear for him" (Mann 47). The text's pleasure, if I can put it that way, in placing Aschenbach at the mercy of respectable society in the form of a judgmental narrator accommodates easily the darker pleasures Aschenbach seeks. That is—and now we begin to understand just how shaken but perhaps secretly delighted the world was by Aschenbach's fall—love's passion is fueled by the sadistic pleasure the narrator derives in watching culture's one-time darling disgrace himself. The humiliation and dejection that drove Aschenbach to Venice, that masochistic urge for perfection met now with rejection and scorn by a once-adoring public, pushes him over the abyss. "I go. You stay . . ." (Mann 47).

Figure I.2: "Could they not see that he was old, that he had no right to wear the clothes he wore or pretend to be one of them."

The narrator, however, does not have the last word. As Cohn points out, the narrator protests too much; an unclaimed space or position is opened up by the gap between the narrator's indictment of Aschenbach and the text's ultimate position(s) vis-à-vis its protagonist. In other words, a space emerges between the narrator and Aschenbach, not because the narrator's disdain registers the text's condemnation of Aschenbach's moral failure, but rather because the narrator's own intractable morality creates a textual blind spot or no-man's land that beckons to Aschenbach: "I go. You stay." Is he returning to a place as inhospitable to polite society as the miasmic origins of the plague? And what possibilities for a different moral order, a different kind of love, might be bred from diseased origins? Or to pose a question asked by others: "Is not art, which so peremptorily dismisses 'sympathy with the abyss,' incomplete?" (Pike 120–41).

Possible answers to such question take us back to Tadzio's pose and enigmatic gesture that draw from Aschenbach his last breaths. "It seemed to him the pale and lovely summoner out there smiled at him and beckoned; as though . . . he pointed outward . . . into an immensity of richest expectation" (Mann75). What does it mean to follow that gesture, where might it lead, what potentialities remain unrealized or beckon with messianic hope? Luchino Visconti's film of Mann's novella in 1971 offers some profound clues to what this other moral order, or rather, amoral order might promise in terms of love. For one, whatever distancing devices and tropes employed by the narrator hardly function in the same fashion as they do in the film. Mahler's stirring adagietto from the fifth symphony attracts rather than repels, invites spectators to follow Aschenbach to the abyss. The free, indirect discourse of the novella always held out the possibility that the narrator could just pick up and leave, drop in a few quotation marks and return to a language separate and ethically barred from the pleasures of a dissolute and dying man. But if Aschenbach's final monologue no longer carries credibility for the narrator, do the attachments summoned by the music of the film draw Aschenbach so completely outside the moral purview of any respectable person that the narrator's retreat in the novella marks less an unwillingness than an incapability to follow Aschenbach?[2]

Like the origins of the plague, Aschenbach's new dwelling allows for no "human" to approach. "A photographic apparatus, apparently abandoned, stood on its tripod on the edge of the ocean, and a black cloth, spread over it, flapped and clapped in the colder wind" (Visconti 58). The camera applauds what it has blinded and distanced itself to: a world free of masters and men (herrenlos) at the edge or on the verge of something it is not prepared to take in. The abandoned camera or surveillance device expresses, as it were, the exasperation of the panoptic gaze, the futility of any narrative posture absorbing what is just about to unfold but never quite does, or rather, what will not have not happened.

If we take seriously the role of free indirect discourse, that part of speech intended to signal the subject (Aschenbach's) participation in an amorphous community of speakers with a shared language, then the film marks Aschenbach's retreat from such a community of speakers with what Gilles DeLeuze would call "free indirect images." Without a master narrative to dictate proceedings, images and voices and sound can circulate and form connections that defy the panoptic order. "Cinema releases us from connecting images to form a shared external world, rather we see imaging itself, freed from a fixed point of view" (Deleuze 19). But do they? Perhaps. To be sure, another camera stands behind or over and above the dysfunctional one on the beach. But in that interstitial space something remarkable happens. As the panoptic moves outward or distances itself from the subject, things get fuzzy and out of focus. Tadzio's initial appearance on the edge of the sea—after surviving a playful but sadistic tussle with a companion—is dappled. While the music finds a second breath and moves toward a crescendo, the image of Tadzio appears about to dissolve in the mist of the sea. For at least that moment the mechanisms of surveillance cannot find purchase or focus. When Aschenbach attempts to lift himself from his chair and grasp with what energies remain him the fleeting figure of the beloved, this momentary freedom from life and death, from narrative commentary, from condemnation or just observation, leads him to an "immensity of richest expectation" (Mann 75). What can await him, whose boundless love for a forbidden beauty left him no means to express that poetry or passion save to summon and succumb to the very vapors which now come to shield and enshrine the beloved?

As we know, it takes little time for the narrator to reestablish a perch above or apart from the deceased and allow respectable society to pay its muted tributes before closing the book on this sordid tale. It is the purpose of this book to reopen and explore the possibilities foreclosed by the reestablishment of panoptic surveillance before such immensities could even be articulated. What I am proposing is to view the last scene as an assemblage or mosaic of immensities that threatens to exceed the limits of the panopticon and does so, paradoxically, only when the narrator severs all ties. In other words, Aschenbach can take the final leap into the abyss and escape whatever controls narration might impose, when even the seeing eye of the respectable world must avert its glance from the disgraceful acts of its subject. "And, as so often before, he [Aschenbach] rose to follow" (Mann 75). This time, however, is different, and so it is my aim to explore those differences with an eye turned toward what might have been or could still be. For reasons to be explained below, my focus will be on mostly German texts written around 1800 and their interlocutors, often belated as in the case of Roland Barthes's reading of Johnann Goethe. Mann's "Death in Venice" is offered as a trenchant example for opening up such a discussion if for no other reason than that the trajectory of love moves in a direction quite distinct from current gay politics and its agenda of marriage equality, a goal achieved, of course, as we proved ourselves to be good liberal consumers keenly committed to preserving family values. But in what other directions might queer love lead? Precisely, what historical possibilities foreclosed for queer love in the past two centuries might be remobilized according to the indices established by "Death in Venice"?

I have chosen to postpone providing a summary of the chapters to provide first an overview of much of contemporary queer theory. By presenting the theory before the literature, the former articulates possibilities for the messianic that are left to the literary texts to actualize, which, as we will see, means to echo. The theoretical, however, not only defers representation of the messianic to the literary but also precludes the actualization with which it charges literature. In response—and the general summary of the chapters provided at the end of this introduction will speak more to this—the literary produces something unforeseen but underwritten by the theoretical. That is, the theory both fosters and disables articulation of the messianic, offering only echoes instead. Just as important, proceeding in this fashion underscores how the messianic possibilities of the literary still echo today and offer indices for a politics removed from the nationalisms and hierarchies of gay politics. The extended discussion of contemporary queer theory that follows thus brings together work from various disciplines to offer a map of where we stand today. It also presents a different narrative that seizes upon the messianic character of these thinkers as a direct challenge to the current state of affairs. Indices and literary articulations are all that the messianic can present of itself; in each instance it refuses conceptualization. Before concluding with a map of the argument, I review some of the more recent attempts to normalize same-sex desire to underscore why the movements that got us to the SCOTUS decision are neither tenable nor desirable and thus necessitate a look backward to restore a lost dimension to the theoretical work discussed in the earlier parts of the introduction. The November 2016 election of Donald Trump as president of the United States and the immediate rollback of newly won protections for LGBTQ people signals the failure of our current politics to prevent a recrudescent homophobia from obtaining. The early targets of the new administration are many—immigrants, refugees, women, people of color, Muslims. Whatever successes the last decades have brought, they also have made it politically incorrectly correct to see all forms of difference as suspect and threatening.

Queer Temporalities: The End of Empty, Progressive Time

"We are always already dead," so Judith Halberstam quipped in a published symposium devoted to queer temporalities (Dinshaw 194). Of course, she is referring to Lee Edelman's insistence upon no future; that is, resisting the refuge of the good, linked among other things to procreation and future generations. Carla Freccero puts it this way, "I often work on the dead, and as time goes by I have begun to think of myself as a future dead person writing myself out of my time while time is running out" (Dinshaw 183). The dense remark, and we will have occasion to explore what kind of love future dead people might still have time to discover, prompts the rather bold question by Christopher Nealon:

> In writing about "time" and "history, we definitely [. . .] are writing about the possible forms and destinies of queer community

[communities?]. . . . How are our theorizations of alternate temporalities legible not only as attempts to think through the possibilities of movement and community but also as attempts to think through or around or against the dominant form of the social organization of the time, that is, the time of the commodity. (Dinshaw 186)

To live as one already dead, or rather, to love as one already dead or always about to die is the central conceit of this project. Before investigating the theoretical possibilities of inhabiting, in the language of Giorgio Agamben, the time that remains, or rather, the time that will have remained, let me position the project in terms of current theoretical debates, after which I will return to discuss what kind of temporalities might be foreclosed and opened by readings of texts from around 1800, texts that prepared the ground for the predicament and pathologies that continue to challenge queer thinking

What necessitates such a project, I believe, is the emergence in contemporary Western societies of homonormativity. As one-time sexual outlaws whose threats to the bourgeois, nuclear family might well have mobilized different relations of power and knowledge, the contemporary, and particularly American, gay subject has achieved "equal" status by committing to late capitalism's agenda of consumerism (i.e., "the time of the commodity") in service of the middle-class family of four. The precise concern of this project is to identify textual moments in selected texts that speak of a potentiality, not something that is on the threshold to actualization but rather something that could be or might never be. These moments of radical meaninglessness or textual stuttering speak to a different kind of gay politics free of the nationalisms and hierarchies of contemporary heteronormativity. Stated otherwise, what might (or might not) be realized in those regions (where the plague originated?) becomes a lost horizon of gay politics that I am trying to recover or reinvigorate.

My use of potentiality draws upon Agamben's philological recuperation of an obscured but decisive aspect of the term.[3] Precisely, potentiality is an entity in itself freed from the binary logic that prescribes an entelechy for potentiality. That is to say, potentiality is itself queer, insofar as the entity resists all attempts at conceptualization and defies traditional markers of being; it both is and is not. Not surprisingly, the apparent opposition of its defining characteristics, the not-yet-real and the never-to-be real, offers a productive grid upon which to map or read the current debates surrounding queer theory in the American academy. The refusal of any thinking that accommodates a future or possible actualization of potentiality is most forcefully proposed by Lee Edelman. In the appropriately entitled, *No Future: Queer Theory and the Death Drive*, Edelman baldly avers that the future is "kid stuff" (Edelman, *No Future* 4). As an emblem of the nuclear family's hope for a future in which the divisions constitutive of the subject are overcome, the child and the promise of its future reduplicates the social order and its hierarchies in service of a future forever deferred but preserved through the child as a carrier of meaning and hope. The charge is for a nonrelational thinking/being in which the queer subject, traditionally linked to Freud's death drive, threatens the social order as a stubborn marker of the non-sublatable difference and disorder announced by death or a present with no future. At the other end of the spectrum are those who imagine queerness as something yet to be realized; a true future, unhinged from the social structures of the present, is for these scholars, truly queer. Among these utopian thinkers is the late José Esteban Muñoz who seeks to redeem futurity, if for no other reason than that current conditions, particularly for queers of color, are intolerable. Recent attention paid to police violence in particular underscores the need to recognize the added dimension of misery that people of color face. As President Obama made clear in his visit to the El Reno Federal Corrections Institution, poorer people of color end up in an endless cycle of incarceration for doing pretty much the same "stupid things" all teenagers do.[4] That is to say, queer people of color are already living a life with no future.

Drawing on the utopian impulse that underwrites the thought of Ernst Bloch, Muñoz in *Crusing Utopia: The Then and There of Queer Futurity* argues that queerness has not yet been truly imagined. A queer future brings to consciousness those missed or repressed possibilities of the past in such radically reimagined or unimagined ways that new possibilities, particularly queer ones emerge. The past recaptured has never truly been a lived or actualized past, but remains just out of reach on what I suggested above is a permanent state of being on the threshold. Muñoz, in fact, pushes Agamben's understanding of potentiality to resurrect from the fragments of the past an actualization of a queer future as the dual deixis of the subject of the subtitle indicates. In other words, restoring a utopian dimension to queer hermeneutics transforms or actualizes what has not yet been imagined so that an authentic queerness can appear. But does potentiality, in the process, lose once again its character as a distinct entity?

No future/A utopian future. However absolute the difference between these two propositions may be, queer theory, I argue, is obligated to think of these two positions together, if not simultaneously. "It is not simply that queer has yet to solidify and take on a more consistent profile, but rather that its definitional indeterminacy, its elasticity, is one of its constituent characteristics" (Jagose 1). The origin of the word "queer," derived from the Low German "terk," mandates a project that serves as a torque or pivot to think and preserve this difference, a potentiality that I mark with my use of the word messianic. Without rehearsing Jacques Derrida's distinction between messianism and the messianic, Jagose's further (in)determination of the term "queer" might suffice for now: "I use queer to designate a zone of possibilities always inflected by a sense of potentiality that cannot yet quite be articulated" . . . and never will be, I would like to add (Jagosse 12).[5] The difference lies as much in the impossibility of fulfillment signaled by the messianic as it does in the posture toward being necessitated by such an impossibility. Stated otherwise, what does it mean to listen to or exist in a past whose only evidence of being is that it will have been? Of course, the same has been said and will have been said of homosexuals: not self-declared (until recently) until the lack of progeny says all that need be said but dare not be said about them. The most felicitous formulation of the messianic potential or its impossible possibility comes in the last two chapters of this book: *I will not have not loved*, or in language reminiscent of Munoz: *I will not have not been queer*. This is not intended as a word game. It seeks to elide the trap and trappings of the future perfect that has always predicted the fate of the homosexual. At the same time, the phrase articulates a kind of love that escapes the controls, for one, of logocentric discourse and preserves the elasticity of the queer project. Like the dappled image of Tadzio as he prepares to signal Aschenbach that it is time, the image flickers in and out of focus. Meaning appears to adhere to the phrase, yet it really only approaches it. The double negative does not cancel out to yield a positive phrase that leads us back to a simple, future perfect. But rather, as an echo it decidedly precedes the possibility of the love that it seeks to recapture. Even the double negative offers an unreadable echo of itself. *The "not" resounds before anything has been actualized*. Romance languages, as we know, can only say "no" twice; that is, the use of the double negative is standard practice. If in English saying "no" twice becomes too often "yes," obscuring the indeterminate space occupied by the double negative, my use is intended to hold all possible meaning in play—and none of them. What I am seeking to preserve is thus an absolutely queer space that suspends all and any structures of power and meaning, that leaves the meaning of the phrase, "I will not have not loved," unsettled and unsettling.

The messiah, of course, can never make good on her promise, lest it cease to be a promise. Fulfilled, it would then become something other than a promise since a promise, by definition, must retain the possibility of being broken, its terms never being upheld or actualized. Important is not that the messiah will always be delayed, held back and paradoxically announced by the catastrophes of history, but that she might still come. As long as time has not yet ended, who can say?[6] A promise, after all, is a promise. In other words, *she might not have not arrived*. Yes, she will never arrive, but she could. And given the outside chance that she will—which of course she won't—one must be ready. How pathetic, it seems, for the messiah to arrive—and not be prepared! As Hamlet reminds us, "The readiness is all." (Act V.2, 237) That is the impossible proposition that grounds my response to the theoretical poles of queer thinking represented by Edelman and Munoz. Central here is less the semantics of the impossible, but rather the kind of queer being in the world summoned by such readiness, which, to cite Agamben again, is living in the time that remains. As Gershom Scholem says of the messianic idea in Judaism, one is compelled to live a life of deferment in which nothing can be irrevocably accomplished (Scholem, *Messianic* 35).

It cannot be stressed enough that the focus of queerness in this project is less about sex or sexuality and more about a subjunctive masculinity that has not actualized and certainly would not be structured along the same lines of a binary distinction that censors, ignores, or erases the female body and her sexuality. In this regard, the argument seeks to open up new possibilities for exploring the female (same-sex) desire and its obscured history. While I do not take this up directly here, there have already been some very interesting readings in this regard, such as the remarkable work of Katrin Pahl.[7] Moreover, all the readings here are reparative rather than strictly interpretive. In other words, they seek to provide what Eve Sedgwick-Kosofsky has called a reparative rather than a paranoid reading. While the latter focuses on exposing hegemonic or dominant relations of power, reparative reading seeks its pleasures in assembling fragments from the past and discovering or uncovering dormant potentialities that could have unfolded or unfolded differently: "Because the reader has room to realize that the future may be different from the present, it is also possible for her to entertain such profoundly painful, profoundly relieving, ethically crucial possibilities as that the past, in turn, could have happened differently from the way it actually did" (Sedgwick-Kosofsky, *Paranoid* 146). What I described as strictly interpretive are those readings that offer maps and guides to the past but fail to reconfigure its pieces of knowledge or interpretive bounty in any ways that challenge the past and seek to alter queer histories going forward.

Secularization in the West prompted a dismissal of the restorative aspects of the messianic idea in favor of Enlightenment ideals. These ideals were linked to a progressive notion of history with the aim of humanity perfecting itself (Scholem 37). The recasting of "Death in Venice" as perhaps the first modern gay-plague novella emphasizes the restorative rather than purely utopian impulse of my understanding of the messianic. In the examples to follow, as well as in the Mann novella, the eruption of the messianic can occur at any moment, suddenly and unexpectedly and, especially, when hope has been abandoned. Scholem's understanding of the messianic is also instructive here: "Jewish Messianism is in its origins and by its nature—this cannot sufficiently be emphasized—a theory of catastrophe" (Scholem 7). It is "transcendence breaking in on history, struck by a beam of light shining onto it by an outside light?" (Scholem 11). On the one hand, the messianic is always looming off-scene (after the camera has been discarded) as something obscene, while the narrator avoids it like the plague because it is the plague. On the other, it is the dazzling mix of sun and sea that captures, transforms, and enshrines Tadzio's last gesture, all the more irresistible for its flickering and fleeting instantiation of classical perfection. In this regard, we might recall the words of a rabbi cited in the Talmud: "May [the Messiah] come, but I do not want to see him" (Scholem 13). Such words could easily have been uttered by Aschenbach's narrator or the upstanding folk appalled by the obscene. But not by us. Given the intense backlash over the SCOTUS decision legalizing gay marriage and the registration of that backlash in the 2016 presidential election, we need to be ready.

Soteriologies of Disease

One of the more instructive and lurid possibilities prepared by this confluence of the messianic with the plague is presented by Leo Bersani in *Intimacies*, as it explores the soteriological potentiality of Paul Morris's video *Plantin' Seed* (48). The video shows bottom's receiving fluids from those penetrating him. That community is enlarged by the number whose fluids are mixed into a Tupperware container and then funneled into the bottom's rectum. More than demonstrate the kinds of queer communities that can emerge in the space of potentiatlity signaled by Tadzio, they also highlight the nervous tension between literature and life, the complex but necessary boundary that delimits literary exploration or narrative from actual life. The uneasy space that separates literature from life, the impossibility of bridging the two as in this example, may also reserve a space for something fully other to emerge, a fully other kind of community.

Barebacking practices exemplify the complex political significations of a love that transgresses the bio-political regimes and its obsessions with bare life or the homo sacer. "What is at stake isn't the survival of the individual but the survival of the practices and patterns, which are the discoveries and properties of the sub-culture." (Bersani, *Intimacies* 46) What Paul Morris intends with sounding the summons to barebacking in dangerous times is, as Leo Bersani notes, a literalization of the death drive. "It is as if barebackers were experientially confirming a specifically Freudian and Lacanian notion of sexual desire as indifferent to personal identity, antagonistic to ego requirements and regulations and, following a famous Freudian dictum, always engaged in group sex even if the actual participants are limited to the two partners of the socially approved couple" (Bersani, *Intimacies* 43). All of the isms necessary for perpetuation of the future under the watchful eye of a camera *oscura* or even the NSA vanish, but so, it seems, would the practitioners of such unsafe practices. In the lingo of a particularly provocative group of practitioners, there are the bug chasers and the gift givers; and HIV, of course, is the gift of choice. Bersani, who admits to wincing himself at the health implications of such practices, cannot resist reflecting upon the odd spirituality of the bug chaser as perhaps saintly: "For him, their identities ["the nameless and faceless crowd"] that have infected him are nothing more than viral remains; his willingness to allow his body to be the site of their persistence and reproduction is not entirely unlike the mystic's surrender to a divine will without any comfortably recognizable attributes whatsoever" (Bersani, *Intimacies* 53). As a lonely carrier of the "stigmatized remains" of those who preceded him into death, the saintly bug chaser is absorbed into his beloved until his disease is passed onto another for consumption.

The introduction of PREP (pre-exposure prophylaxis), whereby sexually active gay men (not exclusively) take a daily dose of Big Pharma's Truvada, changes the dynamics of barebacking, even if bug chasers specifically have no interest in the potentially life-saving protocol. Most dramatically, it extends the reaches of the panoptic regime as these potential sexual outlaws, so to speak, are now bound to a subscribed regimen, monitored and policed according to sound medical practices. These communities might therefore (and thankfully) survive, but the dynamics completely change when the fatal consequences of the behavior have been greatly reduced, if not eliminated, by the drug, and nothing suggests that bug chasers are not now chasing drugs rather than disease.[8]

Reconsidering the NAMES project (AIDS quilt) in this light offers an opportunity to consider what kind of communities are forged in attendance to those who died before they were to have died, who died for the most part as outcasts and lepers as a genteel public did what Aschenbach's did and turned away. The quilt panels create communities as diverse as the loved ones of the many deceased. Each individual panel, stitched to the main canvas, brings that first community into contact with others, if not all the others, comprising what has now become—due to its size—a fragment of the entire quilt, which cannot be held down or displayed in one place. (1,920 panels were included in the first unraveling in Washington, DC, covering a space the size of two football fields. Four months later 3,000 panels arrived in the San Francisco office, indicating both the growing number of mourners and the work of mourning accomplished by quilting.[9] As anyone who witnessed the quilt being unveiled in those early days of the late 1980s knows, the unknown and the famous, the glamorous and the plain, the queer and the straight, the black and the white and the brown and the yellow all share equal billing. "Each quilt panel has its own tale. They tell of people who worked and played, who laughed and fought and are finally remembered" (13). If the initial act of mourning and remembrance was inspired by a need to at least name those who Reagan and Bush were unwilling to acknowledge as beings even deserving of bare life, its afterlife hinges on the new kind of communities that emerge when the already dead, the soon to be dead, the ones living in dire uncertainty, and those completely queer to the queer community rediscover each other. "As one man dying of the disease commented, 'I decided I had to take the lead in order for them to get to know me again and to get to know what it's like for me living this disease, and what it might be like for them'" (*Quilt* 49). If such a plea for community and shared love is based upon the semiotics of disease as a kind of contagion, then its founding members, so to speak, are not just the disease carriers but those who care for them, commemorate them, and stitch their memories into a panel where they are joined to a community of panels whose aesthetics, values, techniques, materials, and messages have only a shared measure in common. The panels are all uniform in size, 3' × 6'; Rock Hudson's is no more easily found than John Trowbridge's or James Mooney's. The book documenting the project carries an introduction by Elizabeth Taylor, but it is the 25,000 unnamed victims that are named and remembered here, not so much because the epigraph preceding Taylor's instructs us to un-forget them (they were never even counted but rounded up or down.), but rather in the very kind of coming together and cancellation of selfhood that Bersani highlights among the gift-giving crowd and their chasers. The borders of the self extend beyond the measure of the panel for no other reason than that the self represented by the quilt is already dead. The dead one inspires the sewer, whose stitching reminds us of how make-shift and "unnatural" or inorganic this community is, that such a coming together is only held together by a promise of certain death and dissolution. All notions that the joining together of so many different kinds of people might leave only a name as a mark of difference is easily dismissed. The rest of a snickering "US" may have defined us wholesale as a group of diseased faggots whose bad end confirmed just how disposable and indistinguishable from one another we were, but as the quilt unfolds, such monolithic assertions dissolve; the vast variety of elements comprising the panel and its sheer scope defy a comprehensive or panoptic gaze. One panel may collect several objects or references to objects dear to the deceased; others may offer a message from a mourner; another might offer a playful collage of sex paraphernalia; or some, a nicely stenciled epitaph with name and dates of the deceased.

The style and material of one panel thus establishes all sorts of random connections with those of another. Consider the following note accompanying a panel addressed to the lover of the deceased: "Please know my intent, when making this panel, was not to invade your memories or life with David. I have no memories to share of him but I do share one thing with you. On October 23, 1986, a pain went through my heart that was unbearable. A loneliness for the loss of a complete stranger—a *potential* friend. To this day I cry when I think of how you must miss each other." (*Quilt* 63; ital. added). The signature block of the panel prepared by Cindy reads, "For your lover, from Cindy, he loves you very much." Who is Cindy in this affair? How does she come to be a part of this community? What potential for friendship might such a threesome have offered?

Adjusting a reading of the quilt to accommodate Bersani's understanding of the gift-giving crowd and their beneficiaries cannot help but fail at the crucial moment. The mourners wandering the periphery of the quilt hardly harbor hope of finding someone to funnel the collected semen of a group of anonymous donors into their anus. Most are still terrified of the disease, many already have it and know it, others have it and don't know it, and still others just know someone who does. Simply stated, those connected via the quilt are unlikely to have been chasing the bug and would eagerly debug themselves as quickly as possible. Still, as Cindy suggests above, a different kind of coming together, which will never obtain save as a potentiality informing and structuring that union, seems ready to present. Two other examples from the quilt point as well to modes of relating that help to understand the sorts of queer love that might have emerged around 1800 and can serve as indices to direct inquiry into that earlier period.

Wayne Hadley learned from his landlord that a man dying of AIDS was moving in next door. He would sit "on the couch and gaze out my bay window and wonder what he was doing [. . .]. And then I'd get frightened and angry and then just wait—and I knew he was doing the same" (*Quilt* 64). Waiting for a cure that will not come and, depending upon whether it is pre- or post-1994, will not have not come, such is the mode of readiness that brings these two together. Hadley never met his neighbor and doesn't even know if he ever saw him. His panel features a silhouette of a single figure whose shadow extends across the yellow background. Above the shadow's end, written in purple, are the words, "Our brother next door." Their friendship, never actualized and existing only in waiting, extends beyond the death of the one to forge a brotherhood of or in shadows.

The story behind the panel for Clarence Robinson, Jr., (Quilt 23) also lends energies to different and unlikely forms of advocacy and friendship. Clarence was placed in an open hallway, avoided by all except for one nurse. His panel features a McDonald's hamburger and a milkshake. Afraid of his fate and of dying alone, Clarence would extend the stay of his visitors by requesting the above junk food. The oddness of breaking bread under these conditions with the least auratic of foods is nonetheless occasion to celebrate or acknowledge a different coming together. Clarence's sole advocate was his divorced father, a burly phosphate miner who often broke into tears while pleading for proper treatment for his son. The person who sewed the panel never met Clarence. Of course, no one should allow the pathos underwriting these unlikely relationships diminish the massive grief that occasioned such coming together. Regardless, the quilt offers a different kind of temporality, interrupted, disjunctive, restorative, and always just outside consciousness or on the other side of it.

A most trenchant analyses of a being unto death before one's time—and thus also a reflection on Heidegger—is offered by Alexander García Düttmann in *At Odds with Aids* (*Uneins mit AIDS*; 1992). García Düttmann considers what the plague means in terms of embracing one's finitude and more specifically, in terms of how it forces us to re-think being unto death and the horizon of subjective unity that underwrites Dasein. As we will see, the interrupted life, the life that mourns its loss before it has been lived, allows García Düttmann to re-read or adjust a Heideggerian understanding of Dasein in concert with Jacques Derrida's assertion that AIDS is an event, "an Ereignis, [that] one could call *historical* in the epoch of *subjectivity*, if we still give credence to *historical*, to *epochality*, and to *subjectivity*" (García Düttmann 90). Here then is the rub and the reason for the title. The subject, to be brief, has always already died. The three highlighted terms have long been discredited, and yet their half-life extends as means to measure to what extent AIDS is an event by not being an event, or a pure event, as García Düttmann emphasized. "At its core, anxiety about AIDS consists of nothing but anxiety about dying before one's time" (García Düttmann 2). Baldly stated, one has been pronounced dead before one has constructed any serviceable horizon for Dasein, (with respect to the three terms Derrida invokes above). The AIDS patient is at odds with a subject that has never been there, only mourned.[10]

If the death of the subject is the event that marks the death of a subject whose only evidence of being is having been or having always already been, then the deployment of AIDS's destructive forces is a compelling paradigm. By definition, AIDS pits one at odds against oneself. The virus engineers control of the immune system to leave the host defenseless. Opportunistic infections, diseases against which a host capable of defending itself would easily defeat, prosper. The self is turned against itself. The body is refused the right to be for itself. Lurking in the deepest recesses of the body, a latent virus can be reawakened, eager to prey upon the unsuspecting. As such, the AIDS virus bears a striking similarity to the one conjured by the travel agent and fed to Aschenbach. One is born and always potentially activated in the forbidden and murky reaches of "the Ganges," where paradoxically no humans dare tread.[11]

To be at one with AIDS, to accommodate, accept, and resign oneself to a linear and highly accelerated narrative of death by disease is then to seek to suture the rupture, which by definition the disease introduces. In other words, being at odds with oneself and the disease, as shown above, is inseparable from the Event that ushers in the death of the subject, to the extent that "ushering in" as understood in this instance disavows any claims to epochality. Aligning one's identity with the disease is foreclosed by the fact that the disease preempts any attempt to construct a unified subject. Succumbing to the disease now means that the never-to-be subject seeks what is unrecoverable, if for no other reason than it was always already mourned.

Fighting the disease, for García Düttmann, never consists in confessions of guilt since confessions presume a subject to issue such self-recriminations. Aschenbach calls forth the disease and seeks to obliterate his subjectivity as an expression of unqualified love for one too perfect to be defiled by a fallen artist. This makes for an uneasy dialogue with García Düttmann, as if the charge were for gay men to become bug chasers. On the one hand, such incompatibility may well result from the incompatibility of literature with life. At the very least, it calls for new forms of cultural production such as the NAMES project. On the other hand, all share a call to imagine new ways for the subject-less to relate. In this instance, the love that dare not speak its name does not because of any taboo (although ones certainly still exist), but rather because such love is speaker-less. Naming our love, if we dare to demonstrate our lack, produces a plenitude of names, a promiscuous mixing of potential partners.

Stated otherwise, to be at odds or not one with AIDS (*uneins mit . . .*) one has no time to live life following an avenue that eventually leads to death. For Heidegger the horizon of Dasein depends upon the indefinite definiteness of death. It will happen, but its certainty is pushed out into a future that allows for a construction of something like an autobiographical subject. A timeline of one's life can be imagined and constructed. For sure, Dasein is constantly threatened by the definite indefiniteness of death. In such manner Dasein anticipates or projects a horizon under the sign of death to disclose a temporality arising from the future of this possibility. Such would be, in Heideggerian speak, authentic. "One is not one with AIDS to the degree that one is not one with time, to the degree that one exists in the Being-not-one of time and that one is incapable of determining a measure of time that still permits the construction of a lifetime" (2).

That is to say, the destructive character of AIDS has the potential to effect a radical political upheaval. Rather than being the "mummy of 1968" as the French linguist Jean Claude Milner claimed, the illness does not signal merely the dead body politic of the promises of the student revolts, but rather it marks the total dissolution of the panoptic systems that require a subject to trail. García Düttmann can thus proclaim that AIDS is not the mummified body of the failed cultural politics of '68, but rather the event that marks the destruction of character in politics. Exploring just what a politics without character means is certainly one of the tasks of this book. How does the pre-pathologized subject of around 1800 present possibilities for coming together before sexual character determined the character of the individual or his/her fitness for politics? To recall Aschenbach's remarks,

"And from this [a lack of character] you can perceive that we poets can be neither wise nor worthy citizens" (Mann 72).

An alternative articulation might read something like this: what kind of politics could a subject who is always already dead announce or initiate? For García Düttmann, it clearly begins with a marrying of homosexuality with the Cartesian cogito: "I am out . . . therefore I am" (García Düttmann 42). This is a particularly complex assertion. How does one who is always already dead come out? How do the pre-pathologized subjects of circa 1800 return? We must also keep in mind that the identifications that permit declaring oneself queer are really what is being mourned at the time of García Düttmann's writing. As Douglas Crimp writes, what has been lost and is mourned is an "ideal," an ideal of a sexuality whose perverse pleasures granted homosexuals an identity" (Crimp 11). Any recognition of identity, the "massive legibility" allegedly produced by the eruption of the disease (the disease now confirms what we thought you always were), can thus only be tied to a sign or emblem that stands in for the "recognition of destruction." So when García Düttmannn argues for a politics of outing, it is not one that has a subject coming to his authentic self by proclaiming his sexuality publicly. "When fighting the politics of the state, when attacking the indifference with which the suffering and dying of the ill is met . . . the activist cannot avoid the dangers of an equation of AIDS and homosexuality that creates identity, by having recourse to a sexual ideal that has already been mourned." (García Düttmann 54). There is no self to come out and be what he/she truly is. To come out is to come out as not being there, as being already dead. That is to say, I am out: Therefore I will not have not been.[12]

"Sickness is instructive. We have no doubt about that, even more instructive [than health]. Those who make sick (Krankmacher) seem ever more necessary to us today than any medicine men or "savoir" (Nietzsche, *Genealogy* 2). Nietzsche's "Krankmacher," the one who makes sick, seems absurd to summon in the time of AIDS. Sickness is not pure negativity, to recast's Schelling's remarks about evil.[13] For both Nietzsche and García Düttmann disease is like the eschaton that inhabits every moment and threatens to disrupt all forms of succession, leading instead to an upheaval of all social structures, or, in the language of Nietzsche, a trans-valuation of all values. "The virus (which belongs neither to life nor to death) may always already have affected and broken into any inter-subjective trajectory." (García Düttmann 90). That is to say, we are always already dis-eased or, at least, our relations with others are.

We have seen in three instances how such a rupture opens up to an unexplored space that resists conceptualization, instantiation, and realization. To understand that aporia, if I may call it that, consider, as García Düttmann does, Heidegger's essay, "The Word Nietzsche: 'God is Dead' " (Heidegger 1943). The relationship of uttering the truth of metaphysics (God is dead) and the impossibility of relying on a metaphysical structure to grant that statement veracity nicely reflects the impossible possibility of dying before one's time. It has already happened but it "exceeds discursive justification" (García Düttmann 87). Like the already dead AIDS patient, the "epoch" after the truth of metaphysics leaves its mark by erasing that mark. What remains are traces that, as Derrida remarked, infiltrate all social bonds "as a de-structuring structuration." (García Düttmann 91). What happens then? What kind of future is one talking about when such futurity has already been disavowed?

Stated otherwise, linking all three discourses above is an attempt to read disease by attending to traces that lead back to no real origin and offer no real history. Still, my work is clearly restorative, promiscuously assembling traces to recapture a past that might have been but never was and beckons with its marks of self-erasure. The disease of modernity, one with no access to an outside or god, is, to speak with Jean-Luc Nancy, "freedom turned against itself," at odds with itself (Nancy 20). As it has already structured or destructured all relations, disease then becomes the terror from within that ruptures immanence by turning the self against itself.[14] It thereby disables constructions of the homosexual but also opens onto a horizon like that delimited by Tadzio.

Gay before Being a Subject

A recent recuperative approach by David Halperin in *How to Be Gay* attempts to disentangle identity from subjectivity. By revisiting the "secret" signs of a gay sensibility that provided outlets for queer sentiments without ever explicitly showing them, he seeks to recover a gay subjectivity that has been lost due to the ravages of AIDS and the emergence of homonormative regimes. In light of the above, one would have to view such efforts of restoration of the gay subject with suspicion. Under what terms can one re-invent the subject mourned during the time of plague? Halperin refuses to focus on individual subjects but rather mass culture as a "point of entry into non-individualizing, non-personalized, and non-normalizing analysis of gay male subjectivity" (Halperin, *How to be Gay* 103). The other part of the answer is quite straightforward: The gay experience begins before sex. Since "gay experience" includes many dimensions of subject life beyond same-sex eroticism, it is possible to attribute a specific gay experience to a child who has yet to form any clear idea of his eventual orientation or sexual desire (Halperin, *How to Be Gay* 93). The statement, made in reference to D. A. Miller and his crafting of such experience in *A Place for Us*, would seem to devalue the very trait that defines us. Can you still be gay if you don't lie with another man as you would a woman? Or if you have yet to lie with anyone? Yes, so long as one understands that the subject is now not a personalized one, but a milieu, a sensibility whereby the self sees itself reflected in something different from itself. The Broadway musical is for Halperin and Miller quite instructive in this regard. What makes the musical so gay was not that it portrayed gay desire, but rather realized it. Singing at inappropriate times, channeling desire across all sorts of surrogate routes, the musical did not offer queer characters, but it did offer a queer reality. "It denied their identity, but it offered them a world" (Halperin 121).

Hard to overlook is the temporal upheaval inaugurated by the claim that gay subjectivity has always already arrived. Before there was sex, there was gayness. On Broadway the young attendee, not yet awakened to same-sex eroticism, witnesses desire moving in a number of directions that "can be read simultaneously in seemingly opposite ways"(Halperin, *How to Be Gay* 107). The Broadway musical is thus gayer than any one of us could ever be. The homosexual subject, not yet born or awakened, does not mourn a loss of personal subjectivity (as with AIDS) but celebrates possibilities that will come to be mourned once subjecthood is claimed. That is to say, there is a rather queer echo to hear here: an "after" before the "before "or a "before" after the "after"; gay before being a subject (Halperin) and dead after having never been a subject (García Düttmann). Simply put, for queers the times are always out of joint and there is no reason to set them straight. Rather, the charge is to explore the potentialities sequestered in that interstitial space of misalignment.

Both Halperin and Miller describe a specifically gay form of interiority that is the result of oppression but a fount, nonetheless, for gay affect. For the generation born before Stonewall, Miller identifies three interconnected aspects of that affect: (1) the solitude, shame, and secretiveness by which the impossibility of social integration was first internalized, (2) the excessive sentimentality that is the necessary condition of sentiments allowed no real objects, and (3) the intense, senseless joy that, while not identical to these destitutions, is neither extricable from them (94).

The choice of the Broadway musical as a critical cultural touchstone could not be more evident. Out there in the dark, the excessively sentimental but not-yet declared homosexual finds an outlet that deprives him of personal identifications but offers instead a world in which manufactured emotion—bursting out in song and dance, for example—substitutes for a love of one's own. What Lotte is to Werther, as we will see in chapter 4, or the fag hag to the fag, the world of the stage is for the pre-Stonewall generation: a cover but also an outlet to express the kind of love nourished by its impossibility.

Such potentialities, I suspect, are now foreclosed rather than exhausted. Social media renders the stuff of interiority as a tweet or Facebook post. The possibility of an immediate expression or connection short circuits the delays, detours, and dispersions of the pre-Stonewall subject. Today, the Broadway musical is unabashedly gay and gay themed. Even if we sing, dance, and skip, we can be like everyone else. To be sure, here, as in the other examples, a note of nostalgia is hard to ignore. The devastation wrought by AIDS, on the one hand, wiped out the community Miller and Halperin invoke, and, at the same time, the political exigencies of the crisis demanded a declaration of being out. Recall again García Dütmann's formulation of the Cartesian cogito. For those for whom gay history begins with *Will and Grace* or *Modern Family*, personal identifications are encouraged. Come in out of the dark and we can see, monitor, police and protect you. Such was the price for organizing politically to combat AIDS. And while no one I know, at least, longs for the days when the police reacted to hate crimes against gays with complete indifference ("They're just fags," as I was told by one of Chicago's best in 1982), the terms of straight society's endearment have led to a politics of appeasement and not upheaval or disavowal. How different our political strategies and agenda would have been, had our best not died of AIDS!

The attempt to recuperate a radical politics or some form of resistance to heteronormativity requires for Halperin an acceptance of a permanent minoritarian position, which does not mean a disavowal of or participation in popular culture. Mass culture, or rather the reception of it, provides for a depersonalized interiority that is openly expressed and embraced. Since gayness can precede sex, this reconfiguration of a closet, if you will, opens its doors to many not engaged or even considering male-male sex. Sensibility is a more likely a ticket for admission to gayness. Like an allergen, one becomes sensitized to gayness.

A much more narrowly focused but equally significant understanding of gay affect underwrites Kevin Ohi's *Henry James and the Queerness of Style*. Mass culture is clearly not the queer matter at hand but rather the late narrative style of Henry James, not for its coding or suggestion of any kind of male-male eroticism, either in its thematics or its subject matter. Rather, the late prose works of James acquire a queer character by virtue of their belatedness, which, as we might recall from the discussion of temporalities above, serves as a cipher for queer potentiality. For example, early chapters trace the movement of tropes or syntactic structures as they perform a deferral of meaning. Zeugma and syllepsis, which expose an unbridgeable gap in the illogic of the terms joined by a verb or adjective (She broke the mirror and my heart), disable a straight narrative logic but instead serve as traces or remnants of an unlived past that points to future configurations and constellations. The same can be said of James's "reticence" in narrating crucial events. Events are reflected upon; nothing is narrated "by the novel" but rather "in the novel." Retrospection and/or belatedness serve to disrupt the causal chains of linear narrative (Ohi, James 7–11).[15] These short-circuitings and misfirings of consciousness as it attempts to come to terms with what has (for James) always already happened constitute his belatedness of style. The piecing together of what cannot be put back together (like the golden bowl of the title with its crack) would seem then to count as queer. In this respect, queerness as literary style would inhere in all narrative constructions to the extent that no semiotic field is containable, but for James, of course, it is an (dis)organizing principle. And it is this affect to which Ohi assigns a queer erotics. "[N]othing might perhaps affect us as queerer than its disorienting mixing of registers, than its interruptions of presumed representabilities" (58). Queerest thing of all, perhaps, is that one always comes out too late in these late James novels, the consequence of a narrative of retrospection or of style.

Leo Bersani has noted something similar in the polyvalence of the "it" in James's "The Beast in the Jungle" (Bersani, *Intimacies* 22–23). In addition to the "its" with determinable referents and the "it" that refers to a general state of affairs, there is the "it" that speaks to the unnamable catastrophe or law that the two main figures grow old together waiting for. Therewith lies for Bersani the potentiality embedded in James's style: a tendency to "extract all events, as well as all perspectives from them, from any specified time, and to transfer them to a before or an after in which they are de-realized in the form of anticipations and retrospections" (23). In other words, queerness (gayness for Halperin) exceeds the contours of individual bodies or a personal subjectivity. For Ohi, arriving too late "allows one the equivocal opportunity to confront the potentiality of identity," to inhabit subjects without actually being there (68). Identity's potentiality is explored through James's style, which resists or upends stable systems of meaning. It is as unstable as the following reworked but by now familiar formulation: I will not have not come to know. And if one comes out too late (as does Strether in *The Ambassadors*) or only comes to know how to be gay rather late (as Halperin says of himself), there is always time for next Sunday's matinee on 42nd Street, if only Broadway—to recall Sam Delaney's *Times Square Red, Times Square Blue*—were still Broadway.

Sexual Outlaws

While for Halperin and Ohi the body is less in play than sign systems, Lauren Berlant and Lee Edelman have published a dialogue, *Sex, or the Unbearable*, which has lots to say about bodies. The latter is linked to the former, insofar as sex is a burden no one can carry because of the unbearable challenges to selfhood and future selfhood sex poses. "[W]e both see sex as a site for experiencing [an] intensified encounter with what disorganizes accustomed ways of being" (Berlant 11). The Western tradition may decry sex as dangerous and disruptive, but Berlant and Edelman only wish it had lived up to its promise. Rather than link sex to hopes of a reconstituted future through future production of bundles of joy, sex is stripped of such optimism. "One need not romanticize sex to maintain that it offers, in its most intensely felt and therefore least routinized forms, something in excess of pleasure, of happiness or the self-evidence of value" (Berlant 12). Only by allowing sex to perform the work of negativity can we escape the "Panoptimism" that rules us.[16] Instead of attempting to attach worth to any sexual encounter, one should be swept away to a point of no return. The joys of sex have nothing to do with the self-satisfaction tied to an affirmation of one's sovereignty. Instead, one luxuriates in no-longer being one. "It breaks us down in multiple, non-identical ways, all of which are in a complex relation to relation itself "(Berlant 117). Relations are fluid. How could they not be when multiple selves are put into play with no aim at sustaining the relationship(s) and thus disabling the possibility of hegemonic regimes and disciplines? The larger claims, as I just noted, extend to rationality in general; one can only misrecognize an interlocutor, who like oneself is permanently under destruction.[17] That is to say, sovereignty is always in question, or rather, disabled. The power of the negative is embraced.

Of interest for this project is how these claims resonate with the possibilities opened up by disease and the plague as well as the markers of those possibilities around Germany in 1800, when much of the vocabulary still in use today in both psychology and psychiatry found purchase. What is clear from all the scholars presented above is a discontent with the present queer state of affairs. Marriage, child-rearing, picket fences, PTA meetings, and renewed marriage vows of until death-do-we-part stand in bald contrast to the sorts of nonrelationality considered here. Instead of congratulating ourselves on having a seat at the table, we might opt to vomit. Look at what's being served: Babies bred by shopping catalogues for super sperm donors and saintly surrogates. Or more generally, we are merely helping to reconstitute the same relations of power we decried. As celebrations greeted the Supreme Court's landmark decision legalizing same-sex marriage, the White House let the world know that the LGBTQ community was a welcome addition to (inclusion in?) the fabric of American life. So much so that a projection of the Rainbow flag covered the façade of the White House. "America likes us. She really likes us." The irony embedded in that show of apparent solidarity can hardly be missed. The universal symbol of global capitalism gladly displays its gay face. Indeed, there are angels in America.[18] "God Bless America . . . and nobody else." But let's not be fooled by what lurks behind that display of global pride. Backlash has already been swift; recent laws in the name of so-called religious freedom should alert us to just how close we are to losing everything, only one election away in fact. Hardly irrelevant to this display of America welcoming us into its fold is lifting the ban that prevented gay men and women from serving openly in the military. Once we are deemed fit to die for our country and hitch our dreams to that of the American military, we are fit to be paraded and celebrated.

Already in *Homos* Leo Bersani poses the provocative question: can the homosexual be a citizen? Not surprisingly the title for the entire chapter that takes up this question is "The Gay Outlaw." And like Halperin, Bersani is also intrigued by a homosexuality before sex. Gide, the first outlaw Bersani considers, or rather Michel from *The Immoralist*, credits his recovery from tuberculosis with his interactions with Arab youth. Here, we have what appears to be the classic pederast, arrested by the life-affirming beauty of the Arab boys. Except that movement is everywhere. Underneath the layers of colonial constructions of selfhood and citizenship. Michel discovers the surface, the narcissistic expansion of a desiring skin, which is "also the renunciation of any narcissistic self-containment" (Bersani, *Homos* 123). Unlike the typical colonialist traveling in Tunisia who sought to include sexual colonialism as part of the deal, Michel's only sexual relationships are strictly heterosexual. This is a "non-relational" pederasty that desires or wants nothing from an other to complete the self of the predator. "The Gidean homosexuality of *The Immoralist* knows no such demands, and its very emptiness constitutes a challenge to any sexual ideology or profundity" (Bersani, *Homos* 123).

Whatever communities can be imagined through the unleashing of such energies that recognize no other are both one and not one (*uneins*), or rather potentially singular and plural. That is to say, by definition they exceed the boundaries of any nation state's interest. Instead of an enemy, the other is merely cruised as an "opportunity, *at once insignificant and precious, for narcissistic pleasures*" (Bersani, *Homos*, 129). Juxtaposing Michel with Aschenbach is instructive here. While these energies bring Michel back to life (at the expense of his wife and neat heterosexual coupling), those same energies invite the plague to pay Aschenbach a visit. What they also share is the possibility of eliding the controls of the panopticon. "By abandoning himself to the appearances of sexual colonialism Gide was able to free himself from the European version of relationships that supported [. . .] colonialism" and, we might add, its peachy Panoptimism (Bersani, *Homos* 34). Can we say something the same of Aschenbach and the Austrian-Hungarian empire? At the very least, both are outlaws, undone by erotic pleasures that demand a sacrifice of the desiring subject and disable objectification of the beloved. Just as Aschenbach cannot lift himself from his chair, there is no possibility of the two standing straight like subjects towering over their latest erotic conquest. As political subjects, they don't meet the minimum requirement of residency. They are always *unterwegs*, on the way.

The status of the homosexual as outlaw, unfit for civil society, takes a particularly intriguing twist with Bersani's analysis of Proust's, *Sodom and Gemorrah* and its apparent, essentialist understanding of heterosexuality: inverts are actually females who can only long for other males. And who but an invert would have sexual relations with an invert? Thus, the invert can only satisfy his desire by projecting onto the surface of the other, the male, to fill his inner lack as a female. It doesn't take long for Bersani to dissolve the essentialisms that seem to underwrite such a strict understanding of male/female. The following passage refers to the narrator having spied on the pickup scene between Charlus and Jupien. At which time he realizes he was right all along about the Baron Charlus, whose outward show of virility could not completely mask the woman he truly was within.

> The very stringency of these sexual categories thus demands an incessant crossing over from one sex to the other, and it wreaks havoc with the boundaries that usually keep each category in place. For in Charlus there may be two quite different women: the one who has a "manly ideal" and desires the male figure he is not, and the other who, in responding to an effeminate male invert like Jupien is revealing the man "she" really is by pursuing a woman.[19] (Bersani, *Homos* 137)

The madness does not stop there. What about Jupien? Is he tricking himself into believing the baron is still all male, still all straight? Does he respond to the body, to the surface, and ignore the woman lurking beneath? The dizzying possibilities for refiguring inversion in terms of what in the other, the woman masking herself as a man, finds alluring can never present a readable map. Any symmetry (a male masked as a woman desiring the opposite) opens up a world of impossible possibilities; one set of heterosexual attractions is always invaded by an other half, a truer half, if you will. Introduce jealousy into this already confused equation, (i.e., desire as lack) and not only does the object of desire undergo incessant shifts, but desire itself is now also routed through the desire of the other. One desires the other's desire.

Without playing through the endless configurations that now emerge in addition to what was just outlined, two things are clear: The invert is always already a socialized being in search of him/herself in an other. "The sexual dramas of *A la Recherche du temps perdu* metamorphose a fundamental relation between the I and the non-I, a relation in which the subject is condemned to sociality as the precondition of self-identification" (Bersani, *Homos* 144). Any narcissistic expansion of the self, which a fundamental lack demands, means the self can find itself only by engaging an other who will always remain "irreducibly" other. The sovereign subject—an indeed the SCOTUS decision presumes such sovereignty among consenting adults—is only always dependent on a relation to him-/herself that is never self-same. Broadway's anthem of the 1980s to celebrate gay existence ("I am what I am" from *Le Cage aux Folles*) would have to be rewritten: I am what I am not or perhaps, I am not what I am not. In fact, the absurdity of *Le Cage aux Folles*—and here we should recall how overtly gay-themed materials mark the end of the pleasures of gay subjectivity—was recalled by George Hearn.[20] One of its show-stopping tunes, "The Best of Times Is Now," stood in sharp contrast to times in which many members of the company and production crew were dying almost daily.

The other affront to the state is not unlike the dappling on which I commented in "Death in Venice." "The dizzying intersections of essences in Proust's work blur the boundaries that essences are designed to solidify." The declaration or positing of male or female essences only serves to blur all identities and thus disable any "disciplinary judgments." As such, psychology is disabled; the law of the father is challenged since fathers and mothers must also be counted as casualties of such an unreadable interiority. (Bersani, *Homos* 145–46). Moreover, self-declarations are always spurious, or at least affirmative ones. How can the state issue papers to an unintelligible self? Or, to one who can only declare him/herself by what one is not or lacks? How does the state track, sanction, and discipline the subject who declares: I will not have not been me.

Just how awkwardly, at best, the depersonalized self, whose boundaries are nothing other than fluid, exists within the state is baldly apparent if we consider briefly Carl Schmitt's well-known definition of the political: "The specific political distinction to which political action and motive can be reduced is that between friend and enemy" (Schmitt, *Concept* 26). In other words, us against them, the self against the Other.[21] One can easily dismiss the characterization by looking at the source and Schmitt's disastrous political affiliations during National Socialism. Nonetheless, it is hard to deny the cogency of the essay's most challenging insight: "The concept of the state presupposes the concept of the political" (Schmitt, *Concept* 19). Schmitt's critique was aimed at the failing liberal state in Germany, citing the occlusion of the political that had been "negated" by the economic, social, and cultural spheres. That is, the liberal state had weakened the political by denying its basis. Since the political is that sphere concerned with the real possibility of physical killing, it assumes precedence and urgency. In his affirmation of the political Schmitt attempts to re-secure the basis of the failing liberal state, but the proper recognition of the political depends upon recognizing its polemical foundation. Schmitt makes clear that the political, and thus the state, exists only by virtue of the pre-existence of an enemy or absolute Other. "One may say: every 'totality of men" looks around for friends only—it *has* friends only—because it already has enemies."[22] Given the life-or-death stakes that inhere in the political, all political discourse finds its energies in these struggles: "[A]ll political concepts, ideas, and words [have] a polemical meaning; they have a concrete opposition in view, they are tied to a concrete situation" (Schmitt, *Concept* 83). Schmitt's observation that "all significant concepts of the modern theory of the state are secularized theological concepts" underscores the contradiction inherent in the *liberal state that proclaims the sovereignty of the subject* (Schmitt, *Political Theology* 52). The basis for such freedom is tethered to the very principles that secularism disavows. The liberal subject thus comes to be only by embracing a metaphysical stance to justify the friend/enemy distinction. On the other hand, consider the diagnosis vis-à-vis Bersani's or Garcia Düttmann's insistence on a self that has always already vacated its position. The strict boundaries of friend and enemy are meaningless, or we might say, the gay outlaw knows of no Other. The gay self that erects itself upon the liberal concepts of the state can only do so since the state, which exists because of the preexistence of the enemy, is looking for friends. And we are, if nothing else, such gay company. The irony embedded in the White House's display of the rainbow flag merely signaled that we, too, in need of friends as the deadly shadow of AIDS continued to subside but nevertheless haunt our own self-understanding, had found a new enemy. As we will see, that new enemy was the terrorist.

Selling Out

How then did gay politics become so complicit with the aims of the state? An awkward and purely speculative answer would be "protease inhibitors." Ever since the cocktail enabled so many of us to return to our lives of average mediocrity, being-at-odds with oneself and one's disease was an option gladly abandoned. Of my friends still living, we all remember those awful times as a dark void in which we hobbled along day by day, hoping never to have to face the light and the awful carnage of our friends cruelly ridiculed and abandoned by the state. To cite Virgil: "How to tell of carnage beyond telling?" (Virgil 246). For most, the memories have lost any resolution. Rather than go back, we moved on. The political energies harnessed to win badly needed funding and legal protections constructed an in-road to state power that, coupled with the loss of radical leaders, led to an abandonment of our marginal status in favor of a position inside, secured from the enemy without. Shall we consider this new state of affairs one of absolute immanence and AIDS among the enemies kept out? But without working through the potentialities opened up by the disease, which, it would seem, would amount to a work of mourning, we resigned ourselves to a politics of appeasement. Two claims are being entertained here: (1) the good gay citizen now participates in the very structure of the political that was the source of an anguish that peaked during the AIDS crisis, and (2) the rupture opened up by the disease also pointed to potentialties of the past that could be recaptured in service of an outlaw politics. Stated otherwise, if the panopticon signals that there is no transcendence, or rather no transcendence of immanence, then disease or sickness turns out to be a "positive possibility of existence," a freedom that unleashed "turns against itself." The absolute world of the panopticon and its attendant "panoptimism" are threatened within by disease: "In our eyes, AIDS does not come from God, but because it cannot yet be cured, it is seen as a sort of self-destruction of a society at the mercy of its own pure immanence" (Nancy, *Une penseè fine* 29). As a potential marker of an internecine battle of the self against itself, of the body (politic) turned against itself such that friend/enemy distinctions also dissolve, AIDS registered, at the very least, a possibility for restoration of a transcendent or messianic horizon that was quickly foreclosed by the politics of appeasement.

Now that we have won the status of friend, now that much of America is willing to reject claims that we aim to destroy all that's great and grand about the family, now that we, too, can register at Tiffany's, who is the new enemy? If my cynicism seems particularly ill-advised, given how hard we have had to fight to win such basic rights for the *homo sacer*, consider how women, immigrants, and African Americans find their rights under fierce attack. It is as if a game of thimble rigging were being staged, enticing one group to join the party while others feel under renewed and even more rigorous assault. As the staging of the rigging goes on, the class war being fought against all of us and designed to align the state fully with the interests of business gets scant attention. If we are always being distracted, perhaps distraction, i.e., pulling away, offers an alternative. And where better to have once found distraction than at Times Square.

Such is one way to read Samuel Delany's *Times Square Red, Times Square Blue*. The interest here, which cannot be divorced from the agenda realized by the SCOTUS decision, is the destruction brought on by gentrification of an interlocking set of subsystems that brought together people of wildly diverse backgrounds who for reasons far beyond the obvious availed themselves of the adult theaters that at one time defined the Square. What matters for Delaney is how Times Square mobilized a crossing of classes, races, genders, etc. that Delaney insists are necessary for a democratic society to function: "The primary thesis underlying my several arguments here is that, given the mode of capitalism under which we live, life is at its most rewarding, productive, and pleasant when large numbers of people understand, appreciate, and seek out interclass communication conducted in a mode of good will" (Delaney 111). It is difficult to avoid the suggestion that the call is for preserving or reinventing new ways to accommodate oneself to the mode of capitalism under which we live. Except that it is this very mode of capitalism and redevelopment that led to the dismantling of the subsystems intersecting at Times Square. There is a messianic dimension to the mode of being in this mode of capitalism. This relates not so much to its restorative aspect—although the reporting of contacts and experiences in these vanishing subsystems is critical to the project—but as a mode of readiness or preparedness when, to quote Heinrich Heine, "capitalism is finally over." The subsystems are constantly being reconstructed with every encounter among "male and female, gay and straight, old and young, working class and middle class, Asian and Hispanic, black and other, rural and urban, tourist and indigent, transient and permanent, with their bodily, material, sexual and emotional needs." (Delaney xx). An altogether new distribution of power, at times even a suspension of power relations, is detailed in the stories and anecdotes that comprise *Times Square Red*. A politics that eschews the hierarchies of marriage and capitalist production seems an embedded possibility here, even if Delaney regards peep-show encounters as strengthening his own relationship. "You learned something about these people (though not necessarily their name, or where they lived, or what their job or incomes was); and they learned something about you. The relationships were not (necessarily) consecutive. They braided. They interwove. They were simultaneous" (Delaney 57). The final sentences of the quote certainly reminds one of the kind of relationships inaugurated by the quilt and its interweaving of panels that brought together so many from such different places. Both are recalled as well under a sign of mourning for the kind of relationships or coming together that might have been. At the same time, the preservation of those discourses suggests a coming together that might not have not been. Certainly, one can no longer expect to hear such resonances above the din that regularly begins every weekday with the broadcast of *Good Morning America* from high atop the Disney/ABC Studios in Times Square.

Just how marriage, conceived as it is according to the spoken but rarely fulfilled vows of heterosexual marriage, is tied to the apparatus of the state is self-evident. What is not as evident is how other possibilities for different kinds of marriages or arrangements become suppressed. In *The Trouble with Normal: Sex, Politics, and the Ethics of Queer Life*, Michael Warner argues that the struggle for gay marriage was always a regressive one, anything but liberating.

> It is always tempting to believe that marrying is simply something that two people do. Marriage, however, is never a private contract between two persons. It always involves the recognition of a third party—and not just a voluntary or neutral recognition, but an *enforceable* recognition. (Warner, Normal 117)

The privileges reserved for the married have been well documented as the argument for expanding its definition to include same-sex couples made its way through the courts. These range from the control and disposition of community property to next-of-kin privileges during hospital stays. As Warner notes, none of the privileges reserved for married couples recognized by the state need to be contingent upon the institution save divorce and its attendant pleasures. For example, parenting rights among gay people often involve a third adult, an arrangement not accommodated by the state since parenting rights require marriage. Equally disturbing are the sorts of hierarchies that grow up around such institutions. How long before the single gay man in his thirties will have to fret and bear the shame of becoming an old maid?

Deplorable for Warner and many of us is not just the artificial cleaving of specific rights to marriage and thus the controls of the state but also the narrative that accompanied the campaign. Particularly comical, were it not so consequential, was the coming-of-age account offered by Andrew Sullivan. Just too rich are Sullivan's reactions to those who considered, like Delaney, the elimination of the subsystems that promoted casual intimate contact across classes with nostalgia and regret:

> [T]here are plenty of people . . . who prefer to chant mantras of decades gone by and pretend that somehow this is 1957 and straight America is initiating a Kulturkampf against sex in parks and somehow this is the defining issue of our times . . . It is a victim panic, a terror that with the abatement of AIDS we might have to face the future and that the future may contain opportunities that gay men and women have never previously envisaged, let alone grasped. It is a panic that the easy identity

of victimhood might be slipping from our grasp that maturity may be calling us to more difficult terrain. It is not hard to see what that terrain is. It is marriage (as cited, Warner, 136).

With that Sullivan dismissed any attempt to think through all the promises of an outlaw politics as discussed above. Instead, we are retarded survivors of trauma that need to restart our development by clinging to the ideals of married life. For Sullivan, does that mean he has given up his barebacking forays in the night now that marriage offers him all the intimacies for which previous, "immature" encounters prepared him?[23]

The other glaring oversight of proposing such puerile paths to normal is the underlying desire and claim that marriage is a ticket to seamless assimilation. The straight world was not freaked by our sexual orientation but rather by our sexual practices. To be sure, acceptance of queers has shifted dramatically, so long as we are seen as wanting what everybody else wants. The identification of what was once seen as an invisible threat to the wholesome life of the nuclear family has its advantages for reactionary forces in society. Already, the Republican National Committee has thrown its support behind the First Amendment Defense Act (FADA). This would allow those opposed to same-sex marriage and homosexuality in particular to refuse to provide treatment or service to those whose "lifestyle" offends their religious beliefs. Surely, an IRS official could then refuse to process a tax return from a same-sex couple, and those seeking shelter or assistance from federally funded programs would face similar obstacles. Given that America has always seemed to me a nightmare of Protestant making insofar as one's personal relationship with God takes precedence, there is no shortage of religious beliefs, cherry picked from various sources that claim universal validity because God ordained such beliefs in the private sanctuary of one's soul. So, *pace* Sullivan, our claims of coming-of-age to embrace a real and responsible future and to dare tread the sanctified terrain of marriage are rejected by those who would speak for God through appeal to what is cloaked in typical Nazi double talk, namely "religious freedom." Still, many may lament that such foes are simply on the wrong side of history, and they, too, will travel down a path of generational maturation, at which time, I suppose, they will mark the occasion and invite Mr. and Mr. Sullivan to high tea.

Whatever reassurances such mantras may offer, the grounds upon which equality is based are, it seems to me, quite shaky. In 1994, long before a sea change in attitudes swept across the land, legal scholar Janet Halley outlined the stakes for finding legal justifications to expand the rights of same-sex couples. While the analysis is both thorough and insightful, the interest of the article lies in mapping out a position that aligns queer politics with prevailing legal theory based upon legal precedent. In other words, the question that drives the argument is: how can we render assurances that we will be good citizens? That doesn't overshadow, however, what certainly seems to be one exceptional insight: that any tenable position on the origins and causes of homosexuality must conform to historically engrained conceits of a society that understand heterosexuality as the model of productivity and normalcy. Her espousal of behavior constructivism, where the object is given (biology is the cause) but the behavior or the actions inspired by the biologically determined object are a result of social construction is something of a compromise position that carefully hedges its bets by anticipating that a completely constructivist or essentialist position is not legally tenable, and maybe for good reason (Halley 520–40). The risk of biological determinism is the same as any theory that claims biology or bloodlines determine social behavior. Simply bursting out in song to declare we were born that way doesn't guarantee that enough additional behaviors will not be attributed to biology, such as violent or asocial acts, so that the state will feel entitled to exclude those deemed biologically at odds with its interests.

Constructivist strategies do not promise any additional security. Assemblages of power would seem to guarantee that the state and its apparatuses have always already conditioned its subjects according to the essence of the political or the friend/enemy distinction. In other words, legal justifications—other than for behaviors that qualify as promoting an eventual arrival on the mature terrain of marriage—demand an abandonment of communities uninterested in sustaining the myth of the sovereign subject. Or, for those of us whose standing vis-à-vis the laws of civil society are always vexed and fraught, why would we think that culture is easier to change than biology, an observation made quite some time ago by Eve Sedgwick Kosofsky (Kosofsky *Epistemology*, 43). Moreover, any lens that proposes to distinguish between the natural and the cultural is itself a production of culture. How could the natural ever be brought to consciousness of itself without becoming unnatural? That is not to dismiss the importance of political action and non-hegemonic coalition building, but as Halley's analysis shows, a radical rethinking of our political strategies is required. My intent in (re)introducing a messianic dimension is to reimagine possibilities for coming together outside the interpellations of the state. Even if a certain readiness, as described above, does not immediately translate into an activist politics, it necessitates formations of the self that are constantly undone by anticipation of an end with no future in sight. For now, it seems accommodating any and all and possible random causes for or sources of desire makes policing us less certain.

Even those who espouse a biological basis for same-sex desire cannot claim any clear line that links genetics with foreseeable outcomes.[24] Amazon Prime's highly acclaimed series *Transparent* offers an insight into just how complicated and unmappable genetic transmission can become. The lead character, Mora—previously Mort—becomes a woman late in life.[25] Most of the first two seasons track the exceptional dysfunction of Mora, his ex-wife, and their three children with pronounced but not necessarily featured references to their Jewish-German origins. The oldest and youngest, both daughters with a son sandwiched in between, display a remarkable but troubled fluidity of sexual preferences. In the last episodes, Mora's uncle is seen being arrested and presumably murdered by the Nazis during a raid of the Magnus Hirschfeld Institute in Berlin. A previous reference to ecogenetics clarifies the connection.[26] The uncle was a transvestite whose horrific death makes an apparent imprint on the genetic makeup of his sister who is with her brother at the time of the arrest. We are left with the impression that Mora's gender dysmorphia is the traumatic expression of that mutation, which is then passed on to his children. The transmission is highlighted by juxtaposing the raid on the institute with the events that take place at a women's music festival. At the festival, Mora learns that she is not considered a woman, because she was not born with a vagina. The randomness but painful cut that separates Mora from her own sends her frantically seeking out her daughters as the world spins ominously before her. Her panic visually and emotionally mimics that of her uncle several decades before, as do the extreme behaviors of the three children at that precise moment. The son experiences a complete breakdown, exhibited by a fierce road rage that leads him to a full breakdown and to consult his mother's latest interest, an upstanding member of the Jewish congregation. Here, he is instructed to mourn for his father, which he does by weeping in the arms of what is now a surrogate father. However clear the source of the dysfunction might be, the lines emanating from that primal scene are as crossed as the lovers in the series. Mora's uncle might have insisted on her female name, but unlike her descendant, she had no opportunity to become or free the women trapped inside her male body. All four of these characters are doubly traumatized by something carried genetically: (1) the experience of gender dysmorphia, and (2) the Nazi raid witnessed by Mora's mother.

If we consider this transmission—indirect insofar as the lost son/daughter is not the carrier but rather the sister, and direct insofar as Mora's mother experienced the Nazi's destruction firsthand PTSD continues postmortem, transmitted to and experienced by subsequent generations, even if it its paths are circuitous and hardly straight. To the extent that the discovery of being gay has always carried its fair measure of trauma, *Transparent* forces us to question what predictive power such biological approaches might ultimately have. In this instance, an insurmountable obstacle frustrates epi- or ecogenetic tracking in the figure of the transvestite uncle. However strong the desire in the 1930s to undergo some sort of procedure to fix things—the uncle is not a transsexual, even if he insists on having official papers list him as female. There are no surgical options for him. And a gay person was not always "gay." The gene that apparently transmits such knowledge has always already been permeated by different discourses for naming, identifying, and dealing with people given to same-sex desire.

Gay Terrorists

The shortcoming of my analysis to this point is its American-centric consideration of political formations. The global map, as we know, offers a far less halcyon picture of gay life. American exceptionalism is reinforced in the special way that we have come to rehabilitate queers. America's way of life is exceptional because it allows even queers, once they have matured, to share in its dreams and way of life. Likewise, such exceptionalism relies on the same matrices of class, gender, sex, and nationality to re-produce a different kind of queer body in the new and more threatening version of Orientalized terrorists. The recent attack in a gay nightclub in Orlando that left 49 patrons dead demonstrates the dialectic here. On the one hand, the terrorist, a devout Muslim who proclaimed sympathies with ISIS, is seen as an enemy of all humanity, whose unfitness for Western society is his hatred of gay people. Conservatives were reluctant to call this a hate crime, preferring instead to see the murders as an assault on the Western way of life. They even went so far as to call the gay victims "human beings." That rumors circulated that the killer might be gay or at least confused pointed to the supposed differences in the civilizing effects of the two cultures. In the West, we become normalized. Islam, on the other hand, brings out the monster always potentially lurking in the homosexual. In fact, the two are indistinguishable. Islam produces sexual deviants. Also, two weeks before the attacks, the GOP House of Representatives in Florida prayed for God to smite all gay people. Suddenly, which ideology actually underwrites the homophobic terrorist is unclear. No matter where he was living or where he was born, he cannot possibly be really American, lest one weapon in the ideological battle against terror be useless. The stakes in securing his ties to ISIS and not allowing for any of his deadly impulses to be connected with anything American, not even the prayers of his state representatives, indicates how the homosexual has become instrumentalized for purposes of the state.

Jasbir Puar,[27] relying on the work of Rey Chow,[28] traces the connectivities of the matrices noted above to reconstitute the friend/enemy distinction along lines of the properly queer and the improperly queer. Not only has the readjustment, so to speak, of these matrices been reconstituted to resecure the privileged space of whiteness, as Chow maps, but the gay rights movement in America has been critical in rebranding the Oriental as the queer gone amok as well. "[T]he contemporary U.S. heteronormative nation actually relies on and benefits from the proliferation of queerness, especially in regard to the sexually exceptional homonational and its evil counterpart, the queer terrorist of elsewhere" (xxv). Queer needs to be understood as incapable of being normalized, which, in turn renders the queer a wild, unpredictable threat that can only be contained by reinscribing its eccentric course according to a geopolitical map, reorganized around the friend/enemy distinction, or as G. W. Bush put it, those who are with us and those who are against us (xxv). Those against us are terrorists in love with death, and their queers, like the American queers of old, are embodiments of the death drive. The exceptional nature of America is evinced in its unique style of tolerance that transforms the queer with no future into a devoted member of the PTA. And despite the homophobic and racist tactics of the U.S. military, homonormative subjects benefit from American exceptionalism whose brand is strengthened by enlisting in its ranks those formerly thought to be a ticking time bomb inside the American family. As a result, this shift produces an image of Muslim masculinity as terrorist and sexually aberrant: "[M]uslim masculinity is simultaneously pathologically excessive yet repressive, perverse yet homophobic, virile yet emasculated, monstrous yet flaccid" (xxv). Nothing about this figure makes sense except to ascribe to his person a new version of queerness with all the markings of both predatory but also unnaturally feminine and passive traits. He embodies the terror of what exceeds the limits of normativity.

The newly formed or accepted homonormative family attests to how far the United States is willing to go to welcome diversity. If we pride ourselves as a nation on our ability to rehabilitate even queers, who were not that long ago bearers of death and disease, our impotence in the face of the predatory but unnaturally feminine body of the Oriental terrorist, evinces the gravity of the danger (xxv). In other words, it extends the claims of American exceptionalism to include now American sexual exceptionalism. Consider the draconian measures taken against gay men in Uganda. Driving that agenda was the religious right of America.[29] To be sure, many would like homosex to offer just cause for imprisonment or death, but critical is how these different pressures coalesce in patterns that exceed the intention of any one group. In this case, the religious right's disgust of same-sex sex finds an outlet in Uganda, which serves to reinforce the image of the Other as intolerant and brutal and stricken with disease. Meanwhile, our own prison populations, in which rape is not only not uncommon but is also used as a threat during police interrogations, exists, as Foucault described in *Discipline and Punishment*, to displace the scene of torture; it becomes as secret as the War on Terror. And that displacement, of course, eases the displacement of the previous American deviant onto the terrorist.

Map of the Argument

Recently, renewed, vigorous research has appeared reconsidering the early, pioneering work of German sexologists. Robert Tobin's excellent volume *Peripheral Desires: The German Discovery of Sex* looks at a variety of scientific, literary, and political discourses from 1830 to the early twentieth century to chart the origins of the emerging languages of sexology and psychoanalysis. I am seeking to find traces of what was discarded, dismissed, or overlooked in the period just before 1830.[30] Likewise, Robert Beachey's *Gay Berlin: Birthplace of a Modern Identity* makes the bold but convincing argument that the homosexual liberation movement finds its origins and most progressive strains in Berlin, even long before the Magnus Hirschfeld Institute arose to celebrate diverse sexualities. As the editors of the volume, *After the History of Sexuality: German Genealogies with and beyond Foucault*, stress, "Rather more starkly than was the case for sexual science, the emergence of homosexual self-consciousness and political activism was a largely German-language affair" (3). Particularly notable, of course, is Karl-Heinrich Ulrichs whose self-identification as an "uranien" combines scientific inquiry with pleas for liberation. Likewise, Heinrich Hössli's two-volume work *Eros* (1836–1838) reads as well as a defense of male-male love. And any list must include the first lesbian activist, Anna Rüling, (Theodora "Theo" Anna Sprüngli, 1888–1953) who later in 1904 at the Scientific Humanitarian Committee, a group dedicated to liberating diverse sexualities, was the first and only person to acknowledge and address lesbian sexuality, going so far as to come out herself to the group.

For the editors and contributors of the volume cited above, most striking about Foucault's groundbreaking *History of Sexuality* is its essentially Franco-centric perspective. "In light of all this prodigious investment [in Germany] in the deployment of sexuality in its various forms, it is curious that Foucault wrote so little about it directly" (Spector 3). More than merely redirect attention to the German examples, the editors of *After the History of Sexuality: German Genealogies with and beyond Foucault* turn back the clock, looking to extend the genealogical traces of the pathologization of sexuality. Their investigation of proto-formulations of same-sex desire in Reformation Germany, as well as viable arguments for tracing conceptualizations of modern sexuality as far back as the early modern period of the Holy Roman Empire, indicate how complex, fluid, and resistant to any stable tracking a history of sexuality is.[31]

This does not excuse ahistorical approaches to literary and cultural production with respect to this topic in particular. What I propose, instead, is to think seriously about what a queer history might look like. Or rather, how organizing and pursuing messianic echoes offers a disjunctive history, in full display of the provisional character of any trajectory. I attempt to perform and thus offer a genealogy that suggests one way to reactivate a potentiality sacrificed in the quest for citizenship and societal approbation. The organization of the manuscript thus brings together a series of texts and films to track the pathologization of same-sex desire and to explore a queer history by listening for echoes of what it means to not have not loved. This also means that my stated emphasis on strictly German texts from the earlier period is somewhat overstated. The energies that I am tracking can hardly be expected to recognize strict "national" boundaries, especially during a period when Germany was not yet a nation. Rather, such energies are distributed more broadly and include, as we will see, texts such as *Frankenstein*. But the epicenter of my interest is still primarily in German narratives of that period.

The focus on this period needs no other justification than to note, as Beacher does, that the very vocabulary still in use today to describe a variety of psychological conditions finds its origins in this period. Many of the early sexologists, Robert Krafft-Ebing and Sigmund Freud found their most compelling examples in literature. And it stands to reason that the period just before and contemporaneous with the development of a sexological vocabulary would discover in literature a rich repository of examples. I think it fair to say that sexologists bring to consciousness what was exhibited in several of these texts.

The first chapter, "A Man's Best Friend Is His Monster: Mary Shelley's *Frankenstein*," actually looks outside of the strictly German context to consider the significance of monstrosity or monsters in emerging bourgeois society at the beginning of the nineteenth century. More than the creature's fascination with Werther—a connection reexamined in chapter 4—is the power of the monster to expose the ideological pressures that seek to reaffirm family and nationalistic values in the face of a something, hovering about the margins, that threatens such a nice recomposition of the Swiss Family Frankenstein, with respect both to the gendered roles of its members and thus to its legacy. As such, the novel signals in a different direction that remains unexplored or rejected; namely, what would it mean for the self to surrender willingly to its own monstrosity—to the forces that disable family, generation, and the colonialist ambitions of nascent nation states. The refusal of the text to pursue these potentialities finds an apt metaphor in Walton deciding to abandon his quest once he realizes someone has already been there before him. It signals—more than just sympathy for his crew—a refusal to greet an Other on its terms, on its turf.

Before seeking out traces of this other way, I turn to an oft-discussed but easily dismissed text from the traditional German canon, *Peter Schlemihl: And His Wondrous History* (*Peter Schlemihl und seine wundersame Geschichte*) in chapter 2, "Peter Schlemihl's Wondrous Story or the Genesis of a Queer Jewish Outlaw." Interest here lies in the manner in which different social pressures coalesce to produce what can easily be seen as the proto-closeted homosexual. Throughout this introduction references have been made to assemblages of power, how different, even conflicting pressures can be brought together to mutually reinforce each other under the unfailing eye of the panopticon. In this example, the Jew seeking emancipation finds his ambitions at odds with the parochial, nativist traditions of German-speaking lands not yet ready to embrace bourgeois capitalism and of course, not yet a nation. These competing pressures serve to awaken a reimagining of the Jew as queer, as introducing an unnatural desire into society that permanently renders the Jew unfit for interaction with upstanding folk. The attempt to distinguish the Jew, now dressed for success in the West, from his German neighbors leads to a new distinction that sets the Jew up for being pathologically different and a decisive threat to the folkish values of Germany. My interest, of course, is less in what is the eventual fate of the Jew so marked, and more in how it offers one genesis of homosexuality, but by no means an exclusive one. How the other, castigated and demonized in Frankenstein, requires damnation of another sort, once his appearance is less jolting, finds a chartable map in Chamisso's story. But it also sets up the possibility for disassembling that assemblage, for disentangling the strands that come to define and (over)determine the fate of the outsider. It thus allows for the possibility for the outsider to find a proper outside, to escape from the immanence exhibited in Frankenstein.

Framed alternately, to what extent is Frankenstein's creation the not-yet-realized of sexual otherness? One answer to this question is visible in the intersection of power relations and relations of power in "Peter Schlemihl's Wondrous Story." A network of reciprocally reenforcing practices—visible in society's treatment of the Jewish parvenu Schlemihl—generates a new kind of degenerate who over the course of the nineteenth century comes to be identified as the homosexual. This is not the only possible genesis, since a central conceit of this project is the impossibility of presenting a history of sexuality. As a series of acts, numerous combinatory possibilities exist and continue to persist as a potentiality with each act.

Just as significant, the text establishes a framework for consideration of the queer possibilities presented by one of the canon's queerest or most inscrutable texts, Heinrich von Kleist's "On the Marionette Theater." That possibility is explored in chapter 3: "Queer Prosthetics or Male Tribadism in Kleist's 'On the Puppet Theater.'" On the one hand, following the closeting of the "homosexual" in *Peter Schlemihl*, it becomes possible to de-code the text, as one critic has done, to uncover a discourse loaded with innuendo and euphemism. To be sure, the emergence of warm brothers in Berlin—or shall we say a secret society of men with men or boys—would generate a coded discourse.[32] On the other hand, such an approach merely appropriates the fundamental assumptions emerging about queers. It situates "queer" identity on a terrain defined by the prevailing discourse and its inherited values. Instead, I accept the text's invitation to defy the possibility of fixing meaning to any of its many gnomic statements. The terrain is thus prepared to reimagine potentialities that come to be lost once interpretive discourses seek to stabilize the text's playful subversion of interpretive consistency.

The potentiality of that terrain is actualized by Johann Goethe's *The Sorrows of Young Werther*. How is it possible that a text composed thirty years before Kleist's can be thought to have responded to or answered a call that has yet to be articulated? Already established is that the past is recovered or reimagined to redeem a past that never actually occurred but could have. If talk about marionettes could disentangle the interpretive certainty that would link securely sign and signified, Goethe's text comes to exploit that potentiality, one that remained unreconstructed until Roland Barthes's *A Lover's Discourse*. And his reading of *The Sorrows of Young Werther* is the subject of chapter 4, "Queer Echoes Traversing Great Spaces: Roland Barthes's *A Lover's Discourse* and Johann Wolfgang Goethe's *The Sorrows of Young Werther*." Let me clarify. In a book comprised almost entirely of citations and intertexts, Barthes most often lifts from *Werther*. Nietzsche, while not as frequently cited, is an equally important interlocutor for Barthes, specifically Nietzsche's eternal return of the same. Barthes's text thus poses the very provocative question of what would it mean for Werther, whose life ends in suicide, to accept Nietzsche's challenge and embrace a life that will end again and again and again in suicide. These echoes in Goethe's text allow for a reimagining of a lover's discourse in a reconstituted past that gestures toward a love that could never have been realized at the time it was written or, in fact, at any time. *Queer echoes need time to traverse great spaces*, and preserved in that time is a love that never quite speaks its name, never makes any full disclosure.

The final chapter, " 'I'm nothin'. I'm nowhere.': Echoes of a Queer Messianic in *Brokeback Mountain*," is something of a coda, leaping to the present to explore what messianic echoes might be retrievable. To be sure, nothing would seem further removed from Frankenstein's laboratory in Ingolstadt than Brokeback Mountain in the American West. If the expectation was an imagining of a very real politic to counter the current politic of appeasement, none is forthcoming. Rather, the purpose is to understand or hear how such echoes persist into a very different present, preserving the possibility that a queerness will arrive to rupture scenes of marital gay bliss. The fundamental wager of this study is that the energies reanimated in the earlier chapters have considerable and vital resonances today that can help us rethink our current politics. While America, of course, has been the center of the gay rights movement at least since Stonewall, the primary reason for looking at this film in particular is how it recaptures the messianic echoes of the previous chapters and rearticulates them in such fashion that marriage (equality) is already foreclosed, therefore necessitating a thinking about queer relationships that goes in a different direction, that goes West to the undiscovered backside of Brokeback Mountain.

1

A Man's Best Friend Is His Monster

Mary Shelley's *Frankenstein*

In Bill Condon's 1998 film *Gods and Monsters* the relationship between the god and his creation comes undone. If expectations dictate that the surrogate monster or its newest version bear the hideous physical deformities of his predecessor, the figure upon whom the cinematic creator of Frankenstein or the film's protagonist directs his affections inspires thoughts of a beauty so sublime that it becomes monstrous only potentially. As a retelling of the final days of *Frankenstein*'s cinematic creator, James Whale, the film explores the homoerotic affections aroused by a gardener who comes to embody Whale's own monstrous hopes in the form of an angelic monster. The monster's beauty deforms and debases its creator; its masculine beauty combined with a fetching naïveté evinces a god-like simplicity at whose hands James Whale would like to be destroyed. "Kill me, Kill me," he pleads with his monster as he mounts and gropes him in a final desperate attempt to inspire his imagined creation to end his creator's life. The monster, while not the laboratory kind with a massive body and reach, has no trouble refusing the advance and repudiating the one who imagined him as his monstrous creation. In this version, which is really not a treatment of Frankenstein but of his cinematic creator's final days and his attempt to reanimate his long-lost monster, the gardener's physical beauty endows him with monstrous possibilities. Whale's mental decline serves to elevate his new monster to god-like status, but only by merging his image with so many images out of a catalogue of lovers from his past that never were, loves that could never have been. Even the delicate Tadzio—we might recall—is seen as monstrous by his admirer. In other words, divorced from scenes of a family romance, divorced from domestic entanglements, the monster comes to be god-like in its physical being; monstrous is the desire of the beholder. And if Mary Shelley's monster could identify with Milton's Satan, that relation, too, is reversed. Satanic is the homoerotic desire that projects god-like potential, the potential to kill with its beauty, onto a creation of its own making or of its mind's making.

Monsters and homosexuals will hardly be strangers to each other as sexology in the nineteenth century advances in naming its other.[1] But for the original author of *Frankenstein*, the monster's grotesque deformity affrights from the start. There is no courting at the opera,[2] no imagining of god-like beauty in an angel of death. Instead, the monster is hideous. Or, so Mary Shelley described her own creation in the 1831 preface to the novel, it is "supremely frightful," "a horrid thing," and most famously of all in her description of the novel itself, "my hideous progeny (1831, ix)."[3]

Admittedly, the comparison between Mary Shelley's monster/novel and any of its cinematic adaptations is awkward and asymmetrical. Who do we align with whom? In the example above, a film about James Whale is not a film about Frankenstein that might serve as a neat vehicle for comparison. But as Mary Shelley's own description of her work suggests, the monster is viewed through or is a product of numerous screens or narrative frames.[4] Simply put, he or it is as much a product of scrambled mediation as it is of assembled body parts. So, how might it to be that whatever scrambling occurs between the novel's penning and say "Death in Venice" that the monster comes to awe with its beauty? In no way do I mean to suggest that a historical shift that can be documented with respect to numerous texts marking a historical or linear transformation. On the contrary, I set the argument up in this fashion to pose and pursue the following question: to what extent does Mary Shelley's novel propose, foreclose, and delimit possible relations with the monster that are espied by the shift described above? That is, the radical reimagining of relations with Dr. Frankenstein's monster underscores, I argue, two things: (1) monsters have an untapped potential, which (2) comes to be de-potentialized through attempts to reinscribe the body into the social order. Mary Shelley's text, as the vast literature attests, pulls in countless directions, accommodating or speaking to numerous critical approaches and interpretive strategies. Nothing can contain the signifying possibilities of the monster; it exceeds proper registration ("Who can describe their horror and consternation on beholding me?" [1818, 97]). It recalls the textual dappling witnessed near the end of Visconti's film, *Death in Venice*.

At the same time, a pentimento emerges in the text that seeks to confine, exile, or just destroy the monster in service of preserving a nuclear family, wedded to the very institutions that will come to marginalize, criminalize, and demonize the homosexual as a type. While it is true that the "turbulent energies" of the text "overwhelm any ideology we may discern in it" (M. Brown 145), the pressure to relieve that turbulence—to domesticate the monster that is also the text—provides a very early indication of how assemblages of such energies work to construct a rather thoroughly modern monster in terms of its sexual energies and their orientation. This chapter will trace the tensions that run throughout the novel and conclude with arguing how such tensions, left unresolved, offer a reading that resists the pressures of the family and its restoration. In other words, what would it mean to befriend the monster rather than seek to contain or destroy it?

What Are Monsters for in Destitute Times?

The central claim of this chapter is that monsters are not simply a marker of something that exceeds identification and "determinations of truth and falsity" (M. Brown 157), but rather the determinations employed to register such monstrosity reveal a fault line in the social order particular to its time as well. Walton's description of the monster at the end of the novel participates in this attempt to register what he freely admits he cannot. As he confronts the monster, he both disavows any capacity to see or describe the creature and also engages in what he has just disavowed. "Over [Frankenstein] hung a form which I cannot find words to describe: gigantic in stature, yet uncouth and distorted in its proportions" (Shelley1818, 155). Whatever aphasia grips Walton as he beholds the creature for the first time, it nevertheless allows for a rapid recovery of that very language.

The initial description is followed by more detail, save his face, which is covered "by long locks of ragged hair." If prosopopoeia, putting a face on that which one reads, is ultimately what is at stake in this text or any text, the rigging together of collected body parts to create a monster does not allow for it to be read. Whether we consider Victor's attempt to create a superhuman in his own image or Mary Shelley's work as caught up in putting a face to a woman writer who must also disguise or question her own ambition, the face that comes to be put on Frankenstein's monster is not flattering to the self or selves that would seek to get a read on their own creation. Walton's (non)description at the end of the novel is unambiguous:

"Never did I behold a vision so horrible as his face, of such loathsome, yet appalling hideousness. I shut my eyes involuntarily" (Shelley1818, 163). The face that asks to be read and understood, to join in the community of readers, reflects a hideous text that registers the contradictory and overdetermined impulses that underwrite the novel. To be sure, Walton is not Dr. Frankenstein. The monster is not his creation, and unlike the doctor, he has already agreed to listen to his crew and end his mission. But as one who has confessed a special penchant for Frankenstein, who recognizes in Victor a soul mate, the object or creature that accounts for their coming together is monstrous. What allows for Walton to assert that he has found a man, who before his spirit "had been broken by misery, I should have been happy to have possessed as the brother of my heart," is a monster (Shelley 1818, 10). Already, we have a friendship premised on the impossible: Were it not for the monster, the two would never have found each other, but the one who appears to Walton as his soulmate is one who can only be reconstructed or reassembled from the remnants of his broken spirit.

Walton reanimates Victor's lost soul for purposes of claiming the friend that since childhood he has always longed for. That brings him face to face with the monster but only after his soulmate has been crushed. The suggestion is that the attractive and repellant forces that drive relationships in the text not only demand negotiation with the monster but also a ceding of authorship to the monster. In other words, there is a reversal here. The monster appears to be the work of a mad scientist, and if extended to the text, the progeny of a woman author. At the same time, the monster appears to have always been at work in the text, a generative and uncontainable force that exceeds all limits. To return to the concept of prosopopoeia, there are so many faces to be read in the text, so many (auto)biographical tales and traces that any face, any reading, is immediately replaced, eliminated, or transformed by another.[5]

Peter Brooks, for one, has situated the problem in the creature's inability to negotiate the symbolic order through access to an outside imaginary.[6] Having had no mother, Frankenstein never experiences a mirror stage; his entry into language is strictly as a voyeur born of the necessity to compensate for his ugliness. The point is that much stronger when one considers the shortage of mothers in the text, or the prevalence of dead mothers and their surrogates. His hopeless tarrying in the symbolic is recognizable in how he comes to inhabit language. What he witnesses through the peephole and then reports in French is what is taught to an Arab in a German-speaking region rendered in English. (Shelley 1818, 85–105). But whatever attempts the creature makes at self-cultivation, nothing can arrest the horror of his physical presence. Language(s) moves through various modes and styles of articulation, but no law governs its erratic movements. Moreover, the elision of Oedipal nuclei also results in a lack of real sexual difference. In Milton's *Paradise Lost*, Eve, according to Brooks, discovers God's law which is also the law of sexual difference and the rule of the phallus (Brooks 88). For Frankenstein's creature, the request for a bride is feckless, even were she completed. "The wife represents only sexual difference but no imaginary." The result is an "uncontestable metonymic movement of desire through the narrative signifying chain, whose resistance to closure is evinced by the many narrative frames of the novel" (Brooks 97).[7]

Frankenstein is not to be beheld. The lifeless remains of his victims speak to his being or having been, as do his kind deeds performed for the DeLacey's during the cover of night, but his presence remains insufferable, universally so: "Oh no mortal could support the horror of that countenance" (1818, 32). He exists as a trace or "a dreaded specter—just as surely as he tracks Frankenstein and his family (1818, 3). But deprived of an imaginary, that trace threatens full exposure of a monstrosity, or is given full exposure by the doctor.

The Swiss Family Frankenstein

The monster that comes to animate the scenes of the novel also comes to both secure and unsecure family ties, or what the text calls "the silken cord."[8] In describing his life to his new-found wannabe soulmate, Victor explains that his early life was "so guided by a silken cord that all seemed but one train of enjoyment for me" (1818,14). Such days of bliss are enabled or even directed by luxurious woven strands of fabric that bind like with like. Generational continuity is tied to the image of a delicate cord that ropes the family in, keeps them together and on a straight path. "The family is a rehearsal space for the exclusionary attitudes of the privatized public sphere" (Komisaruk 441). While that space shelters those like Elizabeth, who "appear[] of a different stock" from those of her common fellow orphans, the cord does not extend to true outsiders to pull them into a protected space.[9]

No such law or silken cord directs and orients the monster's movements through language and landscape, exposing an ugliness inadmissible and absolutely fatal to the endogamous dreams of family. The threat such a free-floating trace poses is succinctly stated by the monster after the description of his first murder, "I too can create desolation; my enemy is not invulnerable" (Shelley 1818, 97). Nowhere more directly are the stakes of this reversal stated than by the monster upon demanding that Victor continue to prepare a bride for him: "You are my creator, but I am your master,—obey!" (Shelley 1818, 116). And he won't leave: "The form of the monster on whom I had bestowed existence was forever before my eyes . . ." (Shelley 1818, 35). A death drive inhabits the monster once his traces are reanimated as creation and exposes the tenuous bonds that make possible a future or future relations. The monster, as much as he traverses the various sign systems of his tormentors, must be contained or killed off. Truth values must be reanimated if the family's legacy is to continue.

But who really wins, should the monster be killed off? The monster's deadly impulses, stemming from rejection of his outward form, inspire the same impulses in his father or creator. Ridding himself of the monster—by begetting him a bride or destroying him—might allow the doctor "to claim Elizabeth, and forget the past in union with her," but it also requires that he remain "a slave of the creature" (Shelley 1818, 104, 116) who comes to inhabit all the deathly impulses that threaten the family in the same way storms appear in Switzerland—"suddenly and in several places at once" (Shelley 1818, 18). The Frankenstein family needs protection from one of its own creations, and that relation locks them in a life-and-death battle that makes creator and creation, master and slave, interchangeable. If the narrative frames did not already confuse who is really speaking for whom (To what extent is the monster's eloquence Frankenstein's creation, both the creature's capacity for such and its story as reinterpreted by the highly educated Victor?), the monster's wild movement through various sign systems and landscape threatens to affect all:

> The sleeper stirred; a thrill of terror ran though me. Should he indeed awake [. . .] and denounce the murderer? Thus she would assuredly act, if her darkened eyes opened. The thought [. . .] stirred the fiend within me . . . the murder I have committed because I am forever robbed of all that she could give me, she shall atone. (Shelley 1818, 98)

The murder of which he speaks, of course, is that of the young Felix, the son of DeLacey; the new victim is Justine, who rather than being murdered on the spot is set up. Since she does not see the monster, she must presume her own guilt. Once again the visual register prevails, but this time the game of appearances shifts. Rather than see the monster and misjudge his acquisition of and potential for *Bildung* by running in terror, Justine can conceive or fathom the monster only after the fact, from whatever evidence he might have left behind, which, of course, only leads to a wrong conclusion about Felix's murder. The sleeper's stirring stirs the fiend within the monster to act; the transfer of stirring from sleeper to murderer also creates confusion among the victims. Now, Justine and not Frankenstein or his monster must atone. Now, Justine is the thief and murderer. Finally, the unseen monster is equal to the threat aroused by his appearance. The monster is unfairly condemned by his appearance that belies his potential or innate goodness; Justine is condemned for murder because of planted evidence and confusion which is misread as consistent with guilt. The pressures of the text to render visual signs reliable implies that the monster's appearance must reflect his true self. He must be rejected and scorned to ignite his rage and ensure that his acts bespeak the horror of his assembled parts. That is to say, the birthrights of the scion of one of Switzerland's most distinguished families gets something in return from the monster. As we will see, whatever attendant threats the monster poses, something about a family that has as many Oedipal substitutions as this one, ("your cousin who has been like a sister should become your wife"), seems to require the monster to set relationships straight even as he destroys them.[10]

Monsters among Us

The monster has no name; no proper appellation cleaves to that which exceeds the possibilities of language. As such, a plethora of descriptive words stand in for the name: "monster," "fiend," "daemon," "creature," "wretch," "devil," "odious companion" and "dreaded spectre." And insofar as "monster" or "creature" might succeed as a "nameless mode of naming the unimaginable," that gap opened up by arriving at the limits of naming when faced by the monster "forms a space that produces the conditions for the production and proliferation of names. . . . The monster, as an unspeakable (__), constitutes the space that is necessary for writing to begin . . . the writing before writing" (Botting 68).

The observation, moreover, implicates the text, its actual production, as much as it does the monster alone. If the monster preconditions all writing as writing, then he inhabits the very text that sought to exile him. Note how names circulate in the text. Margaret Saville/Mary Shelley is quite obvious. A similar clarity and lack of such occurs with the name(s) or missing name(s) of the author on each addition. And since not being able to name (as Justine cannot) the nameless or unnamable implicates the silenced speaker, the risk attendant to a proliferation of names that fails to name its enabling/disabling power carries serious risks. That identity is very much a legal construct, comprised, for example, of birth certificates, passports, wedding certificates, and arrest records, suggests how tethered to taming the threat posed by namelessness a society is. In fact, the common practice that often mistakes Dr. Frankenstein for his monster indicates that a complete reversal of values or relationships is in the balance. "But where were my friends and relatives? No father had watched my infant days . . . what was I?" (Shelley 1818, 80). Names secure family ties, as do family ties, names. That is to say, both revolve around a center whose name dare not and cannot be spoken. Unhinged from the tethers of a society organized around "rank, descent, and noble blood," the monster is also that which languages have yet to name. He is a representative of something that can only be named by reference to an existing list of substantives; as such, he has no claims to an authorized or authenticated existence (Shelly 1818, 79).

This contagion threatens the entire semantic field, contributing to the upheaval in truth values inaugurated by Frankenstein's creature. As Bernhard Duyfhuizen observes, polypotons, the repetition of words from the same root, are strewn throughout the text. The example he uses is particularly trenchant, specifically the shifting values that come to be associated with the word "wretch," from the Old English *wrecca*, meaning "exile" (Duyfhuizen 483–86). Already it has been noted that the creature is exiled from human society since he lacks documentary proof of his existence and drifts outside communities defined and sustained by bloodlines. But the polysemic traces of the wretch, of the exile, infiltrate virtually every relationship in the text. It is worth rehearsing with some detail Duyfhuizen's tracking of the word's textual migrations. Shelley's conclusion to her introduction, "And now, once again, I bid my hideous progeny go forth and prosper," already advances a metonymic chain in conflicting but telling directions. The apostrophe could refer to the text or to Victor Frankenstein. The monster, whose hideousness is extreme enough to deny him any consideration or kindness, is not a possible referent, insofar that the monster is incapable of prosperous reproduction. Still, even the elimination of any threat of offspring, even the apparent certainty that the monster's lineage ends with one generation, offers no security from the threat. Already, creator and creation/text have become interchangeably hideous, long after the monster has been slain or the novel completed. No wonder Victor refuses the wretched creature's request for a bride. His fear that the monster and his bride might not be true to the monster's word seems less unreasonable but no less unenforceable. Any kind of union with the monster threatens further dissemination of its destructive energies.

The first use of "wretch," however, has nothing to do with the monster per se but rather with his contagion. During his first encounter with Victor, Walton observes, "I never saw a man in so wretched a condition" (1818, 8). Several substitutions are at work here; among them is the transition from hideous to wretched. The origins of hideous are informative insofar as the Greek root "keu" addresses sound but also the Germanic "skow" or to show. The monster, that which shows as it warns, is first hideous; that whose repulsiveness shows itself and is heard becomes wretched or that which is exiled. What obtains, however, is not a wall to prevent re-entry of the exile, but rather a modality of substitutions that is as constitutive of the monster's destructive faculty as the parts or meaning of those parts are. Moreover, Victor's description provides a positive prognosis. After returning from exile to the company of Walton, Victor shows signs of "benevolence and sweetness that I [Walton] never saw equaled" (Shelley 1818, 8). Care "lightens up Victor's whole countenance," which, if maintained or readily summoned, such face would allow him to be in the company of or face to face with others (Shelley 1818, 8). The monster's countenance, on the other hand, cannot show what his benevolent words might communicate. Such words then circulate aimlessly with no facial expression or means of display to anchor them, particularly as long as ugliness of that sort must be hidden. The monster can neither be confronted (his hideousness overwhelms.) nor can he be sent into exile. He can traverse whatever distances, obstacles, trenches, and fences are erected between him and his target; and his presence, as in the example above, is always perceived in his absence.

He inhabits the metonymic chain, or by disrupting that chain he generates uncontainable strains of its contagion. "Wretched," for example, appears in the description of his father's rescue of his "most intimate friend" Beaufort, who after falling into poverty sought recluse in Lucerne where he lived "in wretchedness" (Shelley 1818, 13).

The semantic transfer offers a peculiar distinction. Living in wretchedness, the friend inspires Victor's father to come to his aid. Being a wretch, as is the monster, is instead hopeless. Still, the old man succumbs to his illness, which then allows the father to marry the friend's daughter. How sweet! Wretchedness, at least, sponsors a new family romance. And such romance will eventually allow (depending on the edition) the intimate friend's daughter cum wife to adopt an impoverished child/niece who stood out from the others due to a "celestial stamp in all her features," particularly her hair, "which was the brightest living gold" [like a silken cord] (Shelley 1818, 15). That, of course, is Elizabeth, who in turn becomes Victor's sister/cousin/bride. But whoever has seen wretchedness is, it would seem, forever tainted. Whoever whisking-away from wretchedness saves, e.g., Elizabeth or the waif Caroline, still infects, is still tainted. After all, it is the picture of Caroline, the mother, on the body of the innocent adopted child/servant Justine that becomes the key piece of incriminating evidence. Of course, it is planted there by the monster, who in this instance literalizes his destruction of secured sign systems. The dead mother circulates, as her image now serves to condemn one she had previously saved.

Duyfhuizen's tracking of the numerous other traces of "wretch" is worth citing here:

> After the first naming of the Creature "the wretch" (57), the frequency of the term or its polyoptic derivatives skyrockets with appearances in nearly every chapter—in all, sixty-one occurrences of "wretch" or of a derivative such as "wretched," "wretchedness," "wretchedly" ("wreck" occurs three more times). (Duhuzien 484)

Of course, not merely the frequency of the word points to the wretched one's capacity to spread wretchedness, but also grammatical and syntactical migrations suggest how easily the monster's disease adapts to new environments. Take, for instance, the description Victor offers of Justine's trial ("During the whole of this wretched mockery of justice I suffered living torture . . ." [Shelley 1818, 50]) and the reasons given for withholding from Elizabeth news of Victor's illness after he has faced his creation (". . . How wretched my sickness would make Elizabeth" [1818, 35]). Nothing in itself about either of these usages of the word surprises; they exist as possibilities within language before the wretch himself comes to existence. His traces have inhabited language before he comes to be. What requires asking then is just what is it about the various sociopolitical discourses underwriting the text that brings the monster to creation out of the traces he has always already strewn throughout language and languages? What is it about the wrecked wretch or the wretched wreck (of the West) that calls him forth out of his textual traces at this particular moment of the text's composition, which moment, of course, is already moments, given the text's numerous revisions and editions?[11]

A crossing of registers occurs here. On the one hand, hideousness and murderous acts account for the monster's threat; on the other, that threat disrupts the symbolic order exemplified by the polyoptons noted above. It might suffice then to simply assert that the text performs its own monstrosity or that the actual writing of the text is its own monster, its hideous progeny. That also means, however, that Mary Shelley's monster stages its own genesis amid the contingencies, historical and local, that condition its writing.

While much has been written that casts the tensions that exist between Victor's time away from home creating and pursuing a monster and the apparent domestic tranquility that calls him back home, or between the self-seclusion of one driven to "discover the hidden laws of nature" (Shelley 1818, 16) and the outward magnificence of Geneva and its surroundings, such observations merely juxtapose the blissful domestic complementarity between spouses with the Promethean ambitions of the male spouse seeking "a final cause of all things" (Shelley 1818, 19). But the family's preferred residence on the eastern shore of the lake "in considerable seclusion" (Shelley 1818, 19) suggests that Victor's choice is not as distinct as it might seem; he is to choose between two kinds of isolation. The choice is not between a social and an asocial existence but rather between living among one's own or with oneself and an "other."

This binary is evident as well elsewhere. The monster, as we will see, embodies a battle of the sexes whose governing conflict is between fathers and mothers. For when we factor in that the novel itself is a monster, a hideous progeny, the complementarity suggested by Victor and his long-time friend and future colonialist Clerval may seem neat and tidy, but the scenes of that conflict, the very writing of the novel, already create a family drama in which not all the constituent or psychic parts fit or accommodate each other. The monster can no longer be seen, as merely the embodiment of a desire to exclude the feminine, but one that is also the embodiment of the feminine still seeking a genre or voice of its own. The authority granted the scientist Victor is contested in some fashion by Mary Shelley's own coming to be or writing of herself in the text.

The monster comes to be the expression of the will that seeks its own completion in a mirroring self-sameness. He threatens the domestic front by toppling the patriarch. In a remarkable piece of analysis, William Vedeer lists the order of the monster's victims as they proceed backward through a portion of the alphabet: William, Justine, Henry, Elizabeth, Alphonse. The progression also corresponds to an increased level of familial ties, ending with the father and thus the law of the household (Shelley 152–53). After

Alphonse, there is nowhere else to go. The monster has uprooted the patriarchy, and its remains, as we will see in the course of the next two chapters, come to reconstitute a new kind of monster: the homosexual.

> I arrived at Geneva. My father and Ernest yet lived . . . I see [my father] now, excellent and venerable old man! his eyes wandered in vacancy, for they had lost their charm and their delight—his Elizabeth, his more than daughter, whom he doted on with all that affection which a man feels . . . in the decline of life. . . . Cursed, cursed be the fiend that brought misery on his grey hairs and doomed him to waste in wretchedness! (Shelley 1818, 139).

Shortly thereafter, Alphonse dies in Victor's arms. The implications of the quote are not too complex. Frankenstein has created the wretch whose wretchedness has spread and doomed the father. Just as interesting are the grammatical shifts in the passage: from the past tense to the present tense to the putative and then back to the past tense. If such shifts recall the semantic migrations discussed earlier with "wretch" and suggest a temporality equally in flux, such fluidity contrasts with the closeness of the family romance in which Elizabeth is something more than just a daughter to her adoptive father. As we will see, what Vedeer compartmentalizes as Eros or as a destructive bond between two men, could just as easily be read as marking a series of displacements that hide other unrealized possibilities for coming together. The patricide apparently at the apex of the family drama obscures and also throws into relief the matricides or the making disappear of mothers that supplies the texts with energies that seek to break out of the family romance. Uprooting the patriarchy—and that is how Vedeer sees the monster's murderous acts—presupposes a matricide to foreclose possibilities of fathers producing heirs.

Mary Shelley's Progeny

As effectively as psychoanalytic approaches such as Vedeer's situate the novel in Mary Shelley's own struggle with a husband who exhibited the kind of wretchedness depicted in the novel, anchoring the dynamics of the story in a psychoanalytic biography elides the biographical struggle that, according to Barbara Johnson, is the novel itself.[12] The experiencing of the novel or of its writing points to events that exceed the limits of a biographical approach; Mary is also becoming Mary in the novel, and that Mary becomes a different one with each revision. Such an elision points to an equally critical issue. If for Vedeer androgyny promises domestic bliss, a healthy union of engendered traits, it just as likely obscures or dismisses possibilities outside the domestic sphere that might speak to a different kind of monster, one less tied to a binary opposition of the sexes and their eventual union in marital bliss.

Just how imbricated in each other are the monstrosities of writing and of creaturely creation goes well beyond the author's confession in the introduction that links the hideousness of the novel with that of the monster. As Johnson so eloquently argues, female authorship and an unbridled "male" drive for the absolute each have monsters to show for their efforts. But what further links the two activities is that both offer primal scenes of creation (Johnson 3). If Victor Frankenstein sets out to eliminate the mother by conceiving and giving birth without one, he is also the product of a text that maps the dual struggle of a female autobiographer: (1) "to resist the pressure of masculine autobiography as the only available genre, and (2) to describe the difficulty of conforming to a female ideal that is the product of the male imagination" (Johnson10). More to the point, the monster is over-determined; he is to be Victor's expression of the perfect creation, but at the same time the monster that is the text registers the hideous predicament of women seeking to fashion a self that is not merely a product of the male imagination. As Victor's creation the monster may threaten the family, but the hideous progeny that in the text exposes a monstrosity has already taken root in the family and looks to its own monstrous or hideous self to escape the pressures of conforming to a male idea.

The horror story offers a genre that brings the two, author and mad scientist, together in scenes or acts of matricide. Or rather, the female autobiographer working through the horrors of creation and procreation finds a suitable vehicle for expression in the scientist who dreams of carrying the corpse of his dead fiancée cum mother. That the horror of beholding the monster alive for the first time is accompanied by the dream of holding his dead mother provides a striking image of how monsters and mothers don't mix. As Frankenstein's description of the dream to Walton suggests, he becomes the monster who puts the seal of death on the fiancée/cousin, and as her lips begin to favor the same hue as the monster's, she becomes the mother, dead in the arms of the son who brought to life that which, at least in the dream, substitutes for the plague, namely Victor's kiss. As he imprinted "the first kiss on her [Elizabeth's] lips, they become livid with the hue of death; her features appeared to change and I thought I held the corpse of my dead mother in my arms" (Shelley 1818, 32). Yet this mother, as we recall, is the one who died while nursing and giving a second life to the stricken, adopted daughter Elizabeth. The implication of the dream might well be that the doctor has contracted a disease that kills women; his trafficking with the monster is what gives birth to the plague that has already killed the mother. In other words, the threat posed to mothers by the plague is already implicated in a family drama that has yet to play out. The monster is born only after he has arrived, only thus can the threat be contained or identified. For Verdeer the eventual goal of the monster is to eliminate the patriarch, but preceding the series of murders that leads to Alphonse, a matricide or dreams of one have already taken hold.

Indeed, mothers are at extreme risk in the novel. Johnson's claim that the text is Mary's experience of a woman negotiating the difficulties of fashioning an autobiographical self, which is always already subjected to conventions of male authorship, means the mother is always displaced or silenced. Caroline is without a mother, a condition that allows Alphonse to marry her, once her father's financial ruin leads him to an early death. All of this was made possible because the father had been among Alphonse's most trusted friends. The restoration of some kind of family out of those ruins requires another act of selective kindness to complete what will become the quaint nuclear family of four, namely the adoption of the blond orphan Elizabeth. Of course, Elizabeth repays her adoptive mother by infecting her with scarlet fever, which then results in the death of another mother. The monster's repeated warning to the doctor, "I shall be with you on your wedding night," ensures that the maiden Elizabeth will never become a mother (Shelley 1818, 117). Any hopes for the monster to produce offspring die when Frankenstein destroys his bride. Autobiography, self-creation, cannot abide mothers and brides.

Simply refusing the task is apparently not sufficient. Frankenstein can only recognize the dangers inherent in the monster's wish after he has begun to see the bride take shape. "[O]ne of the first results of those sympathies for which the demon thirsted would be children, and a race of devils would be propagated upon the earth, who might make the very existence of the species of man a condition precarious and full of terror" (Shelley 1818, 115). Such belated recognition of the bride's possibility of becoming a mother supplies the compensatory pleasure of destroying the incalculable female counterpart of his monster and any possibility for producing offspring. So, when Johnson asserts that all the autobiographies inscribed in the text (Walton, Frankenstein, the monster) are mirrors of the character's transgressions, those transgressions are linked to the death or disappearance of mothers.

While reducing the various threats to the family to a singular desire for a kind of matricide risks overlooking the other historical currents that contribute to the instability of the Swiss Family Frankenstein, we need only recall the various familial roles assumed by Elizabeth to gauge the breaks or potential break that the monster introduces in the silken. Her versatility helps preserve the family in the name of agape, a pure love whose purity is anchored in the purity of bloodlines, even if it means that line zigzags through generations as one player plays many parts:

> Alphonse: I confess, my son, that I have always looked forward to your marriage with *our* dear Elizabeth as the ties of our domestic comfort . . . You were attached to each other from your earliest infancy . . . you, perhaps, regard her as your sister, without any wish that she may become your wife. (Shelley 1818, 103; italics mine)

Whether it be mother, sister, cousin, fiancée—there seems to be no variation among the Frankenstein women; they are all ethereal creatures whose kindness and generosity could almost sicken. Agape refuses female difference; mothers are endlessly the same. The threat posed by the monster then is also a potential path out of numbness to difference. What is clear is that the integrity of the family unit depends upon a refusal to confuse attachments, even while family roles remain fluid. Nothing about Victor Frankenstein's response to his father's concerns suggests anything other than securing a self-sufficient or self-contained unit: "My dear Father, re-assure yourself, I love my cousin tenderly and sincerely. I never saw any woman who also excited as Elizabeth does my warmest admiration and affection. My future prospects are entirely bound up in expectation of our union" (Shelley 1818, 104).

However aroused Frankenstein is by thoughts of an upcoming marriage to a cousin/sister, libidinal energies also infuse the efforts of Frankenstein to create his offspring sans woman, whose grotesque appearance repulses even as it arouses and excites ("My heart palpitated . . ."; Shelley1818, 33). At the same time, the homoerotic charges of Walton's attentions to Frankenstein imprint every word about the latter in his letters to his sister, who arguably is an intermediary to redirect some of the erotic sentiments that Walton has for Frankenstein. She keeps him from going too far with Frankenstein by reminding him of domestic duties. Desire, it seems, can circulate about as freely as the monster does through the symbolic. Attractions of all sorts, ones that would be enabled by such wild circulation, are contained by reading the matricide as a need to protect the family rather than an impetus to seek its dissolution. Victor's impending marriage to his cousin attempts to secure endogamy, but the monster has always already invaded that family circle; missing mothers attest to his presence.

Moreover, only marked as already diseased can Victor pursue with all his energies and heart what was supposed to be the ideal male. The dream grants him that license but only insofar as the pursuit is now plagued from the start, or rather, the pursuit is the plague. Having created a monster whose string of murders will extend to the heart of the patriarchal order allows Victor to pursue an Other, who outwardly appears to be male, while all along defending such an escape from the welcoming arms of the family by insisting on the need to protect them from something he dare not name. A reckless pursuit of an Other, whose homicidal tendencies are a result of Frankenstein's experiments and determination to break out from the ranks (of family), allows the doctor to justify a preoccupation with the monster and pursue him with all the passion a slave does his master. He has it both ways; ideally, he gets to kill the family and still speak as its savior and protector. Just as matricide both served as a call to close ranks around the family and to explore territories previously foreclosed, Victor's ambivalent relationship to the monster (to the point of becoming the monster in the dream) exposes the dual character of the monster. His repugnant appearance deprives him of family, but as the embodiment and emblem of matricide, he also gives expression to a nascent Oedipal impulse that infects the family and seeks to dethrone the father. Agape is now monstrously other, eros. Read as wish fulfillment, Victor's dream not only renders the monster and him indistinguishable, but it also ties thanatos to eros. However mightily he claims to protect his family from the monster, his dream identifies the threat to the family as a death drive that inhabits Victor and monster alike. And the power of the dream is enough to suggest that the hideousness of the monster derives equally from exposing these ugly secrets that underwrite the family romance on the cusp of psychoanalysis's birth. Nonetheless, reading the dream according to the economies of the pleasure principle or simply as wish fulfillment is not yet the only way to read dreams. By doing so we will see how the text can be read to accommodate psychoanalysis' pathologization of sexuality as well as expose how the family unit is never discrete, always infected from within by a monster of its own making.

The monster emblematizes the emerging threat to the traditional Swiss family. And that threat expresses itself repeatedly in matricide, which in turn structures and underwrites Mary Shelley's and Frankenstein's efforts. This matricide, of course, is quite over-determined: (1) as an expression of the imminent and inherent dangers to the family whereby the writing or experience of writing autobiography requires the elimination of the mother, and (2) as the intention to eliminate women from the (pro)creative process. Mothers are not needed for monsters to be produced and possibly reproduce. Breaking from the father leads Frankenstein to pursue interests linked to the death or even repeated death of the mother(s). If the emerging science of psychoanalysis proposes that the law of the father means to place the mother out of reach, the novel obliges; but by exposing the ugly secrets that underwrite the family romance, the novel also hands the father and the author of the law over to the very same monster. As agape foundered on the erotic tension that underwrites the family romance, the father succumbs, or eventually succumbs to a law he comes to instantiate. In the beginning the law is divided against itself.

The Ends of Family

The analysis above demonstrates how confused and upended symbolic systems are as a result of the monster's wild circulation through all linguistic orders and topographies. Mothers and fathers, it could be said, are vying to be on top. In trying to sort through all of this pre-Oedipal confusion, I want to point out that at this moment in 1818 matricide is realized or actualized as a textual event. But as Julia Kristeva has argued—and we will return to her at the end of the chapter—matricide is incomplete or unrealized in the nuclear family. In the meantime, we can assert that no mapping of Oedipal desires in the text is all that readable without eliminating a narrative frame or two. Any father/son conflict, which places the mother beyond the reach of the son and motivates the latter to go where no man has ever gone before, arouses feelings of an extraordinary sort in the wayward son as exemplified here by Walton: "There is something at work in my soul, which I do not understand" (Shelley 1818, 4). Understanding it, at least at this point, requires reincorporating those passions into a more familiar one: "I have found a man, who before his spirit had been broken by misery, I should have been happy to have possessed as the brother of my heart" (Shelley 1818,10). Walton comes to see the friend he never had as a member of his family's heart, once the friend has become spiritless. That is to say, passions matter less perhaps than timing. The lack inherent in the family structure finds some sort of fulfillment in the remembrance of miseries that result from having sought to push beyond the boundaries of the social order. But pursuit of the secrets of nature fuel a secret passion or passions that underwrite the law of the father while simultaneously promoting a homosocial structure ("Yet his manners are so conciliating and gentle that the sailors are all interested in him . . ."; Shelley 11), that hardly lacks erotic overtones: "I was easily led by the sympathy which he evinced to give utterance to the burning ardour of my soul" (1818, Shelley 10). A self-destructive passion ("I would sacrifice my fortune, my existence, my every hope, to the furtherance of my enterprise" [1818, Shelley 10]), borne of the family romance and always already doomed to falter on its Promethean ambitions, feeds off of its own belatedness or rear view that bonds male to male only once the new friend lingers in misery. Two things are thus apparent: (1) the object choice of at least the men is in flux; a division between cousin/sister/mother and brother/friend/soul mate begins to emerge that links the latter with death, destruction and unbridled narcissism, and (2) Male/male bonding has no future; more than monstrous, at least one party to the relation, is always already broken. But heterosexual unions fare no better. The fulfilled promise of the monster to be with his creator on his wedding night disrupts the most unambiguous scene of union, procreation and promise of a future. Not just the possibility of producing new Frankensteins is undone, but the fulfillment in generational transmission of values and beliefs is also disabled. The family has no future.[13]

Mary Shelley's response, as measured in the introduction of 1831, aligns well with these notions that the novel is pulled toward a restitution of institutions, a restoration of generational transmission in the wake of the French Revolution. Simply put, inherent pressures in the novel push it to speak on behalf of the family and other threatened institutions. "I am the more willing to comply . . ." she asserts in the opening of the 1831 introduction to the publisher's and presumably the public's wish to understand how she came upon such a horrific idea (Shelley 1831, V). Of course, we must be careful here. The exceptional duress that promoted such conciliations does not indict the 1818 version so much as it indicates how in the interim pressures to comply already reshape the text to harness those energies seeking restoration of the family. After all, the poor woman was desperate for money.[14] As many have previously noted, Frankenstein's culpability appears beyond question in the 1818 text: he could have controlled his quest for the "principle of life." The 1831 edition, however, portrays Frankenstein as incapable of free will, swept away by dreams inspired by the time. "Destiny was too potent, and her immutable laws had decreed my utter and terrible destruction" (Shelley 1831, 23).

What I have been suggesting all along is that pressures to comply—to close ranks around the family, to resist passions that transgress traditional boundaries—are already apparent from the start as a way to bring the monster under control. Frankenstein's dream, read as a testament to the psychological mess driving creation of a sociopathic monster, confirms internalization of guilt as a means to compartmentalize monstrosity. Such guilt may not perfectly align with its future mapping in psychoanalysis, but it is highly suggestive of Oedipal drives whose objects are yet to be codified by psychoanalysis. Nonetheless, such drives still indicate the potential threat posed by men pursuing men. These kinds of men no longer feel at home or have a place at home as Victor's remarks upon returning to his home indicate "I felt as if I were placed under a ban—as if I had no right to claim their sympathies—as if never more might I enjoy companionship with them" (Shelley 1818, 102).[15]

At this point, we might find it helpful to frame the nascent psychoanalytic framework that emerges in the text with Paul Sherwin's precise observation that "the monster's marginal place, neither inside or outside, is thus the place of differences" (Sherwin 893). The text proleptically prescribes the stakes and necessity of securing the margin by keeping the monster fenced out—his presence felt, but not acknowledged. As the site of difference, the monster must come to define his difference or have it defined for him so as to keep difference from differing from itself, to maintain the possibility of securing identity, and to restrict the spectrum of possible differences. And if Paul Sherwin avers, "for the psychoanalyst the creature's return amounts to "a bizarre [can I substitute "queer"] symptomatic return of the repressed . . . a figure that re-doubles Frankenstein's literal unconscious complex, which is already present as an apriori with a determinate constitution," he also admits that the monster is not a psychic entity (yet), but a real figure (Sherwin 893). That is to say, the repressed has not yet returned as a psychic entity; interiority is not yet configured. Vedeer, for example, can point to the feminization and loss of vitality in Frankenstein as he pursues his passion, but the signs that link such desire with impotency (an ineffectual pistol, a discarded oar; Shelley 1818, 95) only come to be encoded as such during the next century. As Jane Brown's remarkable study of Goethe's fashioning of a language for the emergence of repressed passion or interiority, Frankenstein appears at a time when the road toward pathologization has not yet been taken. The pressures of family, nation, and empire all contribute toward the specific shape monstrosity comes to assume, but only after psychoanalysis has established or created an interior space to accommodate and monitor the monster.

Monstrous and Pitiful

To this point, I have offered no reason how the monster's physical beauty comes to seduce in the few examples presented at the beginning of this chapter. No answer, of course, is forthcoming or could be. The many versions of Frankenstein that have appeared, even in the last years, attest to the narrowness but highly suggestive strain of monstrous transformations I consider. Still, the line from Shelley's monsters to gods is helpful. The seductive power of the monster testifies to the emergence of a death drive that attaches to male same-sex desire. A sickness until death (something that we will see already afflicts Werther) at the hands of a monster is the fate that awaits the male homosexual. Or rather, the fetching monster is infectious. Whatever directions, and there are many, that sexology pursued in the nineteenth century, one result is to assign to the male homosexual a desire that negates possibilities of a future. The threat posed by Frankenstein's monster to family, society, nation-building, and colonial conquest reconfigure that creature as a figure of seduction, who like a Pied Piper calls out to the queer to follow the monster out of respectable society into the clutches of death. At the very least, the seduction of the monster allows for society to separate the men from the "men."

By highlighting one revealing shift in the monster's attractive force, I hope to set up the possibility for considering what possibilities were foreclosed by a readings of Shelley's text that attend only to pressures to re-secure the family. Is there something about its push for family values that obscures something other than a death wish, something that awakens a potentiality beyond the margin, beyond the limits of desires? Godzilla, as we know, was the inevitable expression of the atomic bomb and its uncontainable destruction. Frankenstein, likewise, appears as an expression of the social turmoil following, in particular, the French Revolution. But Frankenstein holds out the possibility for befriending the monster, for a different politics of friendship that among men that demands abdication of the father's role in securing a future for the family.

To adumbrate these possibilities, I call attention first to the effusive display of self-pity by each of the figures triangulated in a world unfriendly to erotic drives.[16] Certainly, Frankenstein often appears more distraught over his own misery than that which he has caused others. A few examples can hardly exhaust just how often the doctor's empathy ultimately is reserved for himself:

> Above the picture appeared a vast and dim scene of evil, and I foresaw obscurely that I was destined to become the most wretched of human beings. Alas! I prophesied truly, and failed only in one single circumstance, that in all the misery I imagined and dreaded, I did not conceive the hundreth part of the anguish I was destined to endure. (Shelley 1818, 45)

> I was guiltless, but I had indeed drawn down a horrible curse upon my head, as mortal as that of crime. (Shelley 1818, 109)

> I cannot pretend to describe what I then felt. Words cannot convey an idea of the heart-sickening despair that I then endured. (Shelley 1818, 51)

The monster, while certainly blameless for the hideous fate visited upon him for simply looking hideous, proves equally adept at playing the victim despite littering the field with victims of his own vengeance. "No one can conceive the anguish which I suffered during the remainder of the night" (Shelley 1818, 47), or "Must I be hated, who am miserable beyond all living things?" (1818, 64), or "Everywhere I see bliss, from which I alone am irrevocably excluded" (Shelley 1818, 64). Such self-pity comes, of course, to justify his serial killings: "Can you wonder that such thoughts [of social ostracism from "beautiful creatures] transported me with rage?" or . . . "the murder I have committed because I am forever robbed of all that she could me, she shall atone." (Shelley 1818, 98, 98)

At times, the two seemed engaged in a game of who suffered most: "Blasted as thou wert, my agony was still superior to thine; for the bitter sting of remorse will not cease to rankle in my wounds until death shall close them for ever" (Shelley 1818, 158). These final words of the monster also demonstrate how such contests driven by self-pity eventually inspire a death wish on the part of the monster: "I shall ascend my funeral pyre triumphantly, and exult in the agony of the torturing flames" (Shelley 1818, 158). His homicidal impulses, now directed inward, promise his absence, his leaving the scene only to appear, of course, in different, more fetching guises in the future or, as we shall see in the next chapter, hovering off scene, marginalized or closeted in a space of interiority.

For readers of Rousseau, such self-incriminations and even self-indulgence are quite familiar. They speak to his battle for sovereignty over the emotions, for cultivation of a self that masters through repression storms of emotion. "Passion has always had to be controlled in European culture [. . .]. Special in Rousseau is what is now called 'repression,' the character's insistent belief that they have conquered their passions when they really haven't" (J. Brown 19). And if, as in *Frankenstein*, trappings of the nuclear family with all the joys of homeland form the basis for the law of the father to control and channel passions, then the monster has already been marked as a bearer of unnatural passions or desires from the start. That is to say, Aristotle's definition of a monster as an unnatural being bearing a false resemblance to another creature (Huet 3–4) finds that what is added to the mix or what from the outside adulterates the purity of the species is an unnatural desire that comes, as in "Death in Venice" and, as we will see, in *The Sorrows of Young Werther*, to seek its own extinction.

Let me back up for a moment. Self-recriminations begin to offer a possible space for interiority to take hold, a place to contain what is repressed. The passages to follow indicate that territorializing the monster by confining him to an interior space already begins to anticipate the characteristics that will come to cleave to the homosexual after such an interior space is fully completed or adumbrated by psychoanalysis. We have already noted above some similar passages that point to how the ambiguity of certain statements can be settled, once they begin to refer to the modern homosexual. Likewise, the sickness of the other male or, as Vedeer argues, the eventual sapping of vital life energies that results from Eros or its related pursuits may find confirmation in Victor's comatose state upon being rescued by Walton and his crew, but Victor's new-found companion—outside the bounds of English society—finds enough rejuvenation in that new bond to become alert, voluble, and more or less account for almost all of the novel's material. Confiding to his new mate, Walton, Dr. Frankenstein is revived through storytelling, sharing his deepest secrets to another man. Another way to understand the distinctions I am trying to make is to recall how Vedeer's psychoanalytic reading understands male/male bonding to be absolutely destructive, the energies released by Eros disable any possibility of domestic tranquility, which, he claims, is Mary's aim. But when we remember how the writing of the novel itself is a hideous or monstrous progeny that overlays or at least confuses any clear sighting of the monster, then Vedeer's reading demonstrates how psychoanalysis comes to view the monster as a debilitating influence that makes of male scientists a slave and that needs to be exiled or territorialized. ("You are my creator, but I am your master,—obey!"; Shelley 1818, 116). The emergence of an interiority allows for compartmentalization. Such a retrospective reading of the exchange below reveals how the scrambled or unreadable energies of the text come to mirror the fate of the homosexual, once the nuclear family with the father at its head is (re)configured.

Frankenstein does away with mothers, and the monster can only be what he is by emblematizing the matricide that underwrites the emerging social order. How the opening up of a space of interiority, of an unconscious receptacle of repressed energies, anticipates descriptions of the homosexual is quite legible in the following two passages: "Everywhere I see bliss, from which I alone am irrevocably excluded" (The creature on the ills of being a "fallen angel" rather than the doctor's "Adam"; Shelley1818, 64). To which his creator replies, "I will not hear you. There can be no community between you and me" (Shelley 1818, 64.) The first quote recalls the introduction and D. A. Miller's understanding of a Stonewall generation who never fancied social acceptance and whose pleasure was linked to such destitution, a destitution whose dreams of a mate were unrealizable. In fact, the creature's difference is so fundamental that he comes to recognize himself as "not even of the same nature of man," however noble his intentions might have been (Shelley 1818, 79). Echoes of an unnatural desire linked to the pleasures of resentment threaten to become and do become sociopathic and fatal for the family.

Irrevocably excluded, fallen from grace into the reaches of the damned, and a threat to the established roots of family if for no other reason than central to his creation is matricide, the monster begins to acquire characteristics that anticipate later depictions of the homosexual as the Godzilla of family values. His partner, the doctor, of course, has no problem understanding how the threat of engaging with self-creation extends beyond the horrors of that creation to his own relations and passions: "I must absent myself from all I love . . . and put an end to my slavery forever" (Shelley

1818, 104). Just how unfit for citizenship the homosexual will become, if we recall Bersani, is already embedded in the nativist sentiments expressed by Frankenstein as he returns home upon news of poor William's death: "My country, my beloved country! Who but a native can tell the delight I took in again beholding thy streams, thy mountains, and, more than all, thy lovely lake" (Shelley 1818, 45). And nature's poetry, Clerval, may offer a domesticated alternative to the wild pursuits of the erotically charged mad scientist, but such an alternative involves rape of another sort: "[Clerval's] design was to visit India, in the belief that he had in his knowledge of its various languages, and in the views he had taken of its society, the means of materially assisting the progress of European colonization and trade" (Shelley 1818, 108; as reported by Frankenstein). The convergence of values and interests is clear (family, nation, colonies, and god) which, in turn, renders the monster a threat to the integrity and continuation of the family. But the new assemblage of these interests is well on its way to sequestering that threat in the depths of the unconscious. And any expression of those monstrous or repressed desires makes of that person a bearer of something unnatural who is unfit for human society and who saps vital life energies from those that person encounters.

Another way to see the convergence of such energies to produce a pathologized sexual other is to consider the Christian medieval understanding of a monster as a visual sign of a warning from God. Combine that with Aristotle's definition of a monster as an unnatural being bearing a false resemblance to another creature, and one can see how little tweaking is needed to append that unnaturalness to a sexual other once sexology begins to dominate the scientific discourse of the nineteenth century. AIDS as a punishment from God for unnatural practices among queers is the predictable outcome of such logic. Even Diderot contributes to the thinking that calls for extinguishing carriers of the unnatural: "What is a monster? A being whose duration is incompatible with the existing order" (Huet 89). Little is needed to see how that which is incompatible with the existing order threatens that order by its very existence; in other words, it is a disease that needs to be killed.

The Godzilla of Family Values

In conclusion, I would like to recast the nascent psychoanalytic model that has emerged as a philosophical one, namely to conceive of the monster's creation in terms of Fichte's "Tathandlung." It is important to recall that the unconscious at this time is a null, an emptiness rather than a repository for repressed desires.[17] What Fichte's idealist philosophy does is: (1) explain how the self becomes its own creation or simply posits itself, and (2) prepare a space of interiority for the self that shirks back at beholding itself as other. Given that psychoanalysis has not yet sanctioned an interior space to repress unnatural desires, Fichte's philosophy, it seems to me, is nicely poised between inside and outside, negotiating a margin that has yet to take shape. Most important is Fichte's idealist philosophy that begins with a simple demonstration of identity, $A = A$; that is to say, immune to any sort of variable, this statement of identity insists upon the primacy of the identity between subject and object for any kind of consciousness to emerge. Before any object can present itself to consciousness, there must always already have been an originary act of self-positing, or "Tathandlung," in which the limits of the self, of self-positing are established. This preconscious activity is what allows the self to become conscious of objects that appear outside of itself, for no other reason than the self cannot have itself as an object of consciousness. Without taking up the discussion of freedom that emerges from this initial act of self-positing, it is easy to see how mediation that links or re-links the object to its origin in the subject delays the act of self-recognition, renders in that interval the self in its posited being different, distorted as if in a mirror, or just other. The self appears monstrously other to itself. What attributes come to obtain after such monstrosity is contained or tamed are united by a desire for endogamy, a retreat from threatening otherness. And as we have also noted, the emerging figure of the homosexual poses significant risk, embracing that otherness instead of retreating to some perch to police the margins. But if heteronormativity comes to rely on an argument for reuniting different sexes or some version of happiness or coming together as opposites, the Fichtean model provides a means to question that assertion. Instead of retreating to an interior space to reclaim the self's priority, the self, given to seeking out itself in the otherness that it is, can embrace such abjection, such obliteration in the face of a non-sublatable otherness.

Walton's expedition mimics a Fichtean exercise of the self-reaching its own self-imposed limit and turning back. Walton comes to discover that he will not be the first to reach the North Pole, the monster will already have been there by the time he arrives. The North Pole is no longer unconscious, by which I really mean undiscovered. Heeding the pleas of his crew, Walton turns back. He comes to a limit of an already discovered frontier that horrifies and terrifies rather than exalts. There is nothing to cross; humankind has already been there and done that. His retreat, although clothed in the jargon of compassion and a reawakened empathy for crew, mirrors the circular course traveled by the self in confronting an Otherness that is the self in exile. Just as the self seeks restoration of family and roots, Walton opts to do the same. Exploration turns out not to be his thing.

Frankenstein signals a move toward securing the home front from such otherness. That allows for the recognition of a trajectory—only one among many, for sure—that gives the monster an air of irresistibility, an embodiment of that which is on its way to being repressed, to giving the unconscious content. Simply stated, he bears an uncanny resemblance to the self in search of itself. More important, the self-recriminations, the effusive displays of self-pity require a positing of the self, along Fichetean terms, given how the self requires another self to pity or criminalize. Self-pity becomes disgust with oneself that, as Cohn averred with the shift of the narrator's judgment of Aschenbach, becomes societal disgust of the queer on the prowl for youngsters or, in the case of *Gods and Monsters*, of the creator of the cinematic *Frankenstein*, looking to corrupt the few good men that remain. Frankenstein's self-pity finds a correlative in the self-abnegation that plagues the tightfisted Aschenbach. The Fichetan self, rendered abject by confrontation with the self in its otherness, comes to despise itself to the point that it invites the repudiation of a society hell bent on driving that loathsome being to off itself. Almost. Foucault's repressive hypothesis would have us recognize that the causal chain is reversed; the self's insistence on protecting its selfhood, preserving its borders, and keeping its lakes, mountains and skies pure is what drives these two twentieth-century Frankensteins, Aschenbach and Whale, to go over the edge.

The central argument of this book is that another potentiality remains untapped, unrealized, unacknowledged with the initial act of self-positing. To go over the edge is also to escape the trappings of the family and homeland, to become, at least in part, invisible and beyond the reach of the panopticon. Frankenstein's creatures are beings who signal to their creators to pursue an eccentric course, to go over the edge. Stated otherwise, what if the self were to allow for itself to become fragmented, disoriented, and un-reconstructable in the face of otherness? In coming up against its own self-imposed limits ("Anstoß"), the self succumbs and embraces its state of abjection: "I experience abjection only if an Other has settled in place and stead of what will be 'me'" (Kristeva, 6). The mention of horror and abjection throughout this chapter calls forth the work of Kristeva, for a pre-symbolic language not dependent upon an unrealized matricide and submission to paternal law, whereas in *Frankenstein*, the matricide is completed.[18] The following sentence from the opening pages of *Powers of Horror* finds apt repercussions in *Frankenstein*: "Out of the daze that has petrified him before the untouchable, impossible, absent body of the mother, a daze that has cut off his impulses from their objects, out of such daze he causes . . . fear" (Kristeva 6). Easily deciphered here is a profile of the monster, cut off from the absent body of the mother and arousing fear. But no two selves, as the ceaseless framing of the novel suggests, are entirely distinguishable. The imperative to embrace one's abjectness thus easily transfers to the doctor. "Repudiate the name of the Father" (Kristeva 7, trans. altered). At that point, homecomings are impossible, but for Kristeva a different, messianic possibility emerges: "Abjection is a resurrection that has gone through the death (of the ego). It is an alchemy that transforms the death drive into a start of life, a new significance" (Kristeva 15).

The remainder of this book is given to tracing that transformation, to identifying textual moments that bring into being "monsters" that testify to a return of the shattered self, remnants of a self that have always already been shattered, often rendered mute like a marionette or already dead before its time like the AIDS patient. What Kristeva says of this resurrection in terms of Aristotelian catharsis is particularly instructive: The shattering otherness returns (in the form of the chorus) in sound and rhythm, "trace[s], and concatenation[s]" (29). "Aristotle seems to say that there is a discourse of sex and that is not the discourse of knowledge—it is the only possible catharsis [Recall the Quilt project]. That discourse is audible, and through the speech that it mimics it repeats on another register what [knowledge] does not say" (29); that is, what has not yet not been said but still repeats, and mimics. Rethought under the terms proposed by Fichte, Frankenstein should see in his monster the possibility of a new best friend, pieced together from fragments of the dead in the laboratory and a literal reconfiguration and reanimation of the return of the other(s) as an invitation to hear a different call, a different drummer. The following chapters will attempt to find articulations of those echoes.

2

Peter Schlemihl's Wondrous Story or the Genesis of a Queer Jewish Outlaw

The opening episode in Jiri Weil's *Mendelssohn is on the Roof* recounts the peculiar fate of Jewish-German identity that had riddled Germany's own troubled concept of itself as a "Volk" since the Enlightenment. Julius Schlesinger, a municipal officer and a candidate for the SS, sends two Czech workmen onto the roof to perform a task that Schlesinger's own fear of heights prevents him from doing. The roof, despite its elegant and imposing panoply of statues of German composers, is scarred by a single form, that of the Jew Moses Mendelssohn. Schlesinger, eager—given the suspicions raised by his name—to prove his Aryan origins, orders the workmen to remove the statue. Unversed in the fundamentals of German music and racial science, the workmen have no way to determine which among the many statues represents Mendelssohn. Schlesinger, who has just completed a course on racial science called "World View" and studied a series of slides illustrating the "Jewish difference," instructs the workmen simply to find the statue with the biggest nose and remove it. After a quick survey of noses and their lengths, the workmen put their noose around the neck of the statue with the oddest nose and begin pulling at the rope. Suddenly, the order to desist is given. The statue, as it turns out, was not of Felix Mendelssohn but rather of Richard Wagner.

Of course, the task posed a more difficult challenge than the mere sizing up of noses would indicate. Since 1812 Felix Mendelssohn's parents, Abraham and Lea, had used the name Bartholdy, and with their baptisms in 1822 the name became official. Like his siblings, Felix was raised with no religious education until 1816 when he became baptized at age seven in a Reform Christian Church. Informing his brother of the name change, Abraham, son of Germany's most famous and celebrated Haskalah Jew Moses, made no attempt to hide his complete withdrawal from the fold: "There can no more be a Christian Mendelssohn than there can be a Jewish Confucius."[1] Neither name nor nose would any longer suffice to isolate the Jewish interloper.

As the above episode suggests, traditional markers of Jewish identity and difference had become increasingly unreliable or irrelevant as Jews, emancipated from the ghetto, in the nineteenth century began to participate in the social and cultural life of Germany. Although the events in Weil's work occur at a time when efforts to resecure Jewish difference were accompanied by an unprecedented genocidal campaign, the compulsion to reaffirm the otherness of the Jew surfaced, as we shall see, with the first stirrings of emancipation.[2] In the case of Felix Mendelssohn the most indelible if not visible sign of Jewish difference was also missing. His parents emphatically refused to have Felix circumcised.

Nowhere more effectively is the effort to reinscribe Jewish difference encoded than in Adalbert Charmisso's "Peter Schlemihl and His Wondrous Story." Schlemihl's lack of substance (i.e., lack of a shadow) produces a set of behaviors and responses that give rise to a new way of defining the Jew as outsider. Schlemihl's story charts the new manner in which the so-called "moral deficiency" of the Jews will come to be expressed in the emerging civil society of Germany at the beginning of the nineteenth century.[3] The observation that Schlemihl is a Jew comes so late in the text precisely because the text gives rise and sets in play a new constellation of characteristics to marshal against the Jew. Moreover, the process by which the Jew or *schlemiel* seeks to restore his identity or shadow gives rise to a form of narcissistic and/or homoerotic desire. That is to say, the Jew who found that actions intended to advance assimilation serve only to re-anchor his ethnicity according to a set of revisionist terms also finds that his responses to that redefinition of his character redirect his social urges. The Jew who would be German is aberrant, and, if we read with Foucault, this means that due to the desire produced by such efforts to assimilate, s/he is essentially or essentialized as other.[4]

In the previous chapter the monster emerged as a threat to the social order. Saving that order—or at least preserving the possibility that the monster could be restrained—was enabled by the easy recognition of that threat. Monsters are insufferably ugly. In this chapter, the threat to

German society is posed by one who can pose all too easily as a German. That is to say, as Jews began to attempt to assimilate and adopt the dress and customs of Germans, the monster from within becomes difficult to distinguish from "real" Germans. For a people in search of a (national) identity, identifying the enemy is, if we recall Carl Schmitt, the essence of the political. As such, a new means to mark the Jew as inalterably other requires a different assemblage or a recasting of social relations to link the Jew with a new kind of otherness—as a sexual invert. No longer does the Jew's religion, which s/he can cast off as out-of-date, provide the nascent body politic with its necessary enemy, but rather something potentially more insidious and pathological demands his diseased body be excised from the body politic. There is no conversion therapy for sexual inversion. What this chapter sets out to do is offer a reading of *Peter Schlemihl* that demonstrates how Jewishness and male same-sex desire converge to produce a Jew that could never truly pass as a German.

As an attempt to offer one possible genesis of homosexuality, I hope to demonstrate how the logic of inversion, or the convergence of two kinds of difference, enables the production of a vocabulary or sign system to encode and register the emergence of the modern homosexual. The consequences and possibilities of that sign system are taken up in the next chapter. While the Jewish question is foregrounded—Schlemihl is after all a Jew before he becomes a homosexual *avant la lettre*—an equally important task of this chapter is to understand how the apparatus of sexuality begins its deployment, how assemblages of power reconfigure to produce a new kind of outlaw, securely circumscribed, albeit in the dark, within the scope of the panopticon. Part of that deployment is to construct an interior space—in this instance a closet—that keeps the new emerging monster contained or territorialized. At the same time—and this also explains the choice of Schlemihl—the monster is produced or called forth by the very apparatus that seeks to marginalize and silence it.[5] In terms of the overall theoretical argument, the disappearance of the protagonist at the end of the novella suggests the possibility that this newly born, queer Jewish outlaw exceeds the reach of the West's emerging biopolitical enterprise. Exploring how this fugitive spirit comes to inhabit and unsettle terrain far removed from his apparent temporary abode in the Orient will be the subject of the final chapters of this book. In the meantime, let us recall Puar's analysis of the current geopolitical map that casts the Arab as the sexual deviant or outlaw, a formation whose initial disseminations can be espied in part by Chamisso's text.

Shadows and Reflections

Any attempt to capture the confusion inaugurated by the potential divide between inside and outside finds ample evidence, of course, in the works of E. T. A. Hoffmann. Before discussing the particular junction between Jew and queer in Schlemihl, I want to explore the difficulties posed for narration by interiority in Hoffmann. I do so to emphasize the challenges presented by interiority and how it could be said to call forth psychoanalysis to navigate its minefield. Chamisso's text will then be read to expose pressures of a different but related sort unacknowledged by Freud: the need to re-ghettoize the Jew.[6] Hoffmann's work captures the need to align interior experiences with an external world through some kind of logic that allows, so to speak, the eyes to be a reliable window to the soul. The Sandman's obsession with eyes and his removal of them from his apparent victims literalize the attempt to look inside, to expose the black hole where repressed desire is beginning to seek refuge. The eyes also offer confirmation, should they reveal an interior force that animates them, that the owner of such eyes is in fact a real living being and not an automaton.

The struggle to find a language other than the elusive one offered by limpid eyes occupies, as we know, the opening sections of *The Sandman*. The narrator, in fact, absent at the start save for presenting three letters, two from Nathaniel to his friend Lothar (the narrator) and one from his beloved Clara. Afterward, the narrator explains his dereliction of duty in allowing the letters to begin his tale by insisting that traditional openings of narratives were unable to carry the weight of this new task: capturing the interior life of the protagonist. "No words came to me capable in the least of reflecting the color and luster of that internal image" (Hoffman 131; all translations mine). How could the narrator proceed? For one, disentangling Nathaniel's inner experience from his own is nearly impossible. "All that was marvelous and odd about his story filled my soul." Such an admission of transference or a wish for such suggests that what one ascribes to Nathaniel is first mediated by the narrator as he tries to mediate the feelings aroused by Nathaniel's experience. Nathaniel's first letter falls into the hands of Clara, who dismisses Nathaniel's fears by insisting that the Sandman is a figment of his imagination. That aside, the wayward trail of the letter, falling into the hands of one who denies the reality of the Sandman, indicates how fraught with ambiguity and a lack of clarity such translations of feelings and emotions become.

It does not take long, of course, for psychoanalysis to rearrange the disjointed parts of the text and offer readings that come to be organized around a primal scene. As we know, Freud is in a position of sufficient posteriority to propose as primal the scene in which Nathaniel partially observes from behind a curtain his father and Coppelius huddled around a hearth. That is, Freud's interpretation is psychoanalysis's own experience of "Nachträglichkeit," the coming-to-mean something of events or dreams that seem initially too polyvalent to permit meaning to attach to them. If one examines the language of the scene in question, a certain vocabulary does present itself that aligns neatly with possible psychosexual content. "My father opened the door of what I thought was a cupboard. But what I saw was no cupboard, but rather a black cavity with all sorts of strange instruments lying around. Oh my God! As my father stooped down to the fire, he looked completely different. Some horrid convulsive pain seemed to distort his mild, honest features into a repulsive and ugly image of the devil. He looked like Coppelius, whom I saw brandishing red hot tongs" (Hoffmann 122–23). For Freud, whose concern is focused on the source of the uncanny or Nathaniel's experiences of repetition as both familiar and unfamiliar, Nathaniel's unease stems from repressed desires and fear. Specifically, it is the fear of the Sandman stealing his eyes that leads Freud to the following observation: "the fear of going blind is often enough a substitute for the dread of being castrated" (Freud, SE XVIII 338). Primal scenes, constructed as they are after the fact and through no small measure of projection or transference by the analyst, are always only enabled by a supplement or a non-coincidence of what appears to be the same. In this instance, the scene is narrated by the patient as reconstructed by Freud years later.[7] The dream takes place in many places and many times, yet it is such tergiversations on the part of Nathaniel in telling this particular aspect of his story that convinces Freud of its significance. But even if we grant Freud license to regard this as the primal scene which he then links to fears of castration, that does not eliminate the potential for other readings, other mappings of desire. Melanie Klein, for example, associates the fear not with castration but rather with death.[8] Above all, the text already points to homosexuality as a logic to contain differences on all of these levels. As Hélène Cixous points out, what the text tries to repress but cannot is its homosexuality. Freud only mentions Olympia in a footnote, and further declares that Nathaniel was incapable of copulating with a woman in that same aside (Cixous 537–38). Indeed, not much is required to suggest that the scene describes anal intercourse between two men; the father bending over in pain as he is mounted by Coppelius brandishing red-hot tongs.

The text never says that, and nor does Freud. But if he is seeking to repress the text's movements in that direction, as Hélène Cixous argues, he does nothing of the sort in the third of his *Three Case Studies of Sexuality*, namely the case of the Wolfman or Sergei Pankejoff, a Russian aristocrat who also displayed traits of an anal retentive personality, including the need for enemas. Freud bases his diagnosis on a dream the patient had as a child in which several white wolves are sitting on a big walnut tree with ears "pricked like dogs when they pay attention to something" (Freud, *Three Case Studies* 213). The patient awoke with fear, which in turn signals for Freud that underwriting the dream is a traumatic event: the child witnessing one afternoon, at the age of one-and-a-half, his parents having anal intercourse.

In this instance, there is no effort to repress homosexuality. "It was only when, during the analytic treatment, it became possible to liberate his shackled homosexuality that this state of affairs showed any improvement" (Freud, *Three Case Histories* 260). By freeing "each piece of the homosexual libido" the patient sought out some means to express such pieces of his liberated self to benefit the common good" (Freud, *Three Case Histories* 260). What difference in the two stories allows for the dots to be connected, for anal eroticism and homoerotic expression to come out in this text, whereas the Sandman repressed it? More than the mere failure of the Sandman to accomplish such repression is the pulling back of the curtain that obscured Nathaniel's vision of the primal scene. The Wolfman, likewise, reports that he felt "hidden from the world by a veil" that only tore after an enema had allowed him to evacuate his bowel (Freud, *Three Case Studies* 264). When that veil is removed, when Freud pushes back the curtain, the deferred meanings of these primal scenes become readable, offering a pathology of homosexuality. As Deleuze and Guattari in *Anti Oedipus* remind us, the Wolfman in particular reveals Freud's selective logic.[9] The evidence speaks for itself. Hiding behind a veil or ripping that veil could just as easily circulate metonymically in a heterosexual economy of desire, namely breaking the hymen of a virgin. More to the point is just how many possible primal scenes Hoffmann's "Sandman" offers: the vivid account of the Sandman that issues from the mouth of the governess, the visit of the apparent double of Coppelius that triggers Nathaniel's mental breakdown, or all of the scenes that include an encounter with Olympia. Once a light is filtered through the apparatus of sexuality (as evinced in this instance by Freud), a primal scene is illuminated that comes to allow for construction and pathologization of desire according to the anal erotics suggested by the scene at the hearth and realized by the Wolfman in his crib. As for the Wolfman, he disputed Freud's claim that he had been cured and spent nearly six decades in therapy. Shortly after completing his stint with Freud, the Wolfman developed a delusion; he would walk the streets holding a mirror in front of his face to observe what he insisted was a hole that had been drilled into his nose.[10]

As we recall, Frankenstein's monster never possessed a mirror image and circulated wildly through the symbolic order. Given that Peter Schlemihl loses his shadow, one might predict a related fate for him, namely an inability to cast and behold any mirror image as well as a shadow. In the one story of Hoffmann's that the shadowless Schlemihl does appear, "The Adventures of New Year's Eve" ("Die Abenteuer der Silverster-Nacht"), he has a reflection, (Spiegelbild). The apparent protagonist of the story, Erasmus Strikl, is the unfortunate soul who loses his reflection. The distinctions drawn by Hoffmann, most prominently the one between shadow and reflection, merely underscore what the editor of the opening frame identifies as the Traveling Enthusiast's problem: an inability to distinguish between the inner and outer world: "The Traveling Enthusiast distinguishes his inner and outer lives so minimally that no one can distinguish between the two" (Hoffmann 181). That deficiency is evinced in the Traveling Enthusiast's own framed story of how Strikl comes to lose his reflection to a supernatural temptress who has procured the image for the devil Dappertutto. At story's end, (except for a postscript by the Traveling Enthusiast), Erasmus and Schlemihl meet and attempt to recuperate what each has lost: Erasmus will cast a shadow that Schlemihl will reflect: "He came upon a certain Peter Schlemihl who had sold his 'Schlagschatten.'" Both men wanted to forge a companionship (eine Kompagnie gehen) so that Erasums Spikher would cast the necessary "Schlagschatten" and Peter Schlemihl would in turn reflect the appropriate mirror image ("Spiegelbild"; Hoffmann 114). The curiosities of the passage are numerous and working through them will help us recognize a messianic potential intimated but hardly explored in Chamisso's text. I will return to that potential at the end of the chapter.

At this point, one has to ask what is a *Schlagschatten*, a term that appears but once in Chamisso's text during the protagonist's attempt to have a painter restore his shadow. Since the term is a painterly one, the artist can be expected to know the difference. Also, what enables a shadowless person to cast a mirror image? What kind of recuperation can be expected from this odd mixing of reflection and shadow? *Schlagschatten* can be understood only in relation to the term *Eigenschatten*; the former, which Schlemihl has sold, is the shadow cast by one person or object onto another, a way of throwing oneself or one's image out onto the world. The latter refers to that which is blocked from the source of illumination, such as the dark side of the moon. That is to say, Schlemihl, who will come to be a social outcast, may still possess the kind of shadow that results from turning away from the world, from retreating to a closet or a place of interiority. Such self-possession evidently allows for him to have a mirror image, the bounty of being self-reflective. The devil in this Faustian reprise of sorts is Dappertutto. As his name implies, he is everywhere and nowhere (überall und nirgends), or, as the word also signals, exposed on all sides. Like Frankenstein's creature, he traverses distances quite effortlessly, but his lack of a mirror image is not the result of scientific experiment. He has no aspect to project or reflect. Erasmus's subsequent loss of his reflection to Dappertutto, his loss of the ability to self-reflect as Schlemihl can, occurs during the time which this married father is in pursuit of the temptress Giulietta. The mirror image seems to be tied to a moral or ethical faculty dependent on self-reflection, whereby self-reflection requires one to turn at least one aspect or side of oneself away from the light.

In a story about misalignment between inside and outside, such attempts to develop any kind of logic or symmetry are doomed. The comments that frame the story indicate a need to contain and establish an order to the non-synchronous and asymmetrical aspects of the actual narrative of the Traveling Enthusiast. The editor seeks to become the perspective or unifying aspect that can bring all the misaligned pieces into some kind of order only to be unmasked and called out by name in the Enthusiast's postscript: "What do you see in that mirror: Is it really me? Or Giulietta . . . Heaven's image—infernal image . . . You see, my dear Theodor Amadäus Hoffmann . . ." (Hoffmann 114). The awkwardness of the proposed restored specularity of the two figures, indicated by the odd punctuation, structure, and the possible shift in the antecedent of the pronoun "you," is rendered wholly impossible once the Traveling Enthusiast and Hoffman are asked to gaze into the mirror that was not intended to reflect them. Or was it? At the very least, there is an infinite regress as the self turns to its own reflection and through a series of subsequent reflections (or frames) seeks to recover the lost image of a whole self. As we shall see, the failure of such an effort also restores foreclosed possibilities for the self to escape its own bad reflection.

For now, we can recognize how Schlemihl and Strikl's attempt to form a collective body complete with shadow and mirror image defies all logic. How can Schlemihl cast a mirror image that corresponds to the shadow thrown from a different body? To see oneself in the shadow of another or the reflection of another may correspond to the editor's attempt to suture all the misaligned elements, but the experiment can hardly succeed unless someone's body is cut and spliced to conform to that of the other in the transaction. The last line of the Traveling Enthusiast's framed story is thus wholly expected: "Nothing came of it." (es wurde nichts daraus). His postscript or supplement at the end of this misbegotten experiment testifies to the fecklessness of the recuperative effort, to the effort to restore specularity. In fact, the frames of the story reflect an inability to secure inside from outside, real from imaginary. In the fourth and final section of the story (which is more than a section given the inclusion of the postscript) the Traveling Enthusiast indicates that he is going to tell the story of Erasmus Spikher, based on what the latter left behind but in Spikher's own words. All of this is framed by the editor's remarks at the beginning of the tale.

The text is mediated through so many voices or layers that the odd remarks appended by the Traveling Enthusiast only point to all the loose ends that disable aligning inside/outside, and this extends to the persons themselves. When the Enthusiast specifically addresses Hoffmann in the postscript, it only confirms that any reliable perspective on the events of the text falters on its various, misaligned planes or frames of narration so much so that the mention of Peter Schlemihl at the end of part four gives no indication of his appearance earlier in the story. He is introduced anew. Without a *Schlagschatten* he left no traces of his earlier appearance. As we now work through Chamisso's text and recognize how pressures to solve the Jewish question inform ones about sexuality, a different fate other than the one described by the editor may await both figures. That is, the ability to erase traces of oneself may have its advantages.

Aryan Panic

Peter Schlemihl's name may signal his Jewish origins, but, oddly enough, it is not until the end of the novella when he has taken to the road in his seven-mile boots that any such reference is made. In fact, it is a stunning loss of orientation that betrays his oriental roots. Racing from "east to west and west to east" (63) with an ease shared perhaps only by Frankenstein's creature, he is overtaken by a fever and loses his senses. Upon regaining consciousness, he finds himself in a hospital bearing his name, "Schlemihlium." But it is not his name (he is known only by a number) that designates not his Jewishness but rather his physical appearance. "My name is Number Zero, and because of my long beard I now qualify as a

Jew, which entitles me to be treated no less carefully" (64). For the first time in the light of day since pawning his shadow, Schlemihl is afforded equal rights in his one-time adopted land. Two conditions are fulfilled to allow for such a homecoming: an abandonment of any attempt to disguise his Jewish appearance and a promise, at least implicitly upheld by his recent past and his seven-mile boots, to keep wandering and thus relinquish any claims of a "German-Jewish" homeland. Jewish money, particularly since it is no longer controlled by Schlemihl but by his one-time servant Bendel, is welcome even if the Jew is only conditionally so. "Schlemihlium" is named after its exiled benefactor. Jewish money, however questionable its source, is essential for the improvement or healing of German society. The foundation could not exist without it.

The curious ambivalence toward Schlemihl and his money is apparent throughout the text, most notably when his riches and extravagance allow him to be mistaken for and celebrated as a count, only to be loathed once the source and cost of his riches are discovered. At the beginning of the nineteenth century the Jew in German society undoubtedly confronted a similar ambivalence. His connection to German society was in no small measure an economic one. "Jews and non-Jews lived in two worlds apart, with economic relations forming virtually the only link between them" (Rürup 5–6). By 1820 even the salons, once the locus of interaction between Jews and non-Jews, had been supplanted by houses of titled bureaucracy and the upper middle class (Arendt 82).[11] In an emerging new economy, the Jew had become the essential financier, and in some respects, these so-called "Münzjuden," those conversant in matters of money, were welcome and prominent. For example, the Director of Industry for Berlin in 1807 listed thirty Jewish bankers and only twenty-two Christian ones, and the naturalization registers of Jews for 1809 noted fifty-three bankers, fifteen money changers, and sixteen financial agents. Many of these financiers had come from places outside Berlin, which may have contributed to an uneasiness about their presence (Toury 162). The ambivalence that Schlemihl confronts reflects an entrenched distrust of Jewish business transactions and, more important, of Jewish ethics. Noteworthy is how that distrust is formulated to respond to the influence that Jews began to exercise in German societies. In 1783 Friedrich Traugott Hartmann proclaimed in open debate that the Jew, whether destitute or wealthy, was spiritually and morally a group apart (Hartmann 94-95). Adolf Franz Friedrich Ludwig, Freiherr von Knigge, asserted that the Jew was never inhibited by ethics; gain was his sole concern (Knigge 151–52). Baron Schroettter, serving in the Prussian cabinet, claimed that the greatest capital sums were already in the hands of Jews, who were prepared to resort to any means to attain their objective (Freund 177). The ensuing fear of the German's fate at the hands of moneyed Jews was framed most stridently by Karl Wilhelm Friedrich Grattenauer in his 1803 tract, *Wider die Juden. Ein Wort der Warnung an alle unsere christliche Mitbürger* (*Against the Jews: A Word of Warning to our fellow Christian Citizens*). Grattenauer viewed Jewish emancipation as a "threat to Germans' ability to distance themselves from Jews" and came to what for him was an inevitable recognition of the unalterably and morally inferior character or the Jews. As he writes in that same tract, "Grant the Jews full rights of citizenship [. . .], they will reward you royally for you will stand and tend the flock of Jews; your sons and daughters will become the slave and handmaidens of the Jews; you will work in the sweat of your brow, but the chosen people of God will enjoy the fruits and live grandly!!!" (as cited, Katz 101).

Peter Schlemihl's history embodies those fears, or more specifically, those fears that arise from the Jews' attempt to assimilate. His arrival at the outset of the novella from other shores indicates his nomadic nature. Upon touching land, he attempts to establish himself in the new country by seeking out Thomas John, the man to whom Schlemihl's brother has written a letter of reference on behalf of the new arrival (Chamisso 58). Adequate preparation for presenting himself to his new benefactor requires an extreme makeover: "I opened up my bundle of belongings, took out a new black coat, washed, and dressed in my very best clothes. Then, with my letter of introduction in my pocket, I set out on my way to the man, who I hoped would further my modest ambitions" (Chamisso 18). The desire to acquire riches soon replaces his modest hopes, given the grandeur of Thomas John's lifestyle and the ease with which such comforts and luxuries are obtained. Thomas John, whose rather generic name obscures the bearer's origins, has established himself in society by buying his way into a station for which his name indicates that he hardly has standing. In his circle, money substitutes for character: "A man worth less than a million is, pardon the expression, a wretch" (Hoffmann 18), and thus betrays his real reason for disembarking in Northern Germany. John's sentiment has nothing to do with a reserve of feeling for the land and its people; such sentiment is rather indiscriminately exchanged as is a name or money.

Of course, his name, when reversed as John Thomas, is then British slang for penis. The inversion of his name suggests already a homoerotic inclination, and were the city in Northern Germany identified explicitly as

Berlin, one might venture that the letter of reference was tied perhaps to Schlemihl's suitability for the societies of "warm brothers" that had been formed recently. If nothing else, Thomas John's name also implies ignorance of what is front and what is back or what is first and what is second. The moneyed Jew is thus tangentially or provisionally at this stage linked to a secret society, not of the Elders of Zion (It is too early for that!?) but rather of those whose true secret societies are only revealed when names (almost like one does in Hebrew) are read right to left or inverted.

The chatter of Thomas John's circle indicates just how inverted and questionable the values of the newly moneyed are: "One spoke in earnest of frivolous matters and frivolously of earnest ones" (Chamisso 19). For these parvenus, whose "joking and bantering" constitutes an affront to the values of real society, nothing is truly earned. The spoils of their riches, the signs that they are not "wretches" but rather the "master of millions," is brought about by sorcery (Chamisso 19). Whatever is required for the comfort and entertainment of this coterie—a telescope, a carpet, a tent—is all produced miraculously from the meager pocket of a nondescript man in a gray suit. These folks, who are to initiate Schlemihl into his new world, produce nothing; their riches are fabricated. Money brings them the fixings of nobility—names, titles, and property—but they have no intrinsic worth and can be made to disappear as magically as they were brought forth. That, in fact, is the fate of Thomas John, when he eventually finds himself in debt after having been swindled through some shady real estate dealings by the figure simply known as Rascal. Money has effected a severing of the name from the land, and the transactions that have enabled this severance are impure ones.

Worth remarking is Schlemihl's effort to distinguish himself from "wretches," as noted above. In Mary Shelley's *Frankenstein* the creature was a wretch whose contagion, indicated by the remarkable number of polyoptons, threatened to become a cancer capable of infecting the entire body politic. In this instance, "wretch" has already attached to one whose "immutable Jewish character"—to recall critics of Jewish emancipation—poses a threat greater perhaps than Frankenstein's; he can find a means to hide what for the monster was his hideous appearance. But if the doctor feared creating a bride for the monster might result in a race of such creatures, Schlemihl's mentor, Thomas John, relieves such fear. An inverted penis is unlikely to breed, and no doubt depictions of such an inversion easily accommodated ideas of the circumcised Jew as feminized. Stated in broader terms, the conjunction of femininity and Jewishness asserted by the self-hating Jew

Otto Weiniger in his 1903 work, *Sex and Character*, is already taking shape in the German and German-Jewish imaginary.[12]

Self-Evacuation or Panoptic Confusion

While it is the lack of a shadow that signals the suspicious origins of Schlemihl's wealth and marks him as an outsider or a non-German, the manner in which his questionable wealth or alien status is affirmed exposes a damning deficiency that no Enlightenment program for emancipation can heal or overcome. Programs promoting the state to recognize the equal status of the Jew as proposed by W. von Humbodlt or those promoting *Bildung* as a mean to free the Jews from "his moral degradation" serve only as a means to reaffirm Jewish deficiencies along a different axis (Dohm I, 75, 76).[13] In the end, the progressive Humboldt serves the regressive aims of C. Dohm. For both, Jewish difference is tolerable only insofar as it can be eliminated. Ironically, it is Schlemihl's lack of a shadow that is a sign of ineradicable difference. To be without a shadow is to be totally penetrable. Schlemihl is thus without substance which, in turn, grounds his identity as Jewish. If one links a shadow to that which is with substance or is solid, then Schlemihl is without character because his wealth or that which would allow for admittance into society lacks, like the fortunes of the Jewish financiers, the substance or solidity of established money.[14] If selling his shadow allows Schlemihl apparent entry into society, it also reveals that he is without substance by virtue of his apparent ability to blend in or assimilate. The Jew might seek, through any means possible, to enter German society, but his entry would always be marred by an indelible character deficiency, whose ineradicable persistence would manifest itself in the very attempt to gain entry into German society. In this respect, the selling of the shadow points to something far more troubling for any Jew seeking to assimilate. It is not just an indication of the Jew's irrepressible urge to engage in trade, but it is also a sign of the Jew's absolute absence of character; his character is that he has no character. Trading in religious traditions of millennia for the comforts and conveniences of the present reveals the Jews' lack of substance: "Assimilation did not, as its advocates had hoped, dispose of the Jewish question in Germany; rather, it shifted the locus of the question and rendered it all the more acute [. . .], [Germans] began to chalk up against the Jews an all-too-great faculty for abandoning their ethnic consciousness" (Scholem, Jews 77).

The shift in the locus of the Jewish question, whereby the Jew's non-identity becomes the basis of fear, is linked to several factors displayed by Chamisso's text. The most important would be the political conservatism of German-speaking lands that followed the Congress of Vienna in 1815. The increasing urgency to ground German identity in the myth of the "Volk" necessitated a re-securing of the signs of that identity.[15] How Schlemihl comes to secure his fortune and thus his non-identity threatens those forms of identity that require fixed signs. Schlemihl's ability to tender his shadow, to reduce substance to a set of exchangeable signs and commodities, raises the fear that all signs of identity will run amok. Identities will become unreadable and unreliable, and most disconcertingly for those whose identity is linked to the "Volk" and its soil, "Germanness" might be traded fraudulently. After all, Schlemihl is mistaken for a king and a count. Restoration or maintenance of the old order is thereby thwarted. That is precisely the significance of the remonstrations of his fiancée's father, the land and tree-loving forester, when he confronts Schlemihl about his shadowlessness. The father's vocation, for sure, requires lots of time spent in the shade and its shadows, which now renders him privy to the truth of the charlatan. "Is a certain Peter Schlemihl really unknown to you?" (Chamisso 40). His first words assert the need for names to mean something, a clear if somewhat tangential reference to what for Germans was so inscrutable and unreliable about Jewish practices of naming. The denial of who one is—after all, a name cannot just be a name—must be addressed. Schlemihl, however, is really no name; it merely signifies one who is without substance or who for the sake of assimilation was too eager to pawn his essence: "And if I am that same man?" Schlemihl responds to the question posed by the forester, who responds vehemently, "[W]ho . . . came to lose his shadow!!" (Chamisso 40). The forester's moral indignation emanates at least in part from the inability to name the other or for the other to allow himself to be named. He can only be known by what he last lost.

For Germans, seeking to ground an identity through constructions of the "Volk," each proper name must be the property of someone. That explains why in certain German duchies the conditions for becoming a "naturalized" German included the adoption of a hereditary family name (W. Mosse 73). It also clarifies the significance of the Schlemihl Foundation. His convalescence, since he is a patient in his own hospital, is linked to reclamation of his name, which means as well that he must regrow his beard and allow himself to be recognized as a Jew. Since Schlemihl is not really a proper family name but rather something closer to an epithet, this reclamation is tantamount to the Jew's admission that his presence in Germany is improper.

Owning up to one's name can only mean for Schlemihl the disowning of any homeland. Chamisso's Schlemihl does bear numerous similarities with Ahasuerus, the Wandering Jew.[16] The lack of a shadow is thus the equivalent of a lack of a homeland, a metonymy apparently employed by many of Chamisso's contemporaries.[17] Given that the question of residence had long been an obstacle to Jewish integration (Rürup 16), Schlemihl's decision to sell his shadow was not his own. Shadowed by traditions that set him apart, Schlemihl tenders the marker of those differences as a condition of residency that, as a result of the ensuing lack, constitutes a revocation of those rights of residency. The polyvalent significance of the shadow (e.g., as a marker of substance, of tradition, of a soul, of a homeland, or ever the right of residency) all coalesce and serve as a figuration of the misfortune of the Jew caught in a double bind: to meet the ostensible conditions for residency is to betray one's unfitness for it. What one might call Schlemihl's moral awakening is thus tied to his renunciation of that right, and not as some have argued, to his severing of ties with the man in the gray suit or the devil.[18]

Schlemihl's absence, in fact, structures the text. The story begins with a preface consisting of three letters: one from Chamisso to his publisher Hitzig, one from Hitzig to Fouquè, and one from Fouquè to Hitzig. The letters explain the publication history of the text and how Chamisso comes to possess it. Schlemihl, wearing his seven-mile boots, a black Kurtak, and a long gray beard, had turned up at Chamisso's door and then had given the manuscript to him. Publication is thus dependent on Schlemihl's departure, and he embraces his role as an alien to the point of dressing as one. That is the moral directive that issues from his personal confession. Throughout the text Schlemihl repeatedly remarks that what has brought him to be what he is today, a Jew embracing his alien existence, is a product of strict moral reflection: "I have imposed several strict sentences on myself" (Chamisso 49). And the severest sentence that he passes upon himself is, despite its consequence, one that liberates the heart: "I sat there without a shadow or money, but a tremendous weight had been lifted. I was cheerful" (Chamisso 57). A clear Jewish conscience can be achieved only by foreswearing a homeland and the money illegitimately acquired in residence there. A Jew who once pursued integration into civil society learns the importance of confession, which returns him to himself, an eager wanderer groomed once again to be a Jewish alien, but now, at least, a shadowless one.

Degeneration

If this dialectic charts moral ascendancy according to regressive characteristics, it also crosses with another metonymic chain. The *schlemiel* who substitutes for the Jew without a shadow will also substitute for one who is sexually degenerative and nonreproductive. As we shall see, the second chain produces a dialectic of its own. On the one hand, it serves to remark the Jew as "other" along an axis of sexual degeneracy. For even if Schlemihl exposed the moral degeneracy of the "assimilated" Jew by forfeiting millennia of tradition, he also exposed the unreliability of traditional markers of Jewish difference. Sexual errancy might thus prove to be both more reliable and damning. The text does not assert that such errancy is inherent in the character of the Jew. Rather, the closeted existence that the Jew is forced to live as a result of being without substance redirects his desire. His introversion surfaces as sexual inversion. Inversion, as Gerd Hekma points out, is a familiar trope for homosexuality in the nineteenth century (Hekma 213–40). Sexual deviancy thus serves to differentiate the introverted Jew from outsiders. He is a different kind of different, which will not be fully formulated until the end of the century and the birth of psychiatry. On the other hand, Schlemihl's history also revivifies the very Enlightenment ideals that threatened the integrity and purity of the "Volk" and necessitated the ostracism of the Jew for the sake of that concept. In other words, what one might call a dialectic of Enlightenment is the return of Enlightenment taxonomies that serve to reclassify the Jew along the very lines that the Restoration sought to annul.

Ironically, what calls for the discarded taxonomies of the Enlightenment is the inability of the Restoration to account for or name Schlemihl's particular type of deviancy. If his misfortune or "lucklessness" can be attributed to the avarice of a Jew seeking admittance to civil society, his moral deficiency is also evident in a nascent sexual orientation. Schlemihl's deviant desires are clearly not in the foreground during his early adventures; they result from the life he is forced to live as a result of his shadowlessness. As one who would be a good German citizen, so to speak, Schlemihl seeks to adhere to the "positive injunction" beginning around 1800 for "all citizens to be (hetero)sexually active and to marry"(Hull 409–11).Guaranteeing the newfound privacy of the family means that the state has to protect the integrity of the family unit (Hull 411). While punishment of errant sexual practices is eased and sometimes eliminated with the emergence of civil society, the need to foster the family as a procreative unit gives new rise to new forms of deviance that come later in the nineteenth century to congeal around a specific type of deviant (Foucault vol. 1, 44–45). Just as the otherness of the Jew serves to lend obverse meaning to the mythical entity of the "Volk," civil society protects the family by producing the sexual deviant, who, for the sake of that society, needs to be criminalized and marginalized. Protecting the integrity of the family generates its threat; that allows for it to be policed and thus protected from the enemy, to once again recall Schmitt. This disdain, in turn, is the expression of the moral authority required, paradoxically, for the protection of civil society. "I will not accept anything from someone who does not have a shadow," the servant Rascal exclaims as he "turns his back to Schlemihl" (Chamisso 40). This renunciation of Schlemihl allows Rascal, in turn, to marry Schlemihl's fiancée and thus enter civil society, however questionable Rascal's own ethics might be. While the manner in which the shadowless Jew and the sexually criminal are linked still needs to be worked out, its logic could be summarized as follows: According to Hull, "only those unfortunates deemed incapable of participating in civil society remain[ed] sexually non self-determining: the celibate and those stigmatized as either criminally or sexually 'subordinate'" (Hull 409). Chamisso's text legitimates that stigmatization. It is Peter Schlemihl's unfitness for civil society, however, that generates perverse desire. Instead of being sexually self-determining, he is forced to seek himself; his desire emanates from a lack of substance or selfhood without which he is unfit for civil society. That, in turn, renders him sexually criminal. As we shall see, the emergence of same-sex desire in Schlemihl is structured as a narrative, a process that constructs its own pathology. That pathology is the invariable consequence of the mannerisms effected by the Jew seeking assimilation.

Bad Company

The *schlemiel* is no stranger to sexual errancy. While Chamisso and Heine, for example, cite different origins of the term, both link the *schlemiel* to illicit sexual activity. Chamisso cites the Talmud as his source (Chamisso 770). The *schlemiel* is one who had sex with a rabbi's wife, was caught, and then killed. Heine's *schlemiel* has a different origin. In "Princess Sabbath," part of the *Hebräische Melodien*, Heine refers to the Biblical figure Schlemiel ben Urzy Schadday, who is accidentally killed when Pinchas seeks to slay the nobleman Simri, who is having sexual relations with a woman of the Caananites (Heine 3/1, 123–72). Heine's version, often contested, is nonetheless instructive.[19] As witness to a forbidden sexual act, he is killed; guilt, or at least the stigma that accrues to the name *schlemiel*, is transferred onto one who is more or less an innocent bystander. Heine's long discussion of the *schlemiel* in that same work seeks to demonstrate the false appropriation of the term by "Christianized Jews" (Gilman Self-Hatred 182). Heine's questionable exposition of the term's etymology highlights how the *schlemiel*'s act is less significant than the transferability of the stigma associated with the act. A Jew who merely witnesses illicit sexual relations is subject to the same misfortunes as if he had engaged in such relations. As we shall see, a component of Schlemihl's deviancy is a similar kind of impotence; he can only watch hopelessly as his former fiancée is wooed by Rascal.

Although it will be decades before the term "homosexuality" has currency, recognition of homosexuality as "a primary sexual deviancy" and the homosexual's segregation as a "special subclass" was already taking hold in the early nineteenth century (Gilman, Degeneraton 159). In fact, the 1790 *Briefe über die Gallantereien von Berlin auf einer Reise von einem österreichischen Offizier* documents the supposedly new types of friendship that are developing among men (Tobin, *Warm Brothers* 15). The letters are significant not only because they speak of cults of "warm brothers" but also because they give public expression to the opprobrium directed at such acts. For example, the author of the letters, assumed to be John Friedel, writes, "It was impossible to watch the spectacle for very long. The thought alone aroused feelings of horror ("Grauen")—and the actual sight—wouldn't you have the same reaction?" (as cited Tobin, *Warm Brothers* 145). As the citation suggests, anti-Enlightenment sentiments have begun to crystallize around an incipient homophobia. While the punishments for illicit sexual behaviors may have been eased if not eliminated with the introduction of the Napoleonic code (Steakley 173), a critical component of determining what should be forbidden was the sentiment of the public; civil outrage could mandate severer punishments for sex between two men (Lautmann 172–75). Important to note is that the vocabulary of illicit sexual relations is changing as the state's role in policing the family in civil society is being redefined. The public's outrage, which is directed against the Jews, for example, in the Hep-Hep riot of 1819, is also summoned to define the limits of sodomy, which, not coincidentally, is being redefined as sex between men (Hutter 189–91).

The Jew and the man desirous of other men are joined through public sentiments of outrage. The *schlemiel* has a new set of behaviors to which he can conform and thus fulfill the promise of his name. That, moreover, explains Chamisso's description of Peter Schlemihl as *ungeschickt*, a description shared by the painter whom Schlemihl asks to restore his shadow: "Through what clumsiness (Ungeschicklichkeit) does one come to lose his 'Schlagschatten'?" (Chamisso 14–15). *Ungeschickt* is how the author of *Lucinde* described himself and may refer to same-sex relations among men in the vernacular of the day as well (Helfer 176–77). Peter Schlemihl's social clumsiness now assumes a sexual character.

Peter Schlemihl's sexual errancy, however, is not just the result of associations linked to the term *schlemiel*; it is explicitly worked out in the text as well. The wonderful history generated when Schlemihl tenders his shadow for forged or queer coin is precisely one that at least since the Renaissance had linked counterfeiting (or usury), heresy, and sodomy (Bredbeck 5). Although Schlemihl initially has designs on women, his lust for riches immediately awakens a curious desire. He describes his first encounter with the man in the gray suit as follows: "I trembled with fear as I looked blankly (stier). I felt like a bird hypnotized by a snake" (Chamisso 21). The masculine image of the first clause (stier) is quickly sexualized in the next. "The man in the gray coat himself seemed to be very embarrassed" (verlegen: Chamisso 21). The man is both embarrassed and mislaid (verlegt) or soon to be mislaid. The latter sense of the word is apparent only later, when Schlemihl leaps upon the man from behind, who by dint of a bird's nest had become invisible. Schlemihl is a bird seeking his nest in another man's behind, one who had enchanted him like a snake. Sex with animals, of course, has long been one of the behaviors associated with sodomy, but sex with or among animals is now suggestive of sex between two men. The ensuing confusion of who is the pursuer and who is the pursued (Schlemihl or the man in the gray suit, the bird seeking its next prey or the snake entrancing the bird) anticipates the confusion surrounding which role the male sodomite assumes. It signals a sexual inversion much like the inversion of values that characterizes Thomas John's coterie.

This newly awakened desire assumes more definite contours through the reactions it elicits and the dream that is produced in response to those reactions. As one without a shadow, Schlemihl is fully penetrable, thereby suggesting an overt feminization. It is thus no surprise that he is greeted with disdain by the first boy he sees: "With much hilarity he betrayed me . . . to the whole group of street lads, who began to curse and throw shit (Kot) at me (Chamisso 24). The incipient sodomite, whose murky secrets (düstres Geheimnis) is betrayed by a suspicious boy, is the target of shit (Chamisso 26). The continued derision and disdain that Schlemihl sustains from men and boys that same day overcomes him to the point that he finally surrenders his manhood and falls asleep atop his coin: "At night I found myself lying atop my coin, at which point sleep overwhelmed [overmanned] me" (übermannte; Chamisso 24). The dream produced by sleeping upon his queer coin is telling. He dreams of Chamisso, briefly surveys the books on Chamisso's study, and then returns his gaze to Chamisso, who is not breathing and is dead (25). Schlemihl, "overmanned" by sleep, thus dreams of a cadaver. Desire for dead bodies and magic are thus part of the psyche of the penetrable man, elements of the dream landscape of one who is now occupied with how to re-stick it, e.g., his shadow, to himself.

Schlemihl's affections are for himself or for the author of his self, Chamisso. Stated otherwise, the public humiliation that ensues from selling his shadow or pawning his Jewish heritage forces him to mimic the desire of the man in the gray suit, who upon propositioning Schlemihl for his shadow remarked: "I only request that you allow me here and now to stick the shadow on me, how I do that is my concern" (Chamisso 22). Mimicking the desire of his antagonist, seeking to re-stick to himself that part of himself that has been traded away, is thus a form of self-affection. And that affection is related to dreaming one's author, since, from a literary perspective, that is what Chamisso is. Seeking or dreaming oneself in the form of another may posit a self to be the object of desire, but that desire is related to being entranced by a dead self as other. Desire for oneself in the form of another, in the form of another man (and a shadow is nothing but a form) is now linked to necromancy. The historically linked practices of sodomy, usury, heresy (or being a Jew who sells his shadow), and sex with the dead and animals are all subsumed under and as forms of self-affection. It should also be pointed out that the other books upon the desk in Chamisso's dream are by Haller, von Humboldt, and Linnæus. The Enlightenment is thus implicated in this reclassification of shady or aberrant desires. Anti-Enlightenment or anti-Napoleonic sentiments are projected onto the Jew, who sells his shadow in the hope of gaining entry to civil society but who thereby is given to sexual errancy, the many forms of which are expressed by male-male same-sex desire as a form of self-affection.

If we regard narcissism as a form of self-affection, the text proleptically recalls Freud's early text on homosexuality, "On Narcissism." In that essay Freud specifically linked narcissism with homosexuality. The narcissism expressed by homosexuals, according to Freud, was the same as the primary form in which a child cathects itself as whole with a parent without differentiation. Homosexual narcissism occurs at a later stage, when the subject's original narcissism confront the "admonition of others," which is likewise accompanied by the awakening of critical judgment. That is, the subject's primary attachment to itself is shattered by the criticism of others and is later reformulated or recuperated in new ego ideals. The subject thus seeks an ideal completion of himself in another male (Freud, SE vol. 14, 88–94) and comes to recognize what he himself would like to be, such as a Jew becoming a German.

Although any reading of *Schlehmihl* through the lens of psychoanalysis and a language specific to homosexuality is anachronistic, Freud's text does help illuminate, by its very different but similar pathology, the genesis of same-sex desire in Schlemihl. The key difference is that what is provisionally termed Schlemihl's self-affection is engendered by the specific climate of Jew-hatred that surrounds his attempt to assimilate. It is, after all, the need to jettison religious tradition, figured in the trading of one's shadow, that forces Schlemihl to confront the "admonition" or ridicule of others. As a result of that ridicule, Schlemihl closets himself, "As long as the sun was shining, I locked myself inside with Bendel. And it was said that the count has retired to his cabinet" (35). If his actions are shady, it is because he is forced to operate and live in the shadows. The desires bred by a closeted existence might not be directed initially towards an object of the same sex, but this predicament is what renders him impotent to pursue or consummate any interest in women. He is unable to leap across the so-called gulf (die Kluft überspringen, 32) that separates him from Minna when they first meet. And it is what prevents him, in contradistinction from Minna, from truly loving, "She truly loves" (36). The inability to love truly the woman whom he would make his wife is what he finally admits is the curse that has fallen upon him. ("A curse stood upon me," 37). In fact, he lacks any language to describe what he has become: "[A]nd do you know it, this curse, do you know who your love is—what he—?" (Chamisso 35).

While he may not yet be possessed by a love that dare not speak its name, the blanks in his confession indicate that what he is or what he has become cannot be named. He is the homosexual before the homosexual has been named (Halperin, *100 Years*, 15–40). This same linguistic gap informs his response to Rascal, when the servant accuses him of being shadowless: "But Rascal, dear Rascal, who led you to think such an unfortunate thing, how can you think—?" (Chamisso 39–40). He who has sold his shadow has become the unspeakable; it has brought one to the idea of something heretofore unqualified by language. If this is the case, it is important to note the sequence of events. The selling of his shadow for the sake of assimilation engenders in Schlemihl a self-affection. Ridicule and disdain transform that affection into a desire to seek himself (his shadow) under the cover of night. That, in turn, forces him to spend much of his time working in his cabinet, locked up with Bendel. Finally, such an existence compels him to forgo the affections of women or to be disdained as something unspeakable. In such fashion the text offers a genesis of forbidden desire.

If to become a German Schlemihl needed to shed his Jewish substance, which, nonetheless, betrayed the Jew as too substance-less to be German, then the ensuing pursuit to recapture his shadow or the tendered portion of his self can only be described as a queer pursuit or one that turns back on itself and follows a tortuous path. As Schlemihl remarks, "He who frivolously set foot off the straight (gerade) path will suddenly be led astray down a different path that pushes further and further astray" (Chamisso 49). That, he adds, is his curse. The recognition of his aberrant course follows the description of the event that most dramatically marks his desire as aberrant as well, namely, his pursuit of the man rendered invisible by a bird's nest.

The scene begins with Schlemihl sobbing to find relief from a "nameless" weight upon his heart (44). Although he has no name for what ails him, he drinks furiously (mit grimmiger Durst; Chamisso 45) the poison that the unknown had poured into his wounds. On the one hand, the animal urges, suggested in this instance by his thirst and devouring of wild fruits, hint at a sodomite's proclivity, but only insofar as the subject is also becoming feminized. The first signs of that feminization are his weeping and his wound(s). On the other hand, the effects of that poison awaken in him a mighty urge (ein mächtiger Trieb; 45) to leap upon the invisible man. Since only the man's shadow is visible, he seeks to make himself the master of that shadow: "O shadow, I thought, do you seek your master. I will be him" (Chamisso 45).

His queer path is also marked by gender confusion or a mixing of feminine and masculine traits. This poison arouses in his partially feminized self the desire to become master of another man's shadow or substance. To become such a master he must chase or stalk that which reveals itself to be another man only when Schlemihl has jumped the shadow and threatened to take him. "Like the lion in pursuit of his prey, I shot forth with a powerful leap in order to take possession of it" [the shadow, the man, the prey?] (Chamisso 46). Having traded away his shadow, the aggressivity and desires associated with being a "Herr" are no longer aroused by women; he leaves the women in his life since he cannot "really love." Rather such desires are now summoned by the chase and the urge to be the master over a masculine shape: "A terror pulsed through my heart, enflamed my desire, gave wings to my flight [. . .]. I got closer and closer to the shadow. I had to reach him." The apparent success of the chase is rewarded with a bashing: "I then received the worst blows to the ribs that any person has ever experienced" (Chamisso 46). The affect of his ostracism and self-recrimination is horror, the affect of which is to give his desire an object. That object, which simultaneously repulses him, turns out to be the man in the gray suit whose "Tarnkappe" is drawn over both of their heads and at whose feet his shadow and Schlemihl's peacefully rest side by side (Chamisso 47). "The effect of that shock made me struggle desperately to hold down my opponent. I plunged forward and fell to the ground; beneath me, on his back, was a man whom I held firmly but was no longer invisible" (Chamisso 46).

The man's "satanic smile" also defines Schlemihl's predicament in which he can only watch impotently as his former servant Rascal woos his former fiancée. (And here we might recall Heine's etymology of the term *schlemiel*.) Of course, the civil society to which Schlemihl sought admittance has yet to define his condition. As such, he swoons or exits consciousness (Chamisso 50). When he comes to, his "despised companion" (verhaßter Begleiter) curses him: "Isn't that just how an old hag would behave! Get up and act like a man. Finish the business you started. Or perhaps you have second thoughts and want to continue whimpering?" (Chamisso 50). A pathetic old woman, one who cannot complete what she has resolved to do, is the phrase that this text attaches to a man whose absolute penetrability sends him in pursuit of another man. And while his irresolution may signal feminization, that indecision also opens, as we will see, by its very undecidability, onto a utopian horizon.

The Exception Queer or the Emergence of the Sexual Outlaw

In the chapter "Jewess and Schlemihl" from *Rahel Varnhagen*, Hannah Arendt describes the impossible predicament of the "exception Jew," the one who "struggles against the fact of having been born a Jew" and comes in the end to struggle against oneself:

> For the possibilities of being different from what one is are infinite. Once one has negated oneself, however, there are no longer any particular choices. There is only one aim: always, at any given moment, to be different from what one is; never to assert oneself; but with infinite pliancy to become anything else,

so long as it is not oneself. It requires an inhuman alertness not to betray oneself, to conceal everything and yet have no definite secret to cling to. (57)

Peter Schlemihl is this exception Jew as well. Having jettisoned his tradition in the vain attempt to win acceptance, he has forfeited all choice. His infinite resources or recourse to magic offers him an infinite pliancy but only to acquire identities that mask his own lack of one. He must conceal his lack of a shadow, but the secret that he clings to is without any precise or definite meaning. "In the end it was only a shadow, nothing more than a shadow" (Chamisso 41). The maintenance of that secret and the "inhuman alertness" required so as not to betray that secret, however vague the significance of a shadow might be, makes Schlemihl well-nigh a criminal: "Late in the evening I threw a coat on and sneaked out of the house like a criminal" (Chamisso 40). When he approaches his fiancée's family after learning that his secret has been exposed, he presents himself "as a criminal before the judges" (40). Civil society has lured the Jew with the promise of citizenship only to criminalize him. His secret, despite attempts to closet himself in his cabinet with a servant, has always only been an open one.

The exception Jew, however, also has exceptional possibilities. Once the ideal he has set for himself becomes unrealizable, this non-sublatable difference between what he is and what he would like to be gives rise to a critical faculty or judgment (Urteil). Just as Arendt argues that Varnhagen accepted her pariah status in the face of recrudescent Jew-hatred (Arendt xii), Schlemihl, armed with a new-found faculty for critical judgment, decides to retain his soul rather than trade it in for his shadow—thus precluding any possibility of assimilating. "I looked upon myself as a new character who had to be dressed for the world; my suit was a very modest one" (Chamisso 58). He looks upon himself without denying who he is. His self-affection, necessitated by loss, leads to a division of self that generates a critical judgment, the result of which is an appreciation or even apprehension of a soul. The dissonance between his shadowless self and his shadow fosters a new axis of difference, and the living out of this difference between what the Jew would like to be and what he is becomes the embodiment of that soul. He is the wanderer: "I got up and began wandering" (Chamisso 58). The unbridgeable division that rends the exception Jew renders it impossible for him to take up residence: he is always elsewhere. The Jew who would be rid of his past for the sake of becoming German is a divided one, given in his self-affection to male-male, same-sex desire. He is thus criminalized, and the ethical judgment that issues from recognizing the true nature of his soul is self-ostracism. The difference that inhabits his soul produces the text, which is nothing less than Schlemihl's self-assessment addressed to Chamisso. The text is then the document of a Jew coming to ethics, via this newly awakened critical faculty and same-sex desire, so as to abandon Germany.

If by joining two metonymic chains the text fulfills a wish to remark the Jew so as to exile him, it also resurrects the very terms that threatened civil society with integration of the Jew under equal terms. As stated above, civil society sought to police the family. Difference or acceptable difference was constructed along an axis of gender. For psychoanalysis, gender is the phenomenology of difference (Warner 200). Schlemihl or the difference that is Schlemihl undermines that phenomenology, and that necessitates his exile. But such difference is productive. Schlemihl becomes a scholar, demonstrating that ineluctable variation is constituent of all existence. Roaming from the arctic Iceland to tropical Africa—with an ease equaled only by Frankenstein's monster—he charts the geographies of inner Africa and the lands around the North Pole, noting the effects of the magnetic fields as well. He writes *Historia stirpim planatarum utriusuq orbis*, a system for mapping the natural systems of plants that increases its known types by at least one-third (Chamisso 66), and plans before his death to leave the completed manuscript to the University of Berlin. He draws upon the botanical sciences of the Enlightenment, something already anticipated by his dream through references to works by Linnæus and Humboldt. Difference is thus marked by genus and species, in which related organisms, in line with Lennæus's binominal classification according to genus and species, are capable of interbreeding. In other words, difference is not marked by race and gender. Hot/cold, north/south, flora/fauna, genus/species, and the vast category of things in-between remap the conditions of understanding and identity. Chamisso may seek to trivialize Schelmihl's scientific writings by rendering them socially irrelevant and hopelessly incomplete: "And so it was, that already from the beginning everything I would gather and put together was doomed to remain a fragment" (Chamisso 61–62), but their fragmentary character ensures the endlessness of the pursuit. The Enlightenment categories that Schlemihl reintroduces are thus inexhaustible ones that also serve to destabilize the phenomenology of difference that sought to stabilize a Jewless civil society around gender and sexuality. The very conditions of exclusion designed to free society of the Jew engender endless possibilities for the Jew's (re)entry into that society via the Enlightenment and its forms of taxonomy. Ironically, the terror that such possibilities of uncontainable difference evoke is proleptically signaled by Schlemihl's occasional residence: a cave, not in Afghanistan but nonetheless in the desert of Thebias or in the Middle East, guarded by a poodle.

If we return for a moment to the enigmatic transaction between Erasmus Spikher and Peter Schlemihl as presented in Hoffmann's tale, the outcome is perhaps not as feckless as the narrator leads us to believe. As noted previously, the effort to restore specularity through a joining of one man's *Schlagschatten* to another's reflection is destined to fail. Not just the outlines of each would hardly reside seamlessly atop or beside each other, but also the snipping away or suturing required to make the shape or shapes fit their new bearers would result in a self or selves hardly recognizable to that self itself. So, when the narrator of this frame of a multiply framed tale remarks, "*es wurde nichts daraus*," "nothing" is just as likely a displaced substantive that frustrates tracking. That is to say, what came of this experiment is something pushed beyond the boundaries of recognition or policing, an entity that registers as a nothing, escaping the narrator's judgment and purview.

The possibility of a new-found freedom on the other side of narrative consciousness is perhaps best formulated in a different genre about the same Peter Schlemil, i.e., the Volksgedicht: "In der Tat, Schlemihl hat seinen Schatten verkauft, dabei seine Seele verlor'n/Danach hat man niemals mehr von ihm gehört, und niemand weiß mehr, daß er einst gebor'n"[20] ("In fact, Schlemihl sold his sad and thereby lost his soul. Thereafter no one ever heard of him again, and no one no longer knows that he was even born"). In other words, the space of interiority necessary for any self-reflection is evacuated; it becomes a nothing that loses sight of its subject as if that captive being, once captivated by his own reflection and interiority, never existed. We will now turn to exploring the messianic potential of this de-territorialized self.[21]

3

Queer Prosthetics or Male Tribadism in Kleist's "On the Puppet Theater"

Given the almost impossible array of interpretations "Über das Marionettentheater" (On the Puppet Theater; 1812) has succeeded in entertaining, it is nothing less than expected that it should be asked to respond to questions of sexuality.[1] If a text can put into play so many signifieds, it is only because its performative character is so seductive or enchanting that the text comes to be enamored of itself, sufficiently flattered by all suitors to welcome their numerous advances. The text is personified to the extent that the virtuoso performances of the interlocutors are foregrounded as much as the argument itself. Nothing the text says, or rather does, can really mean anything precisely because it *can* mean anything, and this "meaning-so-much" is an irresistible invitation to queer inquiry. For queer studies, the emergence of a queer subtext in "Das Marionettentheater" is not necessarily a good thing.[2] For one, it reinforces the regrettable conceit, as Michel Foucault noted, that the real or hidden truth of a text is always a sexual one that assumes the form of a confession, not all that dissimilar from Herr C—'s for the dissolute pleasured offered by *Gliedermänner* (men of members) or the narrator's for an ephebe in distress. For another, it aligns queerness once again with dissemblement.[3] He, who not unlike Kleist's text, can evince any number of contradictory gestures, who can present himself in any number of guises, is how one comes to designate the homosexual, if for no other reason than his/its essence, which would link, clarify, and assemble the effusion of affects, is missing, hidden, or closeted.[4] Do we really know anything, for example, about the narrator, save that he observes and engages strangers who frequent theaters of ill-repute and bathhouses where boys pose before mirrors? But how would we speak of same-sex desire or same-sex sex acts without the epistemological crucible of the closet, even if the content of that closet is now widely accepted as an open secret?[5] On the one hand, a queer reading that seeks to maintain a balance between surface meaning and deep meaning reinscribes the very episteme from which it sought liberation. On the other hand, demonstrating how such a reading is pure invention undermines its epistemological power and thus begs the question as to whether we need to take a break from sexuality, to paraphrase once again Jane Halley.[6]

The break is something more than simply eschewing queer subtexts or infrastructural supports that buttress constructions of sexuality. Rather, the break is from those readings that seek to find themselves reflected in the text, that pursue a textual narcissism by discovering their own readerly strategies confirmed by or in the text. Narcissism is certainly foregrounded in Kleist's text, given that its central example, or the example in the middle of the text, concerns an ephebe ensorcelled by his own image in the mirror and chagrined by the failure of that mirror to return the desired self-reflection. What is queerer, we might ask? To admire oneself in the mirror as one dries one's foot and think such beauty is comparable to a Greek statue, as the ephebe does? Or to find that the person in the mirror is not the person one thought one was, which the ephebe also discovers? That means I will be operating with two very different understandings of "queer."[7] The first simply refers to same-sex desire but is embedded in the narcissistic textual practices alluded to. The second is one that disables reading insofar as no logic can contain or otherwise explain the signifying chain of the text or its own reading. If we recall the distinction Freud offered about narcissism from the previous chapter, the former would correspond to a naïve narcissism, or a queer reading that seeks its own reflection in the text. The latter would undermine such self-sameness through a critical reflection that disables any form of self-recognition. Both uses are in play here to resist the self-sameness that queer by definition should disable. That begs the question as to what kind of *Literaturwissenschaft* can operate without a hypothesis that seeks compelling proof of itself. While much of this will become clear below, the most concise answer is a queer one. The essay that follows is thus an attempt to violate the protocols of reading while still remaining readable.

The previous chapter supplied blanks as it attempted to pronounce the abomination that the "emancipated" but "closeted" Jew had become. The familiar anecdote from the essay in which the narrator would assert that a dancer with a prosthetic leg excels at her craft does not exhaust the text's reliance on prosthetics to sustain its argument. As the Andreas Kraß's reading demonstrates, the epistemological crucible of the closet operates as an interpretive prosthetic to overcome an interpretive paralysis that disables resolution of the text's most stubborn ambiguities. At the same time, the use of the term in linguistics is instructive. A prosthesis or prosthetic, as the Greek origin of the term (to add to,) suggests, is a metaplasm in which the addition of a letter or a syllable to the beginning of a word does not change its basic meaning. Romance languages offer several examples; the Latin *speciālis* became *especial* in Spanish and Old French. It is a placeholder, marking or denoting nothing but an affect (or effect?) whose nonproductive contribution to meaning can best be described as queer. What might be described as "apheresis" in *Schlemihl*, the removal of a sound or, as in this case, all sound, now comes to be pronounced or said. The temptation to make such saying mean something is what, I argue, needs to be refused.[8]

Read as such, Kleist's text makes a mess of sexuality. If it responds to an interrogator about sexuality—as I believe it does—it equivocates, but the manner described above as symptomatically and inescapably homosexual. Rather, it invents what might be considered an impossible sexuality—a male tribadism, to anticipate Heine's term for August von Platen's less than closeted proclivities.[9] More to the point, sexuality in the text is an appendage or supplement, a prosthetic device. Any reading that seeks to find itself reflected in the text comes only to be another appendage: a reading of the narrator's reading of his conversation with Herr C—, which is a reading of the interlocutor's positions, which is a reading of where they stand physically and argumentatively in relation to each other. In such fashion, the text—obscured, hidden, or even secured amid a surfeit of readerly affects—creates its own closet. These affects can just as easily be called, to cite the text, the *Ziererei*, the ornamentation that afflicts dancers whose center of gravity, unlike that of marionettes, is decentered and thus renders their performance graceless. The sexual character of the text thus lies in a retreat from self-exposure—and again we might recall Schlemihl holed up in his cabinet—but such a retreat is merely the misprision produced by reading doubling back on itself. The text becomes its own self-ornament or *Schmuck*.

The purpose of this chapter then is twofold: to adumbrate how sexuality comes to be *the* truth of a text and to explore how a queer reading, which challenges the standards of any hermeneutic protocols, is perhaps more promising for queer studies because it renders the text susceptible to unpredictable or even ungovernable temptations. To that end, I apply a seemingly invented term, "male tribadism," to the text to justify that term's use, even if it has no real meaning; it is, in other words, interchangeable with the second use of "queer" cited above. If for the sake of shorthand we summarize Kleist's "Marionettentheater," as tentative proof of the misalignments of knowledge and truth, the (mis)use of "male tribadism" is oddly responsive to the text's own indices. The second part of my essay is a reading of Helmut Schneider's "Deconstruction of the Hermeneutic Body: Kleist and the Discourse of Classical Aesthetics" and, as mentioned above, Andreas Kraß's "Der Stachel im Fleische: Kleists' Marionettentheater—ein Queer Reading" (The Thorn in the Flesh . . .).[10] The point is to demonstrate how a self-proclaimed queer reading reconstructs that body to rescue hermeneutic inquiry. But since Kraß's reading relies on the performative aspects of the text, its dialogics, one question that remains necessarily unanswered is to what extent the staging of a queer reading exposes the hermeneutic body as a construct incapable of confession, sexual or otherwise. Finally, I will attempt to demonstrate how a non-narcissistic reading might proceed. What kind of interpretive praxis might be involved? To do so, male tribadism, insofar as it may refuse a binary logic, may be unreadable in precisely the anti-hermeneutic terms described above; the term serves then to describe what cannot be hypothesized.[11] With respect to the previous chapter's description of narcissism, this chapter further explores the two forms, a simple one and a critically mediated one, by linking them to textual practices of reading or of reading oneself into the text.

Let me put this another way. Male tribadism is anything but a telling taxonomic term. Heine's coining of the phrase in the tenth and eleventh chapters of the "Baths of Lucca" to mock Carl Gustav von Platen is intended to name the unnamable, the unnatural orientation of a poet so fey, repressed, and regressive that any form of self-expression is restored only through artificial means. Platen cloaks himself, according to Heine, in the drag of tradition (ghasels), disavowing confident expression of his sexual proclivities. The temptation is to couple his lifeless verse, *geistlos*, if you will, with the lifelessness or *Geistlosigkeit* of a puppet, the *Abgüsse* or copies of the classical statue, the thorn picker, or the physically restrained bear that all serve as models of grace in "Das Marionettentheater."[12] My intention is not to succumb to temptation and look for queerness in "Das Marionettentheater" by deeming it "Platenic" or "Platenesque." What I argue is that sexuality is a default position that is queer, not because homoerotic undercurrents are brought to the surface, but rather only if it truly defaults, if it becomes an indefensible position of last resort, which is certainly reminiscent of the defensive posturing and remarks by the text's interlocutors.[13] In other words, when no other interpretive strategy can be sustained, sexuality becomes the crucible by default for reading the text.

Defensive Reading

The first evidence of being on the defensive is produced by Herr C— in response to the narrator challenging his being sighted at a theater that appeals to the masses (Pöbel) and has recently been denounced by the duke.[14] To defend his guilty pleasures, Herr C— will eventually recite nonsense: "In cases where the movements are crooked [krumm], it appears that the law of their crookedness is of the first or, at most, the second order; and in this case, only elliptically" (Kleist 340) (In Fällen, wo sie krumm sei, scheine das Gesetz ihrer Krümmung, wenigstens von der ersten oder höchstens zweiter Ordnung; und auch in diesem letzten Fall nur elliptisch).[15] When such crooked, or at best elliptical, reasoning fails to obtain, he seeks refuge in the straightforward reasoning of algebra and geometry: "More likely, the movements of his fingers [the machinist's] behave somewhat like numbers of their logarithms or asymptotes to their hyperbola" (Kleist 340) ("Vielmehr verhalten sich die Bewegungen seiner Finger . . . etwa wie Zahlen zu ihren Logarithmen oder die Asymptote zur Hyperbel"). His own excesses or hyperbole suggest that he must go to great lengths to defend what must be indefensible; otherwise, he would pursue a straight or *gerad* line of argumentation. The only point of convergence in this asymptotic reasoning, if one exists, is hidden, in which case the argument and its effects are symptomatic of a secret to be exposed only to the sympathetic. In fact, it is Herr C—'s reading, or rather his performance of such a reading, that invites an outing of what appears to be a secret, and this affect or overproduction of meaning is what arouses the narrator's curiosity. "Since the utterance [that a dancer . . . could learn much from a puppet], by dint of the manner in which it was presented, appeared to be more than mere caprice [*Einfall*], so I sat down next to him [liess ich mich bei ihm nieder] in order to hear more closely the reasons (or grounds) upon which he could support an unusual assertion" (339). His affect seduces the narrator. The latter, if one wants to look for queerness here, could be said to kneel, affirming that he regards all of this as something more than fancy (Einfall) and signaling his willingness to hear or do more by literally getting on his knees (einfallen).

The narrator's *Einfall*, which only occurs after Herr C— ridicules the narrator's disbelief by snubbing his nose at the narrator as he simultaneously takes a hit of snuff, puts the narrator on the defensive. Demeaned, the narrator plays along under the cover of the *Bible* or the third chapter of the first book of Moses. He sets out to prove to Herr C— that he knows what it means to lose one's innocence. He confesses his extended observation in a bathhouse of an ephebe repeatedly performing for Herr C— the drying of his foot in a futile attempt to evoke a Greek statue. When the narrator concludes by asserting that a witness could corroborate his story "word for word," his own hyperbolic gesture (Is it really possible for the witness to repeat the episode word for word?) signals complicity with the tactics of Herr C—. Such hyperbole is replayed at the end of the essay when Her C— asks the narrator if he believes his wild tale about a fencing bear. "Completely! I cried out, with joyous applause [Beifall]; coming from any stranger in that it is so likely; and so much more coming from you" ("Volkommen! Rief ich, mit freudigem Beifall; jedwedem Fremden, so wahrscheinlich sie ist: um wie viel mehr Ihnen!"; Kleist 345) Herr—C's success is complete, due in no small measure to the corroboration of the witness/narrator whom, only pages before, Herr C— had mocked. Their mutual falling (kneeling) for marionettes (Bei-fall) is now a shared secret, the content of which is pure hearsay, reinforced by the indirect discourse of the entire essay. Sexuality, if one aligns the term with the secret of the text, is produced by the effect of defensive posturing, which in turn gives rise to hearsay or rumor. Hyperbole, the central affect of the text, is thus symptomatic of something that comes to be read, as we will see, in terms of sexuality. My other use of "queer" or male tribadism would decouple symptoms from affect; that is to say, the text would become asymptomatic; sexuality/meaning and performance/affect would not intersect. In the language of the text, hyperbole would become asymptotic.

 The most explicitly defensive gesture or gesturing in the text is the parrying of the fencing bear, so we are told, as he humbles Herr C—. He is, of course, the perfect reader. "Eye [in] to eye, as if he read into my soul, he stood there, the claws ready to attack [schlagfertig; more often, it means quick-witted], and if my thrusts were not seriously meant, he didn't move" (Kleist 345; "Aug in Aug, als ob er meine Stosse nicht ernthaft gemeint waren, so rührte er sich nicht"). The perfect reader defends himself by looking directly into the eyes of his opponent or Herr C— such that he can deflect the thrusts of his opponent or recognize when there is no thrust behind the gesture. If this kind of eye contact is a reading of the soul, as Herr C— suspects, then reading beneath the surface is nothing more than parrying and not falling for feints. This link between reading and fencing establishes the performative as defensive and even paralyzed. At its most aggressive, the bearer of grace or the perfect reader is *schlagfertig* or ready to strike.

The emphasis is on a "thrustless" reading, which is nonetheless as quick-witted as the repartee of the essay's interlocutors. Such repartee, initiated when the narrator puts Herr C— on the defensive for hanging around theaters of ill repute, is itself a reading enabled by perfect eye contact. But being eye to eye, being the eye of the other (*Aug in Aug*) is to read oneself and become one's own target, thereby paralyzing the reader. Reading thus needs to miss its target if the reader is to escape unharmed. Misreading is called for, which for a perfect reader like the bear is at best paradoxical. But insofar as his reading is both a delayed response and a deflection, his reflection in the eye of the opponent is off, temporally displaced. "We see that in the organic world the becoming darker and weaker of a reflection is directly proportional to grace becoming more radiant and commanding." ("Wir sehen, das in dem Mase, als in der organischen Welt, die Reflexion dunkler und schwächer wird, die Grazie darin immer strahlender und herrschender hervortritt"; Kleist 345.) If we accept Herr C—'s conclusion, then only a weak and dim (self-) reflection can produce the perfect kind of reader, such as the fencing bear. Grace depends upon poor lighting, which may explain why the interlocutors meet in the evening. These darker aspects of grace will be discussed below. What is particularly curious here is how grace depends on some kind of delay or deflection, but is that inherent in grace or something produced by a self-consciously postlapsarian text? That is to say, even if self-reflection is queered or not the perfectly narcissistic mirroring of the self that would preempt ornamentation, it mirrors perfectly the text's structure of deferral, whether such deferral be the delay in transcribing the discussion with Herr C— or the deferred return to a state of grace. If hyperbole, as the affect (even *Grundstimmung*) of the text, results from the incongruity of the text's rhetoric with its meaning or a misalignment of the two, then the historical moment of which the text declares itself a part guarantees this disconnect.

Stated otherwise, rhetorical embellishment is all any reading can accomplish, which aligns itself perfectly with the misalignment of the text. Is it at all possible then to perform an incongruous reading, which I use here synonymously with the second meaning of "queer"? Or does any execution of such a reading merely reproduce what it sees of itself in the text, its own embellishment? To repeat, the hope for the defensive reader, tied and bound to seeing himself reflected in the text or in the eye of the other, is to misread or miss reading by dint of a delay or a deferral, however graceless he may become as a result. In the next section, I examine how male tribadism as a nonsignifying term, as a placeholder for a practice that has not yet been named and that has not yet become an orientation, might offer a possibility of preserving the incongruity. The approach, if it is to seek a queer possibility in the text, must, in keeping with the indices of the text, be defensive.

Reading Ass Backwards or Entering Paradise through the Back Door

Now, let me defend my reasons as to why male tribadism is appropriate as a heuristic device or rather an asymptotic term. To begin, too much evidence now exists to question the very use of any of the vocabulary invoked today to describe same-sex sex desire. It is not only that the use of homosexuality, or even sexuality, is anachronistic—the term is not coined until the later nineteenth century—but the manner in which we could read any such subtext presumes that the scene(s) of seduction be read consistent with the same semiotic chain that animates more contemporary attempts to disclose the "real" truth, which is inevitably a sexual one.[16] The problem is particularly vexing when one is working with Kleist. His letter to Ernst von Pfuel from January 1805 is instructive: "I could have slept with you dear boy; my entire soul embraced you! I have often observed your beautiful body with truly girlish feelings, when you, before my eyes, entered the lake in Thun" ([I]ch hätte bei Dir schlafen können. Du lieber Junge; so unmarmte Dich meine ganze Seele. Ich habe Deinen schönen Leib oft, wenn Du in Thun vor meinen Augen in den See stiegest, mit wahrhaft mädchenhaften Gefuülen betrachtet). But as Joachim Pfeiffer warns, Kleist's playfulness with such erotically charged tropes cannot be used for purposes of attribution of sexuality, since sexuality has no ontological status at the time (Pfeiffer 217).[17] Rather—and Pfeiffer suggests that this holds for all of Kleist's texts—the letters "prefigure a reality in which people are no longer tied down to fixed orders of subjectivity" (Pfeiffer 227). The dialogic dance of "Das Marionettentheater" in which the two interlocutors repeatedly reposition themselves (i.e., Their arguments are not straightforward) with respect to each other simultaneously articulates a disavowal of any sexual position. If—and I will speak to this later—queer sexuality is tied to what Kraß calls the penetration fantasies of the interlocutors (Kraß 131), their perambulations doom such fantasies. In that case, only the bound and tied fencing bear would be capable of a sexuality, unless we rethink sexuality as merely a textual specter that can be spoken about if its lack of an ontological status is acknowledged, as something that will come to be spoken about once a vocabulary for sexuality is invented. In any case, the text makes a mess of sexuality. Any response to such questions is a recent invention and requires an invented term such as Heine's.

However unprepared our modern discourse on sexuality is to imagine or define something such as male tribadism, using "Das Marionettentheater" to entertain such a definition means—from what was just said in the previous paragraph—that it will have no meaning other than to define or coordinate a field of gestures and affects, to discover, as with marionettes, a *Schwerpunkt* or a center of gravity. The identification of a center of gravity risks granting sexuality ontological status. It suggests a certain inevitability to positing the truth of all secrets as asexual if for no other reason that sexuality offers the text a center of gravity, albeit a specious one. If the discordant effects of the text, the incongruity of its examples (such as the comparison of a three-dimensional dancer with a Teniers painting or the image of a concave mirror after it has passed into and returned from infinity) and the persistent repositioning of its interlocutors can be harmonized by queering them, that new-found harmony is at odds with any language available to the text when it was written. If a *Schwerpunkt* can be said to coordinate the four installments of the text, it is only the reliance on prosthetics—extras, remainders, or affects—that comes to be essentialized around a center of gravity.

So what are these supplements? To begin, there is the dialogic structure that allows the argument to elide its many sticking points. Simply put, the narrator's sudden reversal and enthusiastic endorsement of Herr C—'s startling claims rhetorically settle what logic has not, for example, that those with artificial limbs can dance more gracefully than the famed P— in her role as Daphne and the young F— as Paris (Kleist, 342). The dialogue, moreover, is reproduced as indirect conversation so that it is already a fact, even if the facts of the argument themselves don't all add up.[18] This pattern is apparent in the context. The marionette is hardly self-sufficient; it depends upon a machinist, just as the fencing bear depends upon an opponent and just as the boy in the bathhouse depends upon an onlooker and widely viewed copies of the thorn picker, who likewise depends upon being penetrated by a thorn in the foot. In other words, the extensive reach of the argument from "Genesis" to a return to paradise is really a series of extensions or extended examples that can only repeat the logical impossibilities of the previous ones. The rhetorical power of the argument and its appearance in four installments contribute as well to the interlocutors' dance around what seems to be the missing center or actual topic of the discourse.

To frame this discussion of supplements in the terms of the previous section, do these supplements complement each other to form a perfect whole that embodies grace? Or is the fit imperfect; is there a (temporal) gap that produces a reflection, such as in the case of the ephebe, that is off? In that instance, the supplement is not proper or essential, but rather an ornament or affect whose most striking feature is queer or odd, a linguistic prosthesis. And if the production of such supplements is seemingly endless, is the affect not exaggerated or hyperbolic? Herr C— concedes, at least in the case of the marionette, that there is something mysterious or *geheimnisvoll* (Kleist 340). The mysterious might not be the result of a secret, a unifying truth of which all expression is a perfect reflection, but rather of crookedness or deception. The queer and secret truth of the text is true only insofar as it reproduces not an underlying or deep truth but a deflection, an imperfect reflection that can never be straightened. Like the narrator at the apparent pinnacle of understanding, at that moment when he means to be of one mind with Herr C—, the *Schwerpunkt* around which these affects would collect is itself a bit distracted and dispersed (*zerstreut*; Kleist 345).

Now, how is it that these supplements acquire a homoerotic character? The short answer is that the turning point in the text, the moment when disdain and skepticism are replaced by unconditional endorsement, is its most homoerotically charged scene. The subject matter, a naked young boy drying his foot in a bathhouse with reference to ancient Greece, fuels whispers of something homosexual. The narrator/boy configuration repeats the Socratic model of instruction, which is rehearsed as well by the relation between Herr C— and the narrator. Since "Platonic" served at this time, according to Paul Derks, as a euphemism for pederasty and male-male sex, the essence of the homoerotic in the text is something extra-textual, or at best a euphemism that misnames what it would describe.[19] Insofar as the interlocutors speak from postlapsarian positions, the text is itself an exercise in misnaming. That makes the use of male tribadism all the more inviting.

At this point, it should be clear that male tribadism, as an invented term to describe Platen for Heine's readers, has no justifiable relation to the text, save for an invented one. And that invented relation—dare I call it an unnatural one?—constitutes a "back door" justification for its use, the back door reminiscent of the one through which no one enters paradise, at least under the terms set forth by the text. That is to say, an unrelated term is defined by a text that has nothing to do with the term. Otherwise meaningless, the term becomes the meaning or secret truth of the text. The logic is circular. But so is Kleist's text: the argument is justified once the interlocutors espouse each other's arguments, and that espousal is justified by the arguments. Such circular logic can also be viewed as serial reproduction, particularly since the text appeared in four installments in the *Berliner Abendblätter* (December 12, 13, 14 and 15, 1810). In any case, the text or rather the reading of Genesis by Herr C— and the narrator, the reading of that reading by the narrator in his reconstitution of his conversation with Herr C—, and the reading of each installment of what came before, not to mention our reading of those readings—his endless series of concentric circles calls out for a *Schwerpunkt*, something muted or repressed in the text to keep the text from bleeding. The thorn in the argument needs to be extracted. But once extracted, it is extraneous or as queer to the text as are the actual thorn and cries of the original, injured athlete. In other words, the text is nothing without supplements, and only a queer supplement and/or *Schwerpunkt*—and this is the final component of my reason for importing male tribadism—offers reading "Das Marionettentheater" salvation. It becomes a default hermeneutic to close or rescue the circular logic of "Das Marionettentheater," which is precisely what the text demands. In other words, the use of "male tribadism" questions and renders suspect the very reading it enables. But arousing suspicion gives rise to the very rumors that sponsor a queer reading.

A Prosthetic Return to Paradise

Still, male tribadism must mean something. That is, the long answer to the question posed above needs to show how a queer reading responds to what Helmut Schneider has called the deconstruction of the hermeneutic body in "Das Marionettentheater." Only then will it be possible to offer a different response to the challenge posed by Schneider's reading, one that does not succumb to making queerness the essence of the text's secret. Until now, I have been trying to develop or put into play a dirempted or non-self-identical meaning of "queer," acknowledging that the very use of the term is anachronistic, which is precisely what makes its use so inviting. The text, as evident from the first section, is committed to retrospection or a reading that leads one to the back door. But what does it mean to enter the back door, or to quote the text, to enter "paradise through the back door"? (Kleist

342). We know, from the previous section that it has something to do with supplements that alternate between placing one reader, initially Herr C—, and then the other on the defensive. This alteration aligns one reader with the other, but the alignment is imperfect, subject to deflection. That has two consequences: it invites positing a *Schwerpunkt* (center of gravity) for reflection, and it protects the reader from his own reflection. The question is then whether the use of male tribadism keeps both of these invitations open? Does the tension between a reading that sees itself reflected in the text and one that misses itself by producing a supplement (that is likewise read and misread in the same manner suggested by the remark that there are two routes or lines (of thought) that lead to the back door of paradise? Or is any narcissistic image split from the beginning, pursuing itself from a divided origin? As I move now to track in more detail those two possible routes, I do so, not surprisingly, with two intentions: (1) to show how a self-described queer reading comes full circle and thus restores Schneider's deconstructed hermeneutic body, and (2) to maintain that this restored body is somehow always already unreadable, subject to what I described above as a temporal delay generated, as in the case of the ephebe, by self-consciousness.[20]

The most apt and yet puzzling description of this dual task is found in the text itself: ". . . just as two intersecting lines, converging on one side of a point, reappear on the other side after passing through infinity." (. . . Wie sich der Durchschntt zweier Linien, auf der einen Seite eines Punkts, nach dem Durchgang durch das Unendliche, plötzlich wieder auf der anderen Seite einfindet; Kleist 345). The point (of the argument or the fencer's thrust?) is where the two lines converge, but that point of convergence is on the move, diverging from itself as it betrays itself by going over to the other side. Just think of how the narrator as well betrays his own position by going to the other side, which in a queer context would signal his successful recruitment by Herr C—. And if his convergence is also a kind of divergence, it is no wonder that he is *zerstreut*, distracted or strewn about. Given that the story of the ephebe entranced by his mirror image signals the narrator's successful recruitment by Herr C—, it is no surprise that the mirror serves as another example of perfect consciousness, or rather grace, to follow up on the one about intersecting lines. ". . . [O]r the image in a concave mirror, after it has distanced itself in infinity, suddenly returns dense before us." (oder das Bild des Hohlspiegels, nachdem es sich ins Unendliche entfernt hat, plötzlich wieder dicht vor uns tritt; Kleist 345). Certainly, unpacking this image is no simple task, not the least because the instrument of reflection, the concave mirror, is itself imperfect. Like the description of the marionette's *Schwerpunkt* it is bent or *gekrümmt*. What can be said is that the restoration of its density (*wieder dicht*), which is an expression of perfect grace, is dependent upon a temporal delay, without which repetition (*wieder*) would be impossible. In other words, like male tribadism, grace is anachronistic.

Schneider emphatically proposes a deconstructive reading as a response to the latest wave of theoretical currents that have shaped the hermeneutic understanding of "Das Marionettentheater." He restores a historical context by responding in large measure to the aesthetic values of German classicism, particularly its understanding of grace as articulated by Schiller. Subsequent readings, so Schneider, conformed to the tenets of *Geistesgeschichte*, accepting almost naïvely the text's conviction that a fractured self would be restored at some later date through a higher level of consciousness until Paul de Man undid the text's questionable claims by attending to its rhetoric (Schneider 210). By asserting that Kleist's text inverts the classical model of grace—externalizing through its staging what for Schiller was internalized or spiritualized—Schneider links the history of the text's reception with something already predicted by the text. If for Schiller "grace is the staging of nature by a self-empowering human subject which yearns to reflect itself precisely in that which is beyond its control, [manipulating the body's contingency]," Klest's text, Schneider argues, fractures the phantasm of a unified body (of reading) by constituting its arguments through staging or through the exterior movements that describe the interlocutors positioning of themselves and their arguments with respect to each other (Schneider 212). The text thus comes to question the priority of the signified over the signifier insofar as the mechanics of the argument eclipse the essence of the argument. That potential inversion extends from the *Äusserungen*, the utterances or externalizing of the players themselves, to their physical movements, to the discourse itself. Virtually repeating what was argued above, Schneider asserts that "the rhetorical and gestural appearance of the dancer's speech . . . causes the narrator to draw closer and interrogate him about the reasons for or behind such a statement [the superiority of marionettes over dancers]" (Schneider 214). The point, however, is not to assert that the performative takes precedence or that gesture becomes the argument itself, but rather that it opens up a space that Schneider paradoxically names an "internal space" of "externalized inferiority" (Schneider 214.).

That space is a split that cannot be sutured because it extends to the language of the text, or, as Schneider notes, the "consistent play on the literal meaning of words" (214). The following examples are offered:

Äusserung [making an external utterance], *vorbrachte*, [bring forth or up, present], *Gründe* [grounds, reasons] (Schneider 214.). Decisive here is that the mechanics of the argument respond to the literal meaning of the words all the while asserting, as a precondition of grace, that interiority or what the text calls *Geist*, can align itself with exteriority. But in a postlapsarian world, even Herr C—would have to concede that language as the instrument of consciousness cannot secure such an alignment. This is why the history of the text's reception, its correspondence to a loosely constructed *Geistesgeschichte*, is so compelling; it responds to the text's charge to suture that split, which is every bit as much of a wound as the one caused by the thorn in the classical statue. Through a historical consciousness that in one moment would attend to the spirit of the word and in the next to its literal meaning, one would come, as the interlocutors insist, full circle and attain "infinite consciousness" (unendliches Bewußtsein; Kleist 345), provided all the intervening supplements or readings could be sublated.[21] The phrase encapsulates the problem, since *unendlich* could just as easily describe quite literally an infinite or unending back-and-forth between both modes of meaning and both interlocutors. This back-and-forth further explains the narrator's distracted state at a moment of supposed lucidity. He must occupy two historical spaces at once, the impossibility of which necessitates an interlocutor and a serial delay in relaying his conversation with Herr C—.

In fact, Schneider's reading suggests that over time the fracture only deepens rather than heals. The most telling example for Schneider is the following passage from Kleist: "Und der *Vor*teil, den diese Puppe *vor* lebendigen Tänzern voraus haben würde? Der Vorteil? Zu*vor*derst ein negativer, mein *vor*trefflicher Freund, nämlich dieser, dass sie sich niemals zierte" ("And the advantage that this puppet in advance would have over live dancers? First and foremost, a negative one, my excellent friend, namely this, that there is no self-embellishment"; Schneider 216; Kleist 341).[22] The conspicuous literality or "exterior side of language," literally its "fore-part," represents the "rhetorical décor" or *Zier* of speech (Schneider 217). The linguistic body overreaches, extends beyond itself to the point, according to Schneider, that it breaks apart. The materiality of language becomes its own content despite Herr C—'s passionate repudiation of such. He dismisses Madame P—'s performance of Daphne because she bends as if she were about to break (Kleist 342), but in the sentence just cited, the literal aspect of language, its forepart, can be said to do just that, to bend the argument to its breaking point. The hyperbolic repetition of the prefix *vor* becomes a linguistic filigree, a mere decorative thread that Herr C— cannot help spinning even though such ornamentation (a prosthesis) is at best regrettable. His language is at odds with itself, and while he insists that his consciousness is advanced enough to recognize the split, the expression of such recognition only frays further the thread that links signifier and signified. Schneider is thus justified to remark, "In an act of reverse empathy, the soul is constructed through exterior movements . . . soul or 'Geist' is reduced to nothing" (219). In terms of my reading, the material remains of an argument, whose back has been broken or been reduced to nothing, come back to life once they are queered or call forth a prosthetic so that a calculable logic, call it logarithmic, can account for the dismembered remains of a shattered consciousness. The queer reader inspires or blows spirit back into the limbs of the deconstructed body.

As Schneider's use of such terms as "inversion" and "castrated," as well as the above passage's emphasis of "fore-part" suggest, the next generation of readers in this back-and-forth, give-and-take history would be destined by the text to invert Schneider's reading by clipping its foreparts to preserve interpretive unity. Andreas Kraß's queer reading is such an inversion, all the more queer for its reliance on equating male-male desire with reading itself, or at least the kind of reading that occurs under the sign of a double taboo (Kraß 125). Both the puppet theater and the *Abendblätter* were publicly censored, so that the text was always already castrated, and its strewn (*zerstreut*) foreparts testify to the procedure. It would be more accurate, however, to describe Kraß's reading as a reattachment of these dismembered supplements, which can just as easily be described as prosthetics, as artificial limbs to allow the argument to re-find a leg(s) to stand on. That requires, in keeping with the logic of the text, discovering a *Schwerpunkt*. Such probing with prosthetic devices is, moreover, perhaps the nearest we have come to unifying the manifold uses of male tribadism in this essay around a center of gravity. In other words, a taboo, a twofold taboo—it takes two male tribadists to tango—resurrects the possibility of reading for meaning, which I have aligned, in keeping with Freud's reading of such self-mirroring in the previous chapter, with a simple narcissistic reading. It responds to the text's homoerotic cues for seeing one's grace affirmed in a mirror. It is not the ephebe who does so, but, in a larger sense, the interlocutors who seek affirmation of their positions in their counterparts.

The sexual undercurrent of Kraß's reading is announced immediately. The dialogue between the narrator and Herr C— is redefined as a *Verführung* (seduction but also misleading), which, in concert with the biblical references of the text, leads Kraß to further recast the text as the staging of a seduction:

"The text is about the seduction; about the reciprocal seduction of the main figures, on the one hand, and the seduction of the reader by the narrator, on the other" (Kraß 123). Since the text itself is about a fall from grace, Herr C— is seen—via his argumentative stances—to lure the narrator to partake of the "forbidden fruit in which is concealed an erotic and hermeneutic promise" (Kraß 123). And, if the secret of the text is indeed a queer one, the narrator's invitation to the reader is likewise a scene of seduction. The gesture is remarkable for two reasons: first—and this is not surprising—it couples interpretive acts with erotic ones. Second, the performance of the text, its linguistic or dialogic supplement, is retrieved, but such partaking of the forbidden fruit for a second time so as to retrieve or expose the hermeneutic promise is queer: "it is not a man and a woman who perform the fall from grace, 'Sündenfall,' but rather the narrator and a ballet dancer" (Kraß 123). It takes two men to take the bite for a second time. The second eating can restore interpretive unity to the text only by restaging the fall as a gay seduction scene: "Each interlocutor attempts to read the other, and each attempts to make himself readable for the other. The narrated stores are strategic maneuvers in a game of hide and seek" (Kraß 124). The only way to understand what it means to eat the fruit a second time is to just do it, and the only way to do it is to stage a male same-sex scene of seduction. Remarkably, so many of the text's details now fall into place: why else would the two men meet in an open garden on a winter's evening, when most would prefer "to hole themselves up in an illuminated and heated room"? (Kraß 126). In this context, is there any other way to read the command "Thrust! Thrust!" (*Stossen Sie! Stossen Sie!*) than as a "penetration fantasy" that in turn "alludes" to the statue of the thorn picker (Kraß 131)? And penetration, linked as it is to fantasies of domination by competing fencers and/or interlocutors, is at play in the bathhouse as the narrator-cum-pedagogue seeks to instruct and thus seduce or mislead (*verführen*) the naked boy.

The narrator's sudden conversion is due less to the cogency of the ballet dancer's penetrating insights about puppets but rather to his own conversancy with penetration fantasies. He knows what it means to penetrate and, based on his reaction Herr C—'s examples, to be penetrated. As Kraß writes, "the consternation of the narrator quickly turns to shame, and he lowers his gaze" (128). His shame is his outing; he is exposed. But there is one more twist, one that involves role reversal or inversion. Whereas the narrator's coming-out story allows him to assume the role of pedagogue and dominator, he plays the role of the submissive with the dancer: "[S]o liess ich mich nieder." This is the phrase that signaled his willingness from the start to entertain the dancer's fancies. Kraß pushes the meaning of the phrases still further. The "last chapter in the history of the world," the yet-to-be-written return to paradise, has actually always already been written with the going down of the narrator (Kraß 132). His confession, which is a sexually charged obeisance, thereby becomes the secret or concealed truth of the text, but only if the repositionings of the body (of his argument) are reduced or stabilized through a binary lens of dominator/dominated, mentor/student, and so on. Paradise becomes inseparable from the pleasures of a text that permits wooer and suitor to trust in a winter's garden.

Male tribadism now has a very real textual dimension; it is a queer reading that offers hermeneutics its salvation. It collects the dismembered parts of the deconstructed hermeneutic body and finds new holes in the text to plug them into; that is, the gaps uncovered by arguments such as Schneider's become vessels for a queer content. With each thrust (*Stoss*), Kraß's reading lends Schneider's amputated text a new leg to stand on. But just as Herr C— concedes that those who dance with a prosthetic have a very limited range, a queer reading restricts its signifying potential by converting its content into a secret truth buried in the text. If, as I suggested at the beginning of this essay, the best hope for a queer reading is for it somehow to be unreadable, then the question remains: to what extent is such a salutary hermeneutic "not the last chapter in the history of the world"?

The *Last* Chapter, not the Last Chapter

The second meaning of "queer," which I have linked with male tribadism, now seems at best obscured, lest it can be demonstrated that Kraß's reading signals its own fall from hermeneutic grace. If we return to his reading of the central and most homoerotically charged episode of Kleist's text, it is not so certain that the queer hermeneutic body is as hale as suggested. A reversal of roles renders whatever sexual act that would announce Kraß's last chapter of history unreadable; it points as well to an uncontainable production of difference, including two men, and not a man and a woman, reenacting the fall from grace. Knowledge of the forbidden act thus remains as forbidden as the act itself. One might even say penetration of the text's sexual secrets only multiplies its interpretive gaps. To put it another way, male lesbians have too much to play with.

So much was perhaps suggested by the organization of Kraß's essay, insofar as he devotes a section to each of the four dates on which Kleist's text appeared in the *Abendblätter*. But there is a remainder, an introduction entitled "The Allegory of Reading," that engages de Man's reading while pleading for textual unity to follow. De Man, according to Kraß, fails to consider who/what is the object of reading and, in turn, the subject (Kraß 124). While that opens an avenue for Kraß's own queer take on the text in which the interlocutors seek to read each other, this additional installment, the section that does not correspond to a date of publication precedes everything else. What is extra or supplementary is there from the beginning.

To be sure, this is a minor observation, assignable to the formalities of academic writing as it is to anything else, save that Kleist's text is unthinkable if it is divorced from academic enterprises of reading. More to the point, the extra that is in play from the beginning anticipates several crucial aspects of the episode in question here. According to Kraß, the narrator signals his complicity with Herr C—'s mode of understanding when the former assumes the role of the pedagogue with the ephebe (Kraß 129). If earlier the narrator had fallen (*ließ sich nieder*), which, at least metaphorically, was preceded by the fall of Herr C—' as he deigned to visit the masses at the puppet theater, it is now the young boy who falls from grace and for the antics of a self-confessed, perverse narrator/pedagogue. Sooner or later, everybody falls but also rises. Today's object of derision is soon the seducer, and this give-and-take can only preclude fulfillment of the narrator's final prescription, namely the need to "eat from the tree of knowledge a second time so as to fall back into a state of innocence" (wieder von dem Baum der Erkenntnis essen, um in den Stand der Unschuld zurückzufallen). The problem is twofold. The fallen, even if their subsequent rise is always under the sign of a seemingly permanent fall from grace, keep falling forward and never back. (We should recall Schneider's emphasis on the prefix *vor*.) As a result, eating from the tree of knowledge a second time always occurs with a non-sublatable difference or, to recall the title of Kraß's opening section, it is always only allegorical, or, at least, queer sex is.

And queer sex is queer only when it is allegorical, only when it occurs with a difference. This is all the more evident if one attends to an easily overlooked aspect of the episode in the bathhouse. Judging from the fact that the narrator dates the series of failed rehearsals by the ephebe to three years prior, one can presume that he knew all along the significance of Herr C—'s remarks. Something encouraged him to be less than forthcoming, to lead the dancer on. But once the proper context has been supplied, he confesses his knowledge of how one can be led astray by self-consciousness. That is, once the dancer's argumentative thrust puts the narrator on the defensive, the latter's own self-consciousness allows him, if one follows Kraß's clues, to be mislead or seduced (*verführt*); his attending to the latent agenda of the dancer becomes a rehearsal of the original fall from grace. That the narrator already knows about the "Book of Moses" is expected; sin is original, but the sought-after repetition of that fall is queered. The difference of the self from itself in the beginning replays itself as a scene of same-sex seduction, which is absolutely different from its first or its biblical enactment. As stated above, taking a bite from the apple a second time, its reenactment is queered. Given the narrator's closing observation of the absolute necessity of eating from the tree of knowledge a second time to return to innocence, the path to paradise is a queer one, whereby it is always already routed through difference (Kleist 345).[23] Not only is knowledge of such difference retrospective (there has to have been a "before" to differ from), but also all iterations are always by definition delayed. This delay renders a perfect rendering of the first success or what we referred to above as a narcissistic triumph impossible. It certainly is true when the reenactment involves men only. The serpent's bite in the *Bible* becomes a thorn in the heel in ancient Greece, which becomes, as Kraß argues, the narrator's bite in the foot of the ephebe (seinen Zahn in den Fuß des Jünglings schlägt; Kraß 131).[24] Keep in mind that the narrator intentionally lies to the ephebe and pretends not to recognize the statue in the boy. The narrator thus encourages the boy's failed repeat performances. The narrator queers him by encouraging the boy to keep taking bites from the tree of knowledge. He seduces him to keep gazing at himself in the mirror. What will become of the narrator's own attempted seduction, be that of the boy or now Herr C—, is one that follows upon a lie, his a priori decision to mislead (*verführen*) the boy. The bite in the foot is, likewise, destined to become a different kind of bite when Kleist's male tribadists take their own second bites together.

Since the text is as much about reading as it is about seduction, or the seduction of reading, the question remains: what does all of the above mean nfor reading? The tryst between Herr C— and the narrator depends upon a correct, if not fully forthright, reading of the other's language and gestures. But the reading moves in two directions (we might recall the reference above to two lines passing through infinity), so much so that at the end of the essay, when the two appear to affirm each other's self-understanding, their language withholds something from meaning; it preserves the possibility of meaning nothing at all, of the strangers taking leave of each other at the moment of confirmed consensus or assignation. Queer here only means that two wholly incompatible possibilities coexist and constitute each other.

(Might not the same be said of male tribadism?) The narrator introduces his observation about partaking of the forbidden fruit a second time with the following: "Therefore [*mithin*], I said a bit distracted" (Kleist 345). I have already remarked upon the word "distracted," which also means strewn. The narrator, in other words, has already departed the space from which he speaks, a space indicated, no doubt, by "therefore," or, "literally, "there," or "hither." The narrator's first word seeks to bring the entire argument to a head, to lend it direction if not finality, but how can one who is spread about come to "therefore"? The point of conversion or attraction is already lost; even while it is being spoken, it is "hither." The dancer's last remarks likewise confirm his absence. "To be sure [*allerdings*]," he answered, "that is the last chapter in the history of the world" (. . . das ist das letzte Kapitel von der Geschichte der Welt; Kleist 345). His first word, "allerdings," would appear to recognize a need to reconcile two argumentative threads, to bring several things together. But his concluding thetic statement holds something back; it voids the very space of reconciliation and ensuing seduction. Is there really a last chapter, given that the first was already a rehearsal? If one hears in the word "last" resonances of its meaning in phrases such as, "That is the last person I would believe" or "That is the last thing I would want (to do with you or to do in that position with you?)," the last chapter is not *even* the last, not even a chapter in the history of the world. Everything that has led to this moment has been annulled or invalidated, leaving the interlocutors to grasp for prosthetics.[25]

As I stressed in the introduction, the two chapters to follow provide the most articulate registrations of queer echoes, whose stirrings in earlier chapters were felt but derided and elided, repressed in service of the nascent nuclear family and the emerging nation state. The opening discussion of "Death in Venice" established the central conceit of the project: messianic echoes were distributed broadly and unevenly in the periods following 1800. And given the state of our politics today, it was time to reanimate those energies. To that end, the first three chapters had a dual function: (1) To trace the construction or even invention of sexuality. What literary devices and tropes worked to make of the homosexual a type whose goings-on served to reenforce and extend the reach of the biopolitical regime and its disciplines? (2) To expose the sutures in that narrative and listen for echoes or voices drowned out by dreams of familial bliss or infinitely delayed by the queer paths they follow. The next chapter reads Roland Barthes's *A Lover's Discourse* alongside *The Sorrows of Young Werther* toward a crystallization, if you will, of the faint but still audible echoes of the messianic that were signaled in the first three chapters. In doing so, I work through for the first time the expression of the messianic variously formulated in the introduction but finding its most trenchant formulation as follows: I will not have not loved. The final chapter on *Brokeback Mountain* will thus trace future iterations of that formulation in post-Stonewall America.

4

Queer Echoes Traversing Great Spaces

Roland Barthes's *A Lover's Discourse* and
Johann Wolfgang Goethe's *Sorrows of Young Werther*

Roland Barthes's 1977 *Fragments d'un discours amoureux* seeks to secure a site from which the modern amorous subject, "driven into the backwater of the unreal," can speak (1).[1] But the fragments, which Barthes calls gestures of the "lover at work" (4) are "non-narrative" and "non-integrative" (7). That is to say, the text eschews a hierarchy or vertical structure and embraces instead an endless stream of utterances that form a "horizontal discourse" (7). The book can just as easily be described as a collage of citations that come from at least three sources: "ordinary readings" such as Goethe's *Werther*, "insistent readings" such as those of psychoanalysis, and "occasional readings," based in part on conversations with friends (8). These references to authors, books, and friends are noted in the margins and sometimes in footnotes. If Barthes's discourse is original, it is not so in the traditional meaning of the word, but rather in the manner in which Barthes recites, resituates, and even reinvigorates what has always already been said elsewhere by others. And if, as Samuel Weber has argued, Barthes's earlier *S/Z* depends upon a critically unexamined site from which his reading of Balzac's "Sarrasine" issues,[2] the gestures of *A Lover's Discourse* issue from multiple sources so that the site Barthes would secure for such a discourse is always under (re)construction, if for no other reason than the amorous subject's gestures are performative, with each citation the stage of such performance displaced.

Frankenstein's miserable creature was, of course, also a fan of *Werther*. While it is eager to dismiss the short passage in which the creature praises the novel as the meeting of two tortured souls forced into isolation by an unfeeling and uncaring world, the creature's actual remarks point in a different direction. "This simple and affecting story" arouses strong emotions in the creature, but such sentiments are not his only reaction to the novel. "Many options are canvassed; many lights thrown upon [. . .] obscure subjects" that turn the text into "a never-ending source of speculation and astonishment" (Shelley 122). But if apparent similarities between the two would suggest widespread consensus on these topics, Frankenstein's monster is not so forthcoming; he simply "refuses to ask into the merits of the case" (Shelley 122). These remarks by the creature point to an identification with Werther that is less than complete and that already signals a critical difference. In this chapter, the obliteration of the self in the face of an insurmountable Other, the echoes that return from that pyre—to recall Kristeva—find expression in Barthes's reading of *Werther*. That is, the return of the shattered self (Werther) allows Barthes to pursue through citation echoes that speak to a different fate, a different trajectory for impossible or forbidden love. As we will see, a counter-temporality is constructed to articulate the readiness or potentiality of these messianic echoes. Earlier chapters posited a terrain upon which the emerging male homosexual could be (re)-inscribed within the reaches of the panoptic regime. They also gestured toward something on the other side or outside of this immanence. In Roland Barthes's reading of *Werther* in *A Lover's Discourse* a number of muted queer echoes embedded in Goethe's text come through repetition and recontextualization to sound—or not to sound. From out of this "backwater of the unreal" the amorous subject will not have not been loved.

Nothing is less surprising, therefore, than Barthes's choice of Werther as the amorous subject's preferred interlocutor. Indeed, the expressed aim of Barthes's text—a primary language guided by amorous feeling that refuses "subjugation to the 'Great Narrative Other'" (Barthes 7)—recalls Werther's language of tears that bursts forth not from his eyes but rather from his oppressed heart (Goethe 53).[3] Such a language, Barthes asserts, "produces a myth of grief" that is bearable only because weeping allows the weeper to give his body and not his word to the interlocutor" (Barthes 182). In other words, the language of tears circumvents the word by becoming the body it would otherwise mediate. And since the body Werther would have, Lotte's, is not there or—as he writes in this same letter—is there only in his dreams, they signal the realness of his grief despite the absence of any other body or anybody other than tears. Except that there are bodies everywhere. The primary language of the amorous subject always relies on the fabrications of another: Werther has his Klopstock, Ossian, Homer; Barthes, his Werther, Plato, Proust, Nietzsche, Freud, and in the instance cited above, Schubert. While that hardly exhausts the list, it suffices to demonstrate that what the amorous subject most urgently seeks to confess is only always the language of another. To apply Barthes's terms, the amorous discourse that would preempt any response from the "Other" (Barthes 5) is invaded and occupied by many others, even as it proposes to escape all "forms of gregarity" (Barthes 1). Thus, the words printed in large type as a headline that closes Barthes's introduction, "So it is a lover who speaks and who says," is a dissemblance.

If the example above marks one dimension of the lover's discourse as vexed, Werther's letter from January 20 exposes another dimension of that rift, a brief reading of which will further indicate the direction of the argument to follow. In this letter, Werther addresses Lotte directly: "Dear Lotte, I must write to you . . ." (Goethe 64). He then imagines himself sitting at Lotte's feet, reading about a fairy tale to pacify the children. At that point Werther asks whether Albert is in the room and expresses his regret immediately thereafter for making such an impertinent inquiry. The expression of regret seems, at the very least, to be as direct a form of expression as his language of tears, save that it is off the mark, which prompts Werther in turn to concede its impropriety: "God forgive me that question!" (Goethe 66). More important, such primacy once again recalls a third, in this instance Albert, who rather than enabling the lover's discourse, inspires it only to still it.

Embedded in the letter is also a temporal curiosity that renders all of its claims untenable, but as I will argue later, that same temporal disjunction may ultimately account for Werther's privileged position in Barthes's discourse despite Werther's failure to deliver a real or immediate discourse of the heart. For the moment, it is important to note how the letter of January 20 refers to a time that will have already passed by the time Lotte reads it. Albert will have been by her side and left her side countless times when Lotte finally receives Werther's impertinent remarks. Werther, self-constructing and self-destructing with each stroke of the pen, will hardly be self-same. The Werther Lotte reads will already differ from the Werther Lotte was to have read. Thus, Werther's irrepressible desire to address Lotte ends by anticipating its own end. That is to say, immediacy or circumventing circumlocution not only places Werther outside or in exile from the scene immediacy calls forth but such scenes of immediacy also project their own impossibility. For Barthes, who cites *Werther* more than 50 times, such a discourse is never to accede to the mechanisms of control that police the love story and thus bring it to a satisfactory end (Barthes 1). For Werther, however he wishes his writing to obtain, it ends by submitting itself to the very controls Barthes refuses. Once Werther finally hits his mark dead on with Albert's pistol after it has passed through Lotte's hands, an unnamed editor collects, redacts, and arranges his letters. This de facto executor of Werther's will also conducts a thorough enough investigation of Werther's last days to offer a pathology of the lover's self-described sickness unto death (Goethe 48).[4] Barthes's Werther is at cross purposes with Werther's narrator, and that leads me to conclude the introduction with the observation that cross-purposes may be the precise requirement for hearing echoes of a queer messianic in Barthes's reading of Goethe's *Werther*.

In pursuing those cross purposes, I will first point to the most striking dissonance in Barthes's text, namely his affirmation of Nietzsche's eternal return of the same, a saying "Yes" to life in the face of Werther's unequivocal "No." Barthes's citation of Nietzsche introduces a remarkable difference; the sentimental of the Nietzschean ass replaces the overman. This means two things: (1) Barthes's amorous subject, whose representative is a Werther who says "Yes" to a life that denies life, is conscripted into an order whose borders depend upon a recoding of Werther's desire, whereby plenitude is just as likely a lack. And it is this lack that leads Werther to summon the father and his law. The retrospective that the editor presents of Werther's life, and this holds particularly for how that life is cited by Barthes, invites a queer reading of Werther's effects. Moreover, for Barthes's amorous subject such a reading of these effects has always already occurred. (2) Such repetition produces a radical difference, a difference that is itself an expression of the cross purpose described above. An echo of the name of a different beloved, namely Wilhelm, issues from the space to which Werther always returns and which marks his return to the order of the law. The aural or the acoustical is thus an expression of difference with respect to the spatial. The peculiarity of this site, however, does not end here. It depends as well upon Werther always already having vacated that space over and over again. This also means that the amorous encounter between Werther and Wilhelm never occurs; it is merely an echo of something that was over before it began but is still there as an echo. As such, the echo may remain outside the order of the law. At the very least, the tremulous quality of the echo renders the borders of this space unstable. Finally, this "queer" echo is only one of countless differences produced by an affirmation of the eternal return of the same or the countless rehearsals of what from the beginning has been cross-purposes, but it is an absolute difference that Barthes will affirm again and again.[5] The question that lingers is how to perceive such an echo, if the echo is to be beyond the reach of the law.

Affirmation of the Nietzschean Ass

The discrepancy between Barthes's expressed intentions and the actions of Werther's editor is all the more striking given the preeminent position Nietzsche occupies in Barthes's text. To be sure, Nietzsche is not cited as often as Werther or, for that matter, as often as Freud, Proust, or Gide. But his presence in the text cannot be reduced to the fifteen moments in which the reference is explicit. It is no overstatement to submit that he haunts the entire text. Specifically, it is Nietzsche's eternal return of the same that Barthes seeks to affirm: "Exiled from all gregarity, the [lover's discourse] has no recourse but to become the site, however exiguous, of an affirmation" (Barthes 24). Werther's ambiguous "No" to life becomes the "unreal" site of an unequivocal "Yes" for Barthes, or, in the language of Deleuze, of a double affirmation: "What I have affirmed a first time, I can once again affirm, without repeating . . . I affirm the first encounter in its difference . . . , I say to the Other (old or new); Let us begin anew" (Barthes 24).[6] Even more revealing is the manner in which Barthes reads Nietzsche to reevaluate the amorous subject's suffering as a sign of strength and thus an overcoming of the resentment brought on by rebuffs from the "Other." "Can one, reversing the evaluation, imagine a tragic view of love's suffering, a tragic affirmation of I-love-you? And if (amorous) love were put (put back) under the sign of the Active?" (Barthes 152). To affirm the eternal return of the same is to say "Yes" to all the failed and tragic loves of Werther. Before Lotte, we should recall, there was Lenora, and as Barthes remarks, Lotte is a mere pretext for Werther to identify himself with every lost lover: "I am the one who has the same place I have" (Barthes 129). That is, what is (re)affirmed is a structural operation whereby the tragic lover comes to affirm his fate by occupying the position of every other tragic lover, and the taking up of those positions is an active valuation of their shared fate, a promiscuous reevaluation that occurs with every citation in Barthes's text. The language of tears is *their* tears (his interlocutors) are his tears.

Each section of Barthes's text, insofar as the book refuses a hierarchical classification with a view to an end and insofar as the sections, which Barthes calls figures at work, have no first or last figure (Barthes 8), affirms ever anew Werther's forsakenness and its unbearable intensity. Such intensity, however, only arises because the arbitrary performance of the figures is subjugated to what Barthes calls the arbitrary factors of nomination and the alphabet (Barthes 8). Affirmation of the eternal return of the same depends upon three things: a position always already being there to occupy, a lover having also been there whom Barthes (re)cites, and the willingness of the amorous subject to submit to a structural operation that casts him outside of the order he both enables and disables with his leave-taking. Werther, in other words, is there only soon not to be there so he can be there again.

The double affirmation that subtends Barthes's text relies upon a subject projecting himself in multiple personae for the purposes of denying himself or for the purposes of projecting his own death. In this respect, he has captured Goethe's Werther dead on, who upon reading his duties confesses to Wilhelm that he had predicted his fate from the start. Certainly, such promiscuity echoes Nietzsche; resentment, once affirmed, leads to a second affirmation as it reevaluates (i.e., embraces) the condition of any subject's oppression, and all return or any returning to the scene is called forth by a desire to relive such unbearable intensity. Willing that return renders the intensity bearable.

This subject, however, is not the Nietzschean overman but rather the "Nietzschean ass": "Like the Nietzschean ass, I say yes to everything in the field of my love. I insist, reject all training, repeat the same actions; no one can educate me—nor can I educate myself . . . I persist in a dutiful, discreet, conformist delirium, tamed and banalized by literature" (Barthes 177). Beyond providing the first whiff of the queerness of Barthes's text, the Nietzschean ass demands that we rethink Barthes's recitation of both Werther and Nietzsche. To affirm the eternal return of the same involved a reevaluation so radical that it is a "yes" to the dutiful Nietzschean ass, who "banalized by literature" can only hope to kill himself over and over again. That, sadly, was the fate of many of Werther's most devoted readers, who showed their solidarity with the hero by imitating his suicide, dress and all. Werther's invariable, self-willed path to suicide thus not only poses the most radical challenge to any Nietzschean affirmation of the same, but it also affirms precisely that which Nietzsche was seeking to overcome. It would be an error to dismiss Barthes's reading of Nietzsche via Werther as a deconstruction to expose the ass behind the overman. That would disable the undeniable intent of the discourse to affirm, however, exiguous, the site of such a discourse (1). At the very least, we can concede that the exiguous character of the site points to a difference, or what I have called a rift, inherent in that exiguous site, which such a deconstruction exposes without permitting the coordinates of that site to be fixed. If such coordinates are as displaced as the temporal ones discussed in the introduction, Werther's self-described "pilgrimage" (Bathes 90) acquires a potentiality to be and not to be by abandoning any measure of those dimensions.[7] The site or destination of the discourse could just as easily be marked by the same "X" that is the name Barthes assigns to the beloved.

Barthes's peculiar affirmation of love's failure (Barthes 103) necessitates a consideration of how desire is channeled in *Werther*. As we will see, *Werther* offers a map of how desire's plenitude—its plugging into everyone and everything—is equally a lack, subject to the patriarchal controls that psychoanalysis will come to reify according to fears of castration. There is no need, however, to employ a Freudian vocabulary. Freudian psychoanalysis simply marks the moment, as Guy Hocquenghem reminds us, when desire as lack and the laws governing the object, the choice of which is to compensate for that lack, are codified. Such laws establish a hierarchy of relationships, whereby every subject is derived from filiation.[8] That is, the family portrait that so enamors Werther is possible only insofar as paternity is unquestioned, which it certainly is not for Werther, whose father is simply not around. As desire is mapped onto the body according to the laws of castration or according to who has it and who does not, relations of property are likewise constituted, giving rise to the kinds of class conflicts to which Werther is not immune.[9] If such an improbable economy of desire is at play here (its abundance signals its lack), then the very controls Barthes seeks to elide are (re)-instated the moment they are suspended. The "Great Narrative Other" is not just the editor but the father and his law as well. The doubling of the affirmation of the eternal return of the same affirms a dual character of desire; it is both codified and incorrigible (e.g., the Nietzschean ass). What was alluded to above as cross-purposes is, if this character of desire holds, the impossibly divided essence of amorous desire. At the very least, it is the ineluctable fate of an ass' desire once it is doubly affirmed. To understand this dual essence, it is important to examine how the father's absence increases his allure and structures the trajectory of Werther's desire.

Werther's Eternal Return

If Werther's letters enflame his passion, such inflammation almost always occurs under the watch or imagined presence of Wilhelm, who may offer a compassionate face to the law but nevertheless is strictly bound to its logic of either/or. "Either you have hope with Lotte or you have none." ("Entweder, sagst du [Wilhelm], hast du Hoffnung auf Lotten, oder du hast keine"; Goethe 43). That is, either you have it or you don't. Since Werther's passions are always tied to the scene of writing in which Wilhelm, the addressee, is present in his absence, Werther's apparent transgression seems staged only to recall the father or a representative of his order. In the letter of November 30, shortly before his suicide, Werther makes explicit that the third who had always haunted the scene of passion is the father: "Father, whom I do not know, who has otherwise filled my entire soul and now would turn his face from me" (Goethe 91). The world opened up by his famous turning inward—"I turn inward and discover a world." ("Ich kehre in mich zurück und finde eine Welt")—is thus occupied by the father, no less securely than the estate of the Swiss Family Frankenstein. Such turning inward, in fact, furnishes the father with a space to haunt. In this world, moreover, the father is the only hope, ". . . Only where you are am I well, and before your countenance I will suffer and rejoice" (Goethe 91). Barthes's affirmation of an endless replay of Werther's fate thus might be nothing more than a concession and celebration of the father's will to power. But if such inversions signal an endless return to the father, they also introduce the possibility that the role of the father will change. At the very least, he calls upon surrogates such as Albert, Wilhelm, or an editor to enforce the law. Then to whom else can Werther turn once the father has turned away?

In the same letter there are, in fact, indications that the father is in an awkward position. In the quotation above, Werther could be said to apostrophize himself. He identifies with a madman, who had also loved Lotte and who was never happier than when he was "outside of himself" (Goethe 90). Werther addresses him as though he were addressing himself or even Frankenstein's monster, "Wretched One" ("Elender"; Goethe 90). The identification, however, is not complete. Werther distances himself from the madman, who can find solace in attributing his misery to earthly causes. Werther, by contrast, must look to the heavens for such solace. From within what is supposed to be a site of interiority, the distance from the father proves too great or too real and thus not simply an interior space. The father in his omnipresent absence becomes increasingly fetching. By ending his self-described pilgrimage (Goethe 90), Werther hopes to lock embraces with the father: "Don't be angry that I end my pilgrimage, which according to your plan I should have endured longer" (Goethe 90). The questions that follows is: What happens to the law when the son comes face to face with the father, when immediacy, heretofore conjoined by a third, only means being in the father's face? In other words, what does it mean when Werther proclaims, in anticipation of Barthes's affirmation of the eternal return, "Father, I am here/there again" ("Ich bin wieder da, mein Vater!"; Goethe 91)? On the one hand, it has something to do with the leave-taking necessary to identify with the madman, which is also signaled by the self-apostrophe embedded in the letter just cited. On the other, such being outside of oneself only confirms the need of the amorous subject to answer to the father, even an absent one. Suspension of the law is fleeting at best.

Not surprisingly, Werther's odd self-apostrophe is followed by a more direct one of the heavenly father: "And you, Heavenly Father, would you turn away from him?" (Goethe 91). Not only do these apostrophes confirm the one's presence in the absence of the other; the father is there to address, but only if Werther is not, only if he is about to take leave of himself and commit suicide. (Note as well that Werther's self-reference is in the third person, *ihn*.) Werther's unending displacement also threatens to disable subject/object distinctions, save that the father or his surrogate serves to re-locate that subject, Werther, by soliciting Werther's increasingly fervent appeals. For example, the first word of the letter written immediately thereafter is "Wilhelm," followed by an explanation point. If being in God's face is an impossibility that demands that Werther turn to a surrogate, Wilhelm, the explanation point indicates that desire is not vitiated by such rejection but rather emphatically redirected. In fact, all parties become potential receptacles of desire. The letter, as we know, is prompted by Werther's ambivalent identification with a madman, who is "outside of himself" (Goethe 89) or no longer himself. That means that intermediaries also function as surrogates. Surrogates—and this reflects the difference inherent in self-apostrophe—cannot contain the self; they call the self out everywhere to the point that desire is so eccentrically charged that it does not control or overcome difference via an intermediary, but rather finds in every object of desire a substitute for itself. The surrogate offers the self a new position to occupy but also vacate. "Ich bin *wieder* da, mein Vater!" whereby the "there" is never a "here" or self-same (ital. added, Goethe 91). The interior world to which Werther turns is turned inside out insofar as Werther is always displaced.

The matter explains Barthes's response to Gide, who was so tired of Goethe's here postponing his suicide that he himself "wanted to push him into the grave" (Barthes 219). Barthes responds that the hero is "*real*" because he is "created out of an absolutely projective substance in which every amorous subject collects himself" (Barthes 219). That is to say, Werther projects himself or is projected everywhere, even in the presence of the Heavenly Father, to find himself collected by the projected substance even when it means becoming a representative of the order that seeks to restrict such a projection. Barthes's response thus requires modification; the hero is *potentially* real, which may explain Barthes's placement of the word "real" in italics. As such, the question that must be taken up is already suggested by Werther's confession to the Heavenly Father that he is there again or *wieder da*. Does being everywhere or such an ecstatic projection of oneself confirm the omnipresence of the father and the law, or does it negotiate an exiguous space, to recall Barthes, exiguous because the moment the father looks for Werther he is already elsewhere?

Its temporal-spatial character escapes stable coordinates at the same time it grounds the possibility of such stability by calling upon the father. Is this what Werther means when he writes Albert that he hopes to steal between the either/or of the father's logic ("durchzustehlen," Goethe 43)? Is then every position in which the subject collects himself an "either' that forestalls any "or"? Of course, once the logic of either/or is reinstalled—and Werther cannot help but ask for such reinstallment since his plea to the father demands a "yes" or "no" response—the intensity that such forestalling sponsors alters the relation to the father who is present as surrogate in an interior space turned inside out. But if the intensity is so great that Werther can radically reposition himself with respect to any other being, can he really be killed off? His excesses allow him to take up positions as promiscuously as Barthes's citational practices do for the amorous subject. Very possibly, this explains Barthes's affirmation of the suicidal subject insofar as that subject is really never anywhere to kill himself. He has always already taken off, something to which Werther alerts us in the very first line of the first letter: "Wie froh bin ich, daß ich weg bin!" ("How happy I am to be away:" Goethe 7).[10]

The Eternal Return of the Father

Initially, Werther's disappearing act allows him to float freely on the margins of the family portrait that so enthralls him upon first meeting Lotte. Such disappearing is evident in the manner in which he identifies or occupies the position of his surroundings. "Every tree, every hedge is a bouquet of flowers, and one would like to become a cockchafer in order to float around in a sea of fragrances and find my nourishment there" (Goethe 8). The self, which is never the same from one moment to the next, finds itself everywhere, undergoing constant metamorphosis. So complete is Werther's immersion in his surroundings that he celebrates his own dissolution in the glory of all that he beholds: "But I am overcome, and I submit to the overpowering glory of these manifestations" ("Aber ich gehe darüber zugrunde; ich erliege unter der Gewalt der Herrlichkeit dieser Erscheinungen"; Goethe 9). To be sure, such identifications are not always glorious, since the trajectory of those identifications is tragic, and thus the figures with whom he identifies are, as stated above, tragic lovers. But the intensity that is found in identifying, for example, with a *Bauernbursch* is matched by a delirious immersion in nature: "The overwhelming fullness makes me feel like a god." "My entire soul is moved and invigorated by such beautiful figures" ("Ich fühlte mich in der überfließenden Fülle wie vergöttert, und die herrlichen Gestalten der undenklichen Welt bewegten sich allbelebend in meiner Seele"; Goethe 51). Interiority, *Innigkeit*, does not prohibit entry of/into the world but rather fosters an intimacy whose sponsoring desire seeks neither to possess any object nor to sequester itself in a closet of unpronounced or unpronounceable objects. Two pronouncements the text offers for this condition are *übertrieben* and *überspannt* ("exaggerated but also in overdrive" and "overexcited or over-aroused"; Goethe 34, 47). Such an extension does not permit the self, now in overdrive, to reconstruct a narcissistic or cohesive image of itself, which explains why the passage in which Werther bathes in divine plenitude ends with feelings of complete destitution. The self is present only as premonition ("Ahnung," Goethe 13) or as dark, i.e., unpronounced, desire ("dunkler Begier," Goethe 13). Barthes draws on Plato to define such a condition as the *atopia* of love (Barthes 34), whereby the site of the amorous discourse is so exiguous that it defies qualification or classification. It is only potentially a site.[11]

The object of desire refuses conformation to types, instead undergoing constant metamorphosis in a mimetic economy that acknowledges no natural boundaries. Werther can envy even the canary who gathers his food from Lotte's pursed lips (Goethe 79–80). The scene excites Werther's passion to the point that he must turn away, fearful of his response. Such fear is over-determined. To kiss Lotte is to kiss a lover forbidden him because she is promised to another, Albert, and even if she were to succumb to

Werther's advances, the flightiness of such desire is just as likely to invite advance from a canary as it is from Werther. None of this speaks to the most remarkable aspect of the scene that includes Werther as it excludes him; he also exchanges a kiss with the canary. That is, the canary is both subject and object of desire. That renders Werther's reaction—turning his face away or turning the other cheek as the canary feeds from the mouth of Lotte—disingenuous. For love's atopia that forever displaces the lover and the beloved means that every turning repositions one in a new economy of desire. The radical transformation such repositioning poses cannot be overstated; one moment Werther is wooing Lotte only in the next to play Lotte the coquette, as he weaves a bouquet of flowers during a walk with Albert (Goethe 44). He can fancy himself as Melusine with her sisters (Goethe 9) or find Wilhelm just as worthy a recipient of his rapturous tears. But Wilhelm is available only insofar as he is unavailable: "O, that I not throw myself at him" ("daß ich [Werther] nicht an deinen Hals fliegen . . ." Goethe 56). The letters that incite passion by rehearsing passion depend upon a dual leave-taking: the subject from the object and the object from the subject. Whether the object be Lotte or Wilhelm or Albert or Melusine's sisters and the subject be Werther or the *Bauernbursch* or the madman or Melusine or a canary, the result is the same. If a lover cannot find himself, it is unlikely the beloved can find him, too.

Such a condition has been described as a narcissistic plentitude, whereby the self finds itself everywhere, positioned alongside or as a part of everything it contacts only to not recognize itself as a self since it has no psychology.[12] Werther, as well, understood himself to be scattered, but he depends upon being buffeted about for oxygen: "The light and darkness of my soul are dispersed, and I can breathe again" (Goethe 39). Later, Werther will lament that such distraction is suffocating (Goethe 75). Since breathing is at cross-purposes with itself, desire, not surprisingly, is as well. The aberrant course of his soul might foreclose composition of a psychology, but it opens up the possibility that Werther's desire as well as his core being are errant. How such a core being, or if you will a psychology, comes to be cannot be attributed simply to a turning inward. Without a space already demarcated as the habitat of the soul, such turning would only expose Werther's backside as he repeatedly takes to leaving.[13] The pressure on Werther to collect himself issues not so much from a heartfelt interest to save Werther from himself but more from a need to situate him within the bounds of class and family so as to prevent the obscene exposure of his backside. The Nietzschean ass is more threatening than the overman, save that Werther, even in his most ecstatic moments is already beholden to the father: "Nothing fills me with such peaceful, true feeling as the signs of patriarchal life that I, thank God, can weave into my life without affectation" (Goethe 29).

If Werther is incorrigible, i.e., if he refuses his station, that does not mean he cannot serve to reinforce the family portrait he threatens.[14] Clinging to the fringe, he also demarcates its boundaries in much the same way his grave is positioned to the cemetery: "I will not ask pious Christians that their bodies should be laid next to mine. Oh, I ask that you bury me along the road or in a lovely valley" (Goethe 123). Even before the editor will arrive on the scene to scrutinize every scrap of paper left by Werther and lend order to the life of one who was not of the "common stamp" (93), Werther has already been recruited to delimit and thus preserve the social order that could not countenance his backside.

> Were I not such a fool, I could lead the best and happiest life. Barely do such favorable circumstances come together to delight the soul of a man as those that I find myself in now. Oh, just as certain is that our heart alone creates happiness. Oh, to be a member ("*Glied*") of a family so worthy of love, to be loved by all as a son, by the children like a father, and from Lotte! (45; ital. added)

Werther, judged by this passage, is already lacking what it takes to be a member of the happy family. He is only a part of such bliss by dint of simile: "like a son," "like a father." When some form of immediacy is pursued, as it is with Lotte, he is immediately displaced by a third. The passage continues, "then the upstanding Albert . . . who, after Lotte, is the loveliest person on earth" (Goethe 44). In the first meeting between Lotte and Werther, the word or name "Klopstock" prevented their lips from meeting, indicating that intimacy or *Innigkeit* always depended upon a third. Here, the triangle is reconfigured to preserve the family portrait. Albert can love Werther, almost as much as Lotte, for he knows that Werther assures Albert's position in relation to Lotte. Somehow the plugging-in of everyone and everything of Werther's desire has succumbed to a calculus that secures the social structures that might otherwise be threatened by one who is *überspannt* and *übertrieben*. Striking is how the plenitude of Werther's desire is unthinkable without the presence of the father, i.e., without the threat of castration that restructures such plenitude as lack and impregnates desire with a need to reclaim the lost member (*Glied*).

Since the narrative that the editor presents to explain Werther's strange ways charts a clear progression from bliss to desperation, it offers a documented pathology of his sickness unto death for purposes of securing the family structure. The editor's detective work is exhaustive: "I have been at great pains to collect precise testimonies from the mouths of those who could have known much about his story. And all of their accounts, apart from a few minor details, are in agreement with each other" (Goethe 92). These are not just any witnesses; but ones who have been well instructed (*unterrichtet*) by Werther's story; that is, once it is a story, Werther's life has the potential to be as instructive as a moral tale. Something must be at stake for the editor to carry out such a thorough investigation that he describes as *gewissenhaft*, signaling the convergence of knowledge and morality (Goethe 93).[15] Even bits of paper are subject to scrutiny (Goethe 7), and if Werther's life seemed to go nowhere by his being everywhere, the editor's linear narrative takes Werther straight to the grave. His end, announced already in the editor's preliminary remarks (Goethe 7), provides the narrator with the necessary omniscience to judge and perhaps condemn, save that Werther has condemned himself already. Instead, the narrator—whose authority signals precisely the interventions Barthes decried when he refused the "Great Narrative Other"—offers pity as a salve for the force of the (narrative) law he imposes. "You cannot but offer his mind and character your admiration; his fate, your tears" (Goethe 7).[16] The condemned man can be pitied when his fate is evident from the outset. He can also be pitied because his soul was afflicted; a diseased desire had taken hold of him and affected even his way of thinking (*Sinnesart*; Goethe 98). But the self that was to become the beneficiary of such benevolence is there only as a posthumous construction. It was the progression of Werther's disease, his sickness unto death, that called forth the absolute voice of narrative reason. The Nietzschean ass that Barthes affirms in Werther is thus one whose perversity always summons a voice to pity the absent Werther and to name the pathogen and immunize others against it. "And you, good soul, who are feeling the same anguish as Werther, let this small book be your friend, should fate or guilt prevent you from finding another one" (Goethe 98). According to the logic of the eternal return of the same, it is impossible to speak of a time before the law, before guilt.[17] The temporal disjunction remarked upon in the introduction in Werther's letter to Lotte is repeated here: the wayward Werther is before the law only because he is constructed after the law. This posthumous construction comes to re-mark Werther's errant ways as queer.[18]

The Eternal Return of the Queer

As Barthes notes, two economies are opposed and seemingly at cross purposes with each other: "[. . .] there is the lover Werther who expends his love every day, without any sense of saving or of compensation, and on the other, there is the husband Albert, who economizes his goods, his happiness" (Barthes 65). Barthes names the confluence of the two a simultaneous proffering that is possible only in a "single flash" that refuses the time necessary to draw up an agreement (Barthes 80). That is not to say a lover and a husband are offered simultaneously. Barthes is imagining the possibility whereby lover and beloved utter the words "I love you" simultaneously; as such, no thought of repletion can exist. How can one husband resources if the return, in the form of a response, is simultaneous with the expenditure? The "I" is already elsewhere, unable to receive the proffer. Writing places the subject elsewhere, particularly when the self is a letter-writer who is constructed as something to be sent or posted. But the letter or the vow can never arrive, since it has already been returned as a simultaneous proffering from one who has also left his/her place and sent the return to a place from which the other has already departed. Thus, there arises the need for a placeholder: a Klopstock to seal the first kiss between Werther and Lotte by coming in between them, a husband whom Werther often loves with as much fervor as he does Lotte, or a gravesite to guarantee a final return on incalculable expenditure.

Such placeholders render simultaneous proffering impossible. Reciprocation is delayed, and it always misses the mark. Werther's impertinent kiss of Lotte right before his death may indicate that this economy has been thwarted, since he spends the next hours virtually unconscious, but the kiss is retuned only later and not by Lotte. Rather, the eldest son of the old steward does so as he passes Werther's casket. His passion matches Werther's; he must be dragged away by force as Werther expires (Goethe 124). The son's kiss is a kiss of death, except that the kiss Werther impertinently placed on Lotte's lips the night before was just such a kiss as well. Not surprisingly, Albert, unlike the steward's son, does not follow the body, as he apparently needed to tend to Lotte for whom a fear for her life had been expressed. The kiss of death is a potential pathogen and contagion (see Barthes 136) whereby its spread and containment is regulated by this odd economy of impossible desires. That is to say, the impossibility of a simultaneous proffering summons a third who intercepts the kiss and isolates its pathogen but who, in being turned away, kisses another to summon once again an interloper. As we have seen, such interlopers are as numerous as the Werthers that are in play here, ranging from Klopstock to a canary. "This 'affective contagion' . . . proceeds from others, from language, from books, from friends; no love is original" (Barthes 136).

If the subject is not there to locate or to offer an account of his whereabouts, the structural operation discussed above already has assigned the subject his place, which he will also, paradoxically, already have returned to or, as we have seen throughout this essay, been returned to. But the disavowal of the beloved, necessitated by countless interlopers and indicated as well by Barthes's "X," creates its own site, however exiguous and fleeting, that at least momentarily, in the time perhaps of echo, secures an experience of love outside of this economy. In other words, the tension of this paradox, particularly as it pertains to Werther's whereabouts, retains the possibility that a series of repeated disavowals of the amorous subject will occasion a different rhythm that escapes or steals through the logic of either/or: a logic that marks desire as either plentitude or lack and according to which Werther either submits to the law or he becomes an outlaw only to be subjected again to the law. Such a love might be "original." That possibility, to repeat, resides in a temporal disjunction, which is captured by Barthes when he insists that the primal scene of love has always already occurred, just as Werther's with Lenore had before his story with Lotte began. It is pretextual and spoken in the past tense. Thus, Barthes can confidently assert that the scenes Werther relates always have the vocation of a remembrance (Barthes 217). That is not to say the scenes are merely memories, but rather the scenes are intended from the beginning, even before the beginning, to be lost in the past. "The imperfect tense murmurs behind the present" (Barthes 127).

Such murmuring is evident in an episode Barthes reports in "Soirees de Paris." The episode concerns the calculated rejection of Barthes by a hustler. The calculation is in the form of a payment in advance. "I gave him some money, he promised to be at the rendezvous an hour later, and of course never showed" (Barthes 51).[19] Initially, the calculation seems to be a simple one: sex in return for a fixed sum of money. Of course, it is no sex for money. The manner in which this complicates the calculation is understood by Barthes as follows: "I asked myself if I was really so mistaken (the received wisdom about giving money to a hustler in *advance*!), and concluded that since I didn't really want him all that much (nor even to make love), the result was the same: sex or no sex, at eight o'clock I would find myself back at the same point in my life."[20] Going against received wisdom and paying in advance is the thing one does who knows he will end up at the same point in his life no matter what he does. The either/or that Werther would like to stealthily make his war in-between is rejected here as well. "Either I will have sex or I will not have sex": both options are put in play by the calculation of miscalculation, but it is also clear that disavowal does not fully break with what it disavows. After all, the one who disavows returns to *that* place, but the difference inherent in that return always appears to have been accounted for in advance. If an echo of something absolutely different is to become audible, it will be necessary to think not only what such a disavowal means but also what it means to have staged it in advance. That requires examining how Werther, and thus Barthes's amorous subject, come to be encoded as queer. And even if such encoding merely rehearses once again the rhythm of a return to the father or the order of his law, Barthes's (mis)calculation echoes of a potentiality that never fully registers. It does so by preserving a saying "Yes" to Werther's undeniable "No" or by disavowing the beloved in advance, a disavowal that is possible only because of what I have called a temporal disjunction that underwrites the return to *that* place.

Nietzsche offers a framework for understanding this queer echo in his discussion of the sentimental. The sentimental for Nietzsche is the pathological, the total aberration of the instincts that turns one onto Wagner, who composes "one piece of anti-nature that downright compels a second" ("Eine Wideratur erzwingt formlich eine zweite.").[21] The condemnation of the sentimental is even more emphatic in *Thus Spoke Zarathustra*: "O, you sentimental hypocrites, you covetous ones lack the innocence of desire, and now you slander desire."[22] Thus, the anti-nature that compels a second (to do what?) becomes the motor of resentment, a second sentimentalizing that defiles all desire and eventually leads Nietzsche to speak of Wagner's "incredibly pathological sexuality" that necessitates putting gloves on "when reading the score of *Tristan*" (". . . im Banne seiner unglaubwürdigen krankhaften Sexualität; ich ziehe die Handschuhe an, wenn, ich die Partitur des Tristan lese").[23] If Barthes affirms the sentimental to disable any pathology, its repetition, according to Nietzsche, merely describes how inveterate aberrant desire is. Nietzsche should know, since his repulsion of Wagner is always at cross purposes with his love of Wagner, a love that is enduring enough for him to insist that his own name is interchangeable with Wagner's.[24] But to what extent does unnatural desire attach to the figure, Werther, insofar as Goethe's text is composed at a time when terms such as inversion and homosexuality have no ontological status?[25] The unnatural or sodomitical act—and Barthes identifies the beloved, almost without exception, as male—did not extend to the person; such acts were not part of a psychological substratum that organized the psyche and the self. His editor knows only that such passion is strange, *wunderbar*, and leaves one fatigued and world-weary (Goethe 100), something that no doubt accounts for Nietzsche's disdain. Werther's effusive displays of emotions are thus merely effects, save that they will always only be charged with significance.[26]

Citing a cluster of such effects indicates how queerness or aberrant desire serves as a crucible for encoding and decoding them: His dandified dress that inspired a fashion craze, the comical manner in which his mimetic desire finds him strolling with Albert as he plays the role of a florist weaving his companion a bouquet; Lotte's ribbon, which he famously preserves, and while not in the shape of a triangle, is certainly pink; the ease with which Wilhelm or writing to Wilhelm enflames his passion, which leads to apostrophes such as "Ach Lieber," "Mein Lieber," "Mein Schatz" ("O dear," "My dear," "My sweetheart; e.g., Goethe 17. 63, 75, 98).[27] In fact, this potential superseding of Lotte by Wilhelm is telling in the letter of July 26 in which he asks Lotte directly not to put sand on the notes she sends him as the sand causes distress when he kisses her notes. The addressee of the letter, however, is arguably uncertain or displaced.[28] Such confusion is telling in that he may kiss the wrong notes or seal the ones addressed to Wilhelm with a kiss if such letters, as this one, recall her presence to the point of embodiment. Anyone who professes that it is better to see his beloved through the eyes of another—and Werther confesses a need to see the widow through the eyes of the *Bauernbursch* (Goethe 18)—always comes dangerously close to desiring the one whose desire he desires. Or as Barthes writes, "Show me whom to desire" (Barthes 136), which is precisely what the women in the carriage do for Werther as they describe Lotte in advance of his meeting her.

How such queering accommodates the logic of the "Great Narrative Other" is particularly evident in the first installment of the prequel to *Die Leiden des jungen Werther, Briefe aus der Schweiz*, although it was written much later in 1803. Here, the young Werther is captivated by the sight of his friend Ferdinand's impressive physique, "I made it necessary for Ferdinand to bathe in the sea. How beautifully my young friend is built. What symmetry and measure! What fullness of form! what a youthful glow! what a gain for me to have my imagination enriched by such a complete exemplar of human nature." This is hardly the same family portrait that ignited Werther's love for Lotte, but the emotional charge is unmistakable. So easily does it resonate with Werther's later letters to Wilhelm that one could question what or whom Werther actually saw in Lotte. To what extent did his imagination, so enlivened by the sight of the naked male form whom he solicited to disrobe, find an equal conformation or measure of beauty in Lotte? Did Wilhelm ever offer the same spectacle so that in writing about Lotte to Wilhelm Werther could draw upon his friend's naked splendor to inspire his love for Lotte? That Werther cannot bring a silhouette of Lotte to paper suggests that her form was not as generous in endowing the imagination with gifts as was Ferdinand's. But the diligence he displays in attempting to bring Lotte to paper is not lacking in *Die Briefe*. Werther tries to set things straight by viewing a naked woman, since the absence of Venus renders the scene incomplete: ". . . She was quite fetching as she disrobed, already beautiful as the last garment fell away. She stood as Minerva might have stood before Paris."[29] The erotic charge of the scene, nonetheless, lacks the immediacy of the former. Venus's or Minerva's desire is routed through the desire of another, although Paris is certainly a more seductive third than Klopstock. If her charm arouses desire, it does so by positioning Werther as the voyeur watching Paris watch Minerva. This tortuous route to heterosexuality, if the younger Werther's Swiss *Bildung* is to train the eye to look through the eyes of another (which Werther of *The Sorrows* does), is to trace the fabulous outline of the male nude before assuming a position that opens up to the spectacle of the female form.[30]

Male same-sex attraction may be, as Robert Tobin has argued, a phase for Goethe that one outgrows,[31] but since the prequel is written after *The Sorrows*, male same-sex attraction is always something one potentially returns to. In any case, the most Werther seems prepared to accomplish is to make of his servant a Paris: "Today, I couldn't go to see Lotte. I sent my servant instead so as to have someone around me who had been in her presence today. How impatiently I waited for him! How gladly I would have taken his head and kissed it, were I not afraid of embarrassing myself" (Goethe 39). Less interesting is whether Werther will succumb to kissing a servant. More important is how such a triangulation of desire produces shame, but also conflates a surfeit of desire with lack and absence. Recall how Werther wants to kiss Lotte as she plays the piano and sings, only to reproach himself afterwards for his sins (87). But what are his sins? This letter to Wilhelm is replete with dashes or *Gedankenstrichen*, a practice Werther cursed in a recent post but found unable to resist. His lips, neither pursed for a kiss nor labile enough to articulate, albeit metonymically, desire, mark a site of emptiness and lack. The Swiss prequel already offered knowledge of what Werther's sickness unto death was. Without the naked Ferdinand his lips merely suck air. When he finally is able to kiss Lotte, the pharmakon only releases its toxins; he kills himself thereafter, the most emphatic statement of his absence.

For Barthes such postscripting of desire has already occurred, which leads him to lament, "I am an amputee who still feels pain in his missing leg" (Barthes 39). Barthes experiences Werther's castration as *Nachträglichkeit*. Or rather, he experiences Werther's absenting of himself from the family portrait as castration: "Grant me only a little peace, and everything will be settled," Werther says to Charlotte in a plaintive yet threatening tone. Which is to say, "You will soon be rid of me" (as cited, Barthes 208). For Barthes, Werther becomes the pain associated with a missing appendage so insistent that only an affirmation of that pain might offer relief. The affirmation requires nothing less than a second, given how Werther's threat fails to achieve its purpose, which, according to Barthes, is to have the last word. Werther's redactor usurps that word and offers a frame for understanding Werther's effects. Moreover, the effects come to acquire a name precisely because they lack one, not unlike Schlemihl or the schlemiel. The love that does not speak its name does so precisely by being a cluster of scattered effects. Or as D. A. Miller writes, "It overperforms by not performing as itself," and the polymorphous self is never itself.[32] If Barthes looks to Werther to discover the possibility that such love could refuse nomination—and it is worth recalling yet again that the amorous subject is denoted not by name but by an "X" in Barthes's text—"the name in question is that name, whose diffuse prejudicial effects depend on its not being pronounced, on its being restricted, quasi catachrestically, to a system of connotation (Miller, Barthes 25). Barthes's affirmation of the sentimental, his resentimentalizing of Werther as the modern amorous subject, cannot rescue him from the vicious circle, to reapply Pierre Klossowski's by now canonical description of the eternal return of the same. "In fact, it leaves him all the more destitute for resisting them," (Miller, Barthes, 25) which, in turn, necessitates a second affirmation that only reconscripts Werther in a system of connotation. Nostalgia obtains as loss for the possibility that an affirmation of a moment in which sexuality, lacking any ontological status, could steal between the logic of an either/or, only to discover that a second affirmation is always already part of a hetero/homo calculation.

To escape this order requires refining Barthes's expressed intention of affirming difference a second time. That is to say, an affirmation of the disavowal of an affirmation—and we should think here of Barthes's miscalculation—affirms a potentiality that neither is nor is not, provided it is never fully articulated or echoes from a site so exiguous it defies nomination. Replaying the timelines critical to this essay will render the echo audible since the echo is constructed via repetition.[33]

Messianic Echoes and the Eternal Return of the Queer

The queering of Werther's desire is based upon retrospective knowledge, even if Barthes hears echoes of something not structured by the law that governs such knowledge. This is because Werther's editor, as we know, reconstructs the narrative with a purpose and because Werther's letters are both separate from and intimately bound to the events described. As a citation of the feelings and events in question, they interrupt the economy that has made of him the hysterical outsider who will always only come to be read as queer, but the letters also remain the primary vehicle for the "Great Narrative Other" to weave a moral lesson from his case study of Werther. Barthes's citations of Werther, or his practices of citation, confirm or replay this odd dialectic; they wrest the original from a context that has already been ordered according to the economic constraints of the editor and in response to the need to pathologize Werther, but the citations also confirm Werther's role in that economy. Nietzsche's eternal return of the same serves as a means to affirm and preserve the tension that results from endlessly re-citing Werther. But the uncertainly, the suspension of meaning such re-citing should mark, acquires meaning in a queer context or when knowledge is preterited.[34] The sentimental amorous subject is named and type-cast precisely because he is nothing but citations, as the reference above to D. A. Miller indicate. Barthes's insertion of Werther into the Nietzschean scene of affirmation demonstrates how the entire unfolding of heterosexual normativity is knotted around the absence of one who will become but always only has been queer. The Nietzschean occlusion of the sentimental enables a developmental logic from sickness to health, or from same-sex attraction to so-called opposite sex attraction. Here, it is helpful to recall the young Werther's attraction and deification of Ferdinand in Goethe's *Briefe aus der Schweiz*, an attraction the Werther of the *Sorrows* has outgrown.[35] Barthes's interruption of that development eventually succumbs to that logic—inserting Werther in the economy the amorous subject sought to evade—but it simultaneously, and thus paradoxically, undoes any teleology of sexuality that charts nonaberrant desire as moving through and between same-sex attraction. *The repetition of that rupture, its silence, is what echoes.* But we are not finished yet. The question that remains is whether the preservation of both of these moves or possibilities is a double affirmation that affirms both an "either" and an "or." The answer lies in reexamining the specifics of how Werther's "No" to life rewrites the terms of such an affirmation.

The affirmation of Barthes's amorous subject and of Werther's tragic fate fails because Werther is always already recuperated posthumously by a "Great Narrative Other" that strings together and renders legible the diffuse cluster of his traits: "I am being played like a marionette," Werther laments (Goethe 65). If as a result of that recuperation the amorous subject is always viewed as lacking, as an "amputee who still feels pain in his missing leg" (Barthes 39), a disjunctive temporality is just as likely the source of that pain. "Love at first sight is always spoken in the past tense, it might be called an anterior immediacy . . . distinct, framed, it is already (always again) a memory" (Barthes 194). This then is the difference that is doubly or endlessly affirmed, that was rehearsed with the memory of a rendezvous with a hustler that never occurred. The interminable taking-leave from the scene of the amorous encounter, which has always already occurred by the time Werther writes his letters, may, in one of its endless rehearsals, reposition the amorous subject outside the "Great Narrative Other's" panoptic field of registration. He may come to occupy a space so exiguous, assuming positions inevitably at cross-purposes with each other, that his presence will echo from no identifiable source, his lack of identity disabling nomination. At best, nomination becomes a barely audible echo. While the memory of that which didn't happen may, as Barthes claims, be framed, the edges of that frame, the margins where the amorous subject resides, tremble, since the love that offered memory its frame was dissolving before it even occurred. This also means that the beloved, "X," is a "supplement of his own site" (Barthes 221), placing him and the amorous subject at the limits of language where nothing can be pronounced. Think only of Werther's need for dashes or "Gedanken-*striche*."[36]

But what does it mean to be at the limits of language? "Love falls outside of interesting time. No historical or polemical meaning can be given to it. It is in this sense obscene" (Barthes 178–79). If the future anterior, as the explicit undertone of the lover's discourse, is to exceed the calculations of interesting time, that promise registers polemically. "I will have been" does anything but deflect scrutiny from its subject. It nominates one for homosexuality. The imaginary, coherent body of such reverberations—to rephrase Barthes—indicates, at the same time, that memory of the event precedes the event. What is therefore required is an adjustment to the future perfect that disables or rather destabilizes the frame of the future anterior from the start, from before the beginning, the frame that Barthes describes as, "The impossible moment when the obscene can really coincide with affirmation, with the 'Amen'" (Barthes 179). Affirmation must maintain its impossible character, the impossibility of which constitutes its obscenity. This temporal adjustment thus requires re-casting the contractual impossibilities of paying a hustler in advance. The transaction itself is not obscene insofar as it occurs on the street or inside the café to which Barthes, sex or no sex, will return. What is to take place is obscene, if it takes place, but it does not. "I will have made love" or "I will have loved" becomes "I will already not have made love" or "I will already not have loved." But it could just as easily be, "I will already not have not loved."[37] The last formulation signals a double affirmation of Werther's "No" to life. The double negative does not convert into a positive, but rather it preserves the possibility for love to be and not to be, to restore, in other words, its potentiality. For Barthes's amorous subject, "I will not already not have loved" means that "X" is there in never being there as well as never having been there. For Werther, the only one who is there only insofar as he is never articulated as such, only insofar as his absence echoes throughout the text, and only insofar as a queer echo, like the first letter of the Hebrew alphabet, aleph, could have been articulated but was not, is . . . Wilhelm.[38]

5

"I'm nothin'. I'm nowhere."

Echoes of a Queer Messianic in *Brokeback Mountain*

The final chapter is more of a coda. The messianic promise embedded in the film's melancholia finds it cues in the past, something that is repeatedly emphasized by the film's penchant for rearview images. That is not to say that the texts considered in chapters 1 through 4 reverberate conspicuously or consistently throughout *Brokeback Mountain*, but rather those texts prepare a terrain that moves in a different direction from the politics of normalcy. The first two chapters, as we might recall, looked to understand how family values as well as dreams of endogamy and nation contributed to the eventual creation of the male homosexual as a type, easily contained and identified within the sights of the panoptic regime. While *Frankenstein* makes a mess of sexuality, its energies pull in two distinct directions—toward restoration of the Swiss Family through preservation of endogamy and toward a self that goes outside of itself and thus de-constitutes itself. Peter Schlemihl's wondrous history points to construction of an apparatus to link the Jew and the queer to solidify the outsider status of the "almost" emancipated Jew and to sequester the queer in a closet of his own "Jewish" making. At the same time, something escapes confinement, call it an avatar, that augurs of a sexual terrorism that still haunt the margins of the world from which Schlemihl was exiled. Kleist's "On the Puppet Theater" looked at how the text came over time to invite a queer reading only to reject such a disclosure in favor of disabling any interpretive gestures that could link sexual acts with sexuality or character traits. In other words, the text pulls, as did *Frankenstein*, in two directions. Roland Barthes's reading of

Werther reawakens the messianic echoes of Goethe's text. Through citation and repetition his reading comes to create a counter rhythm that preserves love of different kind.

While it is the purpose of this chapter to fill out the possibilities adumbrated in the previous one, the echoes pursued in this chapter follow a different rhythm or configuration. Repetition in this case actually reduplicates construction of a closet or, to recall Schlemihl, a cabinet. But this constant return to an inside, and even an inside of an inside, strains the limits of interiority until something collapses or just breaks and a new horizon of possibility is espied. We might recall from the introduction the dizzying and ultimately unreadable course of inversion in Proust's *Sodom and Gemorrah*. The reading of the film offered here is actually a collage of sorts that relies on the short story and the screenplay as well. If the previous chapters sought to collect traces of a forgotten or discarded aspect of the texts, the decision to piece together a reading from all three sources follows that strategy. From the beginning, the fundamental wager of this project has been that earlier texts would open onto possibilities for queer readings that translate into surprising but politically productive indices for jumpstarting gay history along a different axis from its current one. Understood as well is that they would be disseminated unevenly. As before, the echoes do not articulate an actualization of a potentiality once heard and now recalled but rather ones whose fragmentary and at times disjointed character preserves a possibility beyond the regimens of the biopolitical. That is, the barely audible announces something in excess of bare life, resistant to the management of the homosexual as a species.

Jumpstarting Gay History

The image on the back of an early copy of the DVD of the movies expresses the predicament, as it were, of gay politics in the neoliberal age. There are four images. At the left margin is Ennis Del Mar; at the right margin is Jack Twist. Center left are Ennis and his wife; center right, Jack and his wife. In other words, gravity pulls even queers to a center occupied by heterosexual unions. What such symmetry means is that gay relationships or love stories are over before they begin; always seen through a rear view mirror; their rear end always in sight before anything begins.[1] While critics may have argued how easily the film's gayness translated into stories befitting straight people, the real question might be if the film is even a love story.² Do a "couple of high-altitude fucks once or twice a year," as Jack laments, constitute a love story? Or is it precisely a gay love story because it never materializes? Half of the film follows the lovers as members of the traditional family and their travails as heterosexuals. Almost every time we see Jack and Ennis together, the following scene concerns life on the heterosexual home front where girlfriends, wives, children, and in-laws both protect and threaten the closet. As the cover of the DVD indicated, the film's understanding of homosexuality appears to be pure inversion, standing in reverse relationship to heterosexual marriage, which governs the center and protects the essence of all sexuality.

To focus, as many early critics did, on the universal dimensions of homosexuality obscures other issues such as class and race. Class is hardly obscured in the film. Jack Twist, the one whose marriage jumpstarts his social mobility, is ever ready to come out and set up house, thereby triangulating class, coming out, and domestication. Ennis de Mar, on the other hand, may live in a mobile home and move from job to job, but he goes nowhere fast. Mobility, at least for him, is a fiction—as is his family name, del Mar. He is "of the sea" or queer to mountain country, and apparently, of Latino origin despite his porcelain skin. The sexual partners Jack finds on the other side of the border in Mexico for backroom, anonymous adventure are mere metonymies for the one Latino who remains forever removed by a border of a different kind. But the love story, if there is one, is over before it begins. Metonymous, anonymous sex fills the void. Moreover, such rear viewing renders class and race inconsequential. Those antagonisms have already been played out.

If the homosexual love story is over before it begins, as it were, then the promise of coming out, the promise of going West to realize the American kind of freedom is rather moot. Such blindness extends to the film itself or at least to its obscured time line. The film begins in 1963 or pre-Stonewall and ends in 1983 or at the beginning of the AIDS crisis. Perhaps that explains why in the middle of Buttfuck, Wyoming, everyone has homosexuality on his mind. In the period during which coming out is essentially a gay narrative, the film, set in a part of American that seems to promise so much physical space *in* which to come out, begs the question: Just where does one come out *to*? To *Brokeback Mountain*, where "stemming the rose," as the ever vigilant sheep rancher Augirre describes it, is already under his watchful eyes.³ To Mexico? Where backroom sex and the specter of AIDS signal the fate of those who would cross real borders and transform coming out into something more than a re-casting of the

American myth, "Go West, Young Man!" Or perhaps to a corner of the Twist homestead, where a gay couple can set up house under the *fatherly* watch of the *stud duck*? (Proulx 2005, 24). Stated precisely, the manner in which male homosexual desire is constructed, understood, and practiced in the film exposes "coming-out" as a myth productive only for the policing of aberrant desire. Given the ahistorical character of the film, the manner in which arguably the most significant period in the American gay movement appears to have already ended before it began, the fracturing of the family unit might restart that history to include the issues of class and race as well.

That possibility emerges in how both Jack and Ennis foreshorten the panoptic gaze by exposing its limits. The myth of coming out is what lures Jack to his death, his enactment of the death drive, even his very embodiment of it constitutes a fissure in the codependent myth of a happy, heterosexual family. His mobility threatens the focus of the panopticon. Ennis, who refuses to come out, who understands from the beginning that he is being watched, pushes the logic of inversion to an illogical extreme, so inverting the panoptic gaze that he recovers an exceptionally exiguous space that opens up a messianic dimension precisely because it does not register or is out of register. What such an inversion withholds constitutes the possibility of a promise or a vow. Since the love story that occasions such a vow is already over before it has begun, the promise remains intact, never fully registered or articulated. The oversight and mapping of sexuality, in other words, can account neither for what occurs on the other side of the border nor for what can be clearly located or marked within its borders.

Seen (Scene) from the Rear

If we recall once more Guy Hocquenghem's 1975 analysis of homosexual desire, the construction of same-sex desire in the film is nothing if not homophobic handiwork: "There is no subdivision of desire into homo- and heterosexual. Desire emerges in multiple forms, whose components are only visible a posteriori, according to how we manipulate it" (1993, 49–50). If desire is thus polymorphous, more adequately defined in terms of plenitude and not lack, then any analysis of desire in *Brokeback Mountain* must attend to how such desire is manipulated a posteriori. I have already mentioned how the rearview mirror is the lens through which the homosexual gaze is captured. Up until the last several scenes, the film's celebrated sweeping landscapes are framed as a series of postcards, something that is already amply apparent from the screenplay. "The thousand sheep, the dogs, the horses. JACK and ENNIS and the mules slowly flow out above the tree line into the vast flowering meadows of the mountainside" (McMurtry and Ossana 2005, 6). No conversation interrupts the flowering visual; the panorama is the story; homosexuals like mules flow into and become a part of the panoptic frame.[4] Several scenes later Jack and Ennis sit around the campfire. The acoustical accompaniment is minimal, only their chewing and a crackling fire. The entire scene is shot at dusk, already subsumed by the flickering visual vocabulary of memory (McMurtry and Ossana 2005, 12).

Two scenes shortly thereafter repeat the pattern, early and amply filling up the photo album with picture postcards: Jack and Ennis are on horseback, "moving higher up the mountain to new pastures" (McMurtry and Ossana 2005, 16). The scene evokes the Greek pastoral; no voices from the present intrude upon the bucolic bliss of the past. And the scene that ends with their only on-screen fuck begins at sunset with Jack singing a Pentecostal hymn, "Water walkin' Jesus." The screenplay describes his rendition as "sad" and "dirge-like," "causing coyotes to yip in the distance" (McMurtry and Ossana 2005, 17). That is, the night of their celebrated love-making is already framed by a dirge-like sadness with Jack asking the water-walking Jesus to "take him away," which prayer will ironically come to be answered (McMurtry and Ossana 2005, 17). The entire homosexual love affair, in other words, always has something of the character of a souvenir, an affair to be remembered before it ever occurs. The most poignant and thus telling souvenir is, of course, Ennis's blood-stained shirt that Jack steals as a keepsake after the first, and what will prove to be the last, summer spent together on Brokeback Mountain. They are never again seen having sex, as if they have always already made love. Their relationship is a series of post-coital-a-tergo intervals, some that last as long as four years. Exchanging postcards is all that is afforded them between those few high-altitude fucks. And if all that they have, according to Jack, is Brokeback Mountain, it is only a postcard of Brokeback Mountain, hung on the inside of a closet door inside a trailer.

What I will call, albeit somewhat ironically, the poststructural epistemology of the story, the coming-to-know who and what is queer based upon an a posteriori manipulation of desire, also seems to undo its own postscript.[5] Such a dynamic evinces itself already in the final scene when the camera shows how Ennis had reversed the order of the shirts and placed his on top. Blood is exchanged in this exchange, at least metonymically, just as Ennis and Jack can be said to have exchanged blood products metonymically in Mexico. This combination of metonymy and inversion opens up new pathways (and pathogens) for bloodlines to redraw the map of desire by becoming as unreadable as the patronymic "Del Mar." Then looking back, manipulating a posteriori the positions of the shirts, renders it impossible to read the trace blood on the shirts, which blood Jack, via Mexico, will already have mixed or contaminated with that on Ennis's shirt. If the reconfiguration of bloodlines that occurs as a result of a poststructural epistemology might serve, in keeping with the liminal function of homosexuality in the story and film, to pathologize same-sex desire, the dynamic generated by its metonymical character de-secures that boundary. Something is not properly bounded, which is not to say that it is unbounded, but rather that its exiguous character confuses those boundaries, and as we come to see, turns in on itself, rendering the homosexual script illegible.

Inversion, as I use it here, means that male homosexuality is a subcategory of sexuality in general, that it exists only in relation to or over and against heterosexuality.[6] As such, it should be calculable, which is to say it should subscribe to a rational or natural order of things and thus ensure that the wife and kids are never really out of the picture. Even if the homosexual act always occurs outdoors, it requires nature, which in turn helps to "naturalize" it. "Stemming the rose" stems from nature, and that eases the transition back into the family, where the family tree can continue to bloom. Homosexuality becomes dependent on heterosexuality; it looks to nature for sanction. But such sanction requires acknowledgment of the priority of heterosexuality and the family. That is one reason why there are more scenes of men screwing women than of Jack and Ennis stemming the rose.

Moreover, homosexuality (or what we see of it) is synonymous with butt-fucking. No reference, let alone filming of oral sex is seen, and no foreplay is ever shown. But if the homosexual is invited into the family via nature, the family boundaries are apparently restored once he is inside, and any precedence that might cleave to coitus-a-tergo or the homosexual way of doing things is quickly reversed and re-coded. As the short story makes clear, the missionary position is to be assumed in the bedroom. "What she [Alma] hated" was anal sex, but when Ennis consents to doing it in a way proper for married couples, Alma insists he use protection. Ennis will do so only if she consents to having more of his babies. She responds that she would if he were able to support them. The homosexual, unable to support his family, prefers to butt-fuck his wife. The short story makes this connection between (re)productive and impoverished sex explicit: "And under that, thought, anyway, what you like to do don't make too many babies"

(Proulx 2005, 16). The sentence's odd construction, whereby "that" can be thought anyway but in a straight way, points to the manner in which homosex is always an afterthought, even if the initial positioning of bodies suggests its precedence. In such fashion, homosex, as the floating signifier of this afterthought, is circumscribed.

The positioning of bodies such that one gaze is met by the other constitutes the heterosexual union whereby children are produced if the father is also economically productive; such reciprocity secures the space in which man and wife come together. Homosex is unbounded insofar, as Leo Bersani notes, both men look out across the horizon in an endless extension of self (1995, 166). Coming out, at least if it is linked to butt-fucking on Brokeback Mountain, has the potential to exceed all boundaries, save that the expansive extensivity of this queer union can only reach as far as the eye, which is not far enough to escape the boss man Aguirre's 10 × 42 binoculars.

Nature, moreover, does not cooperate; early snowstorms end Jack and Ennis's romance on Brokeback Mountain. From now on, their relationship will always be something of a *fairy* tale, a once-upon-a-time moment whose sequels will always be interrupted and discontinued due to family obligations. There are limits to coming out, and such limits are intended to secure the family. Just as the positioning of bodies is as rigid as it is prescribed in the family, the homosexual can only come out insofar as he is positioned alongside, at the margins of, the family. After all, Jack's idea of homosexual bliss is quite filial—setting up house on the outskirts of the Twist homestead. In this regard, Jack's ashes, or the fact that his father, despite all his disdain for Jack and his dreams, will not relinquish his ashes and allow Ennis to spread them on Brokeback Mountain, indicates the stakes in not allowing the homosexual's ashes to be spread across what might be an infinite expanse, particularly should the winds pick up and strew them all across the West. (Jacks widow Lurleen keeps the other half in Texas.) Of course, according to the poststructural epistemology of the film, his ashes are always already everywhere, which not only speaks to the end of their relationship before it has begun but also to a threat which demands that even in death the homosexual take up his place inside the family plot. Reducing him to ashes alone is not enough to eliminate the risk of the contagion, particularly when those ashes will already have been to Mexico.

If, as Ennis fears, the homosexual urge might come upon him at any time ("Bottom line, we're around each other and this thing grabs onto us again in the wrong place, wrong time, we'll be dead"; McMurtry and

Ossana 2005, 52) and if it is so irresistible that it might break out even under the watchful eye of Ennis's horrified wife, it needs to be called out, lest it secretly enter the family as some kind of sleeper cell. But if this strange thing, as Ennis calls it, can happen upon even those who insist they are not queer, what means are there to control what by definition is uncontrollable? Something must elicit its expression. While there is no evidence that either Jack or Ennis do more than keep company with sheep, sleeping with sheep is a means to produce homosexual desire. It does so by fortifying a metonymic chain that for centuries has linked bestiality and male-male desire (Bredbeck 1991, 5). That alone, however, is not enough to induce transgression, save that forcing one of the two herders to sleep in those parts is, as Jack laments, "not right." Unlawful sleeping with sheep thus becomes unlawful sleeping with another man, unlawful insofar as it violates, on the one hand, the terms of the contract with Aguirre and, on the other, it puts sheep and thus, by extension, nature at risk. Since it is not "right," Ennis must do the "right" thing and sleep with Jack.

If Jack and Ennis's affair is then something of a setup, if they are framed for homosexuality, their homosexuality is thus required. But for what? The most obvious answer is for the police; that is, Jack and Ennis commit the transgressions that necessitate surveillance. The law of the father, who in this context is the internalized enforcer of the biopolitical regime, requires homosexuals insofar as they establish a limit without which there can be no law.[7] The dead sheep that Jack and Ennis discover after having abandoned the sheep for each other demonstrates that the law is already in force. The word need not be uttered nor the punishment refer specifically to the act. The force of the law is nonetheless unmistakable: The dead sheep declare that a practicing homosexual has slept here. The homosexual, in other words, can either sleep with sheep or sleep with another man and kill sheep. In both instances he is an instrument of the law, allowing for its expression. If desire, even aberrant desire, desires the law, then the homosexual threat is a welcome one, ensuring that the homosexual can never really come out to anything but an always already delimited space. Even from afar they are within the purview of the boss, Aguirre, who by forcing one to sleep with sheep is getting precisely what he wanted. The real reason he rejects Jack's request to herd sheep the following year is less because of what he witnesses and due more to Ennis's absence. Without Ennis he won't get what he wants. That also explains why both Aguirre and Alma, Ennis's wife, only reveal what they have witnessed later, after the fact or a posteriori. Withholding such information invites repeated transgressions, which, in turn, only serve to reinforce the law.

Such reenforcements are synonymous with rearticulations, which is often enough to have the desired effect. "You ever get the feeling," Ennis asks Jack, "I don't know, when you're in town, and someone looks at you suspicious . . . like he knows. And then you get out on the pavement, and everyone, lookin' at you, and maybe they all know too?" (McMurtry and Ossana 2005, 71). The results of such self-policing are predictably violent, too. When Alma finally confronts Ennis after a Thanksgiving dinner at the home of her new family, his reaction is practically violent. He raises his fist and can barely restrain from beating the one who knows more than she ever gave onto. While he does not bash Alma, he does beat on the truck driver in the next scene, who was forced to brake to keep from hitting Jack. The trucker yells out, "Hey, asshole, watch where you're goin'," at which point, "without hesitation, ENNIS runs around the pickup, punches right inside the open driver window . . . yanks open the driver door, drags the huge man out . . . pummeling him and kicking him" (McMurtry and Ossana 2005, 80). The outed asshole's violent response invites an even more violent response from the trucker, "who doesn't let up" (2005, 80). In other words, he gives the self-policing queer just what he asked for.

Seen in this light, Aguirre's anger is more than the voyeuristic curiosity indicated above. In the film, at least, he doesn't witness the act, but he knows it happened by the mixed or impure herd that is returned to him. In the scene that follows Jack's success in convincing Ennis that storms prevent him from venturing up the mountain to sleep with the sheep, they discover that Aguirre's herd has mixed with a Chilean's herd. Upon their return, Aguirre notes, "some of these never went up there with you" (McMurtry and Ossana 2005, 26). Hispanic sheep and American sheep have mixed. After the fact, there is evidence that Jack and Ennis have exchanged blood products, which is readable both by Aguirre and the unreadable paint brands on the sheep. If Aguirre is truly angry, it is only because fewer sheep returned from the mountain than originally ascended it. Homosexual unions are not only not pure, but they are also nonreproductive. Such unions offer apt occasion for Aguirre to assert his authority. That is not to suggest that Aguirre—whose own name is from the Basque for open pasture and field— is gleeful that they have stemmed the rose.[8] Clearly, he is not. Rather, his anger celebrates the homosexual union insofar as that union supplies incontrovertible proof of the need for the law, which, as it turns out, is nature's law. Aguirre, in other words, is the law's most felicitous expression.

Withholding knowledge about what one has witnessed is less a matter of volition or even fear and more the inescapable condition of how things come to be known, according to what I have called the poststructural epistemology of the film. There is always something belated about the homosexual. Their last time together, after all, is interrupted by a flashback when Ennis embraced Jack from behind on Brokeback Mountain. "They gently rocked back and forth, the shadow of their bodies a single column against the rock." The screenplay is remarkable for what it reveals and does not reveal: "They are wrapped in a closeness that satisfies some shared and sexless hunger" (McMurtry and Ossana 2005, 84).

If the immediate question is why such hunger is sexless, the obvious answer is that such poststructural awareness is intended to de-sex or even castrate those given to male-male desire. But in this instance, the merging of homosexual bodies—bodies that have already been marked by difference through heterosexual unions or through heteronormative exclusion—opens up onto a vastness that the foreshortened gaze inside the tent or the site of their first fuck simultaneously disabled. That shared closeness belongs to the past; it is merely a single shadow, but it may not be entirely irretrievable. If the conditions under which it can be retrieved are unclear at this point, the scene accords to the logic of the postcard. One has already returned from holiday by the time the addressee reads the card, just as this scene of remembered closeness closes with a "childhood song, from some long-ago memory." Even if the postcard is returned to sender, as it is to Ennis after Jack's death, the messages on the card are always an open secret.

Figure 5.1. "They were wrapped in a closeness that satisfies some shared and sexless hunger."

The policing of the homosexual relationship, even if we are beginning to note slippages in those mechanisms, is not limited to declaring the homosexual relationship DOA. Rather, its epistemological structure includes a reliable mapping of same-sex desire, which, in fact, is evident from the opening shot. A cattle truck moves west through a dark background as light begins to surface in the east. The truck's tracks create a line of light that allows for its vector to be trailed. The light also serves to divide the uncharted and heretofore darkened space in two, anticipating thereby how homosexual and heterosexual desire will be viewed in terms of a divide to allow for calculation of what is on the other side of that divide. Moreover, the one who drives establishes the divide. His heeding the call to go West produces a boundary, one that Ennis, the passenger, will frequently cross and patrol. His frequent violent outbursts in the film reveal how homosexuality polices itself; it draws its own line as the cattle truck does in the opening scene. That Jack, unbeknownst to Ennis, will steal the shirt that was stained with blood in what is something other than a lover's first quarrel demonstrates how violence underwrites their relationship, preserving its memory and anticipating, at least, Jack's fate.

Rear Ended

The law governing inversion is most evident in how apparent banter comes to acquire a sexual undertone if the punch line, so to speak, is already known in advance. That is, what in a different context might seem like idle chatter acquires added significance since the temporal inversions of the film render such chatter a snide commentary on what has already happened. Viewers, for example, know that this is a gay cowboy movie, so they are already in on the joke. This is also what confirms the impression that homosexuality is on everyone's mind. A few examples will suffice: Lurleen will lament, "It's funny, ain't it? Husbands don't never seem to dance with their wives. (sarcastic). Why do you think that is, Jack?" (McMurtry and Ossana 2005, 75) Her "sarcastic" tone betrays the secret, which has always been an open one. Jack likes to dance, just not with women. Nonetheless, he takes the bait and dances with Lashawn, the wife of Randall, as if to signal that women are not the problem, his wife is. The open secret still needs to maintain the structure of a secret.[9]

Homosexuality, as the implied double of the entendre is unmistakable. In fact, throughout the first two-thirds of the film. Jack, in reference to his mother, offers his interpretation of Pentecostal Christianity: "I don't know what the Pentecost is . . . Mama never explained it. (pause) I guess it's when the world ends and fellas [no gals implied] like you and me march off to hell." The pregnant pause gives Ennis all the time he needs to pick up on Jack's meaning, "Uh, uh, speak for yourself. You may be a sinner, but I ain't yet had the opportunity" (McMurtry and Ossana 2005, 17). Ennis's remarks follow what the screenplay describes as a sudden loosening of his tongue (McMurtry and Ossana 2005, 15). And since it is not long before they will come to abandon the sheep for each other, the retort reads like a plea to Jack to offer him the opportunity to sin. Retrospective knowledge, in other words, transforms the apparently innocent remark ("It's not right Aguirre makes us sleep with sheep.") into one loaded with homosexual overtones, articulating with increasing force the law of same-sex desire. The scene in the bar, a straight bar, when Jack offers to buy a drink for the rodeo clown who earlier that day pulled him from harm's way, is understood by the clown to be a come-on, although no mention of sex is made. Whatever isn't explicit is explicitly homosexual. More to the point are Aguirre's first words to Jack and Ennis as they await his arrival and a chance for employment, "Get your screwing asses in here." That seems to open the back door for Jack to insist that men's asses are for screwing: "Aguirre got all over his ass after a storm last year led to the loss of so many sheep." Or, "Joe will have your ass" if you let the sheep stray (McMurtry and Ossana 2005, 7). And on that fateful night when Jack convinces Ennis that he's too drunk to journey up the mountain to sleep with the sheep, he reprises the theme, "Freeze your ass off when that fire dies down" (2005, 18). Finally, when Jack steadies his gun to shoot a two-point buck, Ennis remarks, "Was getting' tired of your dumb ass missin'" (2005, 11–12). Such remarks prepare Ennis to have Jack's "missin'" ass. But again, such retrospective knowledge, understood as one form of inversion, is not entirely predictable. Aguirre will not have Ennis's ass; instead, Ennis will have Jack's ass. Reversals, in other words, may not be fully containable, however calculable they may seem.

The visual framing of how retrospection calls homosexuality out needs to be remarked more fully. The first time we see Ennis is after the trucker screeches to a halt to let Ennis out, departing almost before Ennis touches ground and spraying him with dust. In other words, the truck that marked the divide can now dump Ennis. The dust signals that a line has been drawn in the dirt, and Ennis, who is dirt poor and carries only a grocery sack with a shirt and a pair of Levis, is immediately marked as some kind of trade. He stands beneath a sign, "Farm and Ranch Employment Agency," smoking a cigarette and striking what comes to be a homoerotic pose.[10] For once Jack comes to notice Ennis, he "stiffens a little" and then looks away (McMurtry and Ossana 2005, 2). It is now that Jack first uses the rearview mirror in an attempt to shave. The pose that comes to be homoerotic calls forth a rear view that not only teletypes the framing of the relationship that will come to be but also prompts the suitor to tidy up. The furtive glance offered by the rearview mirror of Ennis the Marlboro Man is replayed on Brokeback Mountain when Jack catches a rear view of Ennis, dressed only in boots and socks, "slop[ping] a washcloth under his arms, between his legs" (McMurtry and Ossana 2005, 13). Viewing the behind might cause Jack once again to stiffen a little—although it would be innocent enough if we didn't already know what it will come to mean. Such rear (rare) viewing is all Jack and Ennis have, seldom together and only together under the sign of imminent departure and doom.

Worth noting is that reversal, which term I use synonymously with inversion, apparently extends to sexual positions. Ennis may start out as the top dog, but subsequent positioning suggests otherwise. At times Jack is cuddled by Ennis, at other times the reverse. At least once, the film shows Ennis's head on Jack's chest. Any such knowledge about who plays what role in the relationship, according to the logic of hetero-normativity, is preterited. More than beg the question as to what happens when the symmetrical other of heterosexual partnering engages in a symmetrical reversal of its own, the reversal reinscribes the backward trajectory of any knowledge

Figure 5.2: The pose that comes to be homoerotic calls forth a rear view.

about homosexuality, save that it now sponsors a misprision and threatens to obscure the rearview.

With the appearance of such a misprision arises the urgent need to immobilize the queer. The instruments for such discipline and punishment are clear by now: relegating all homosexual relationships to a thing of the past, linking that trajectory with death, bashing—self-inflicted or otherwise—and if necessary, death. The death penalty need not be executed but merely inferred. That much is clear when Ennis relates what he recalls was the fate of the two old queers, Earl and Rich, who had "ranched together down home" (McMurtry and Ossana 2005, 53). Ennis was not a witness to the bashing in which allegedly "they'd took a tire iron to Earl, spurred him up, drug him around by his dick till it pulled off. Hell, for all I know he [my father] done the job" (McMurtry and Ossana 2005, 53). He comes to know this since '"my daddy, he made sure me and brother seen it." Not only is knowledge about Earl and Rich preterited in this instance, but the omnipresence of the father, as both educator and executioner, attests to the veracity of such knowledge.

His omnipresence, however, is not enough to keep the homosexual in his place. If all of the potential slippages in what can be called the biopolitical regime threaten the border whose crossings are meant only to affirm the limits, then a different kind of fix is needed. In this respect, the film, the short story, and the screenplay are shameless in their reliance on gay clichés to make of the homosexual a type. Both Ennis's and Jack's childhood offer simplistic pathologies to explain and thus contain what happened on Brokeback Mountain or on the others side of the divide. Ennis comes from a broken family or a completely broke one, since his parents left his brother, sister, and him only $24 in a cookie jar after they had "run themselves off the road" (McMurtry and Ossana 2005, 16–17). Since the bank took the ranch, Ennis was already nowhere as a child. And given the manner in which property is attached to the patronymic in a heteronormative society governed by the phallus, Ennis is already destined to not have "it" from the moment his father runs himself off. More predictable is how the internalized presence of his father haunts his entire negotiation of his struggle with the meaning of his sexuality. If Ennis's mode of being in the world is structured by the past in the form of dreams and flashbacks, then such memory is already ruled by the violent and omnipresent memory of the father, who may well have castrated the old queer. And when sons don't have fathers, they end up herding sheep. They come to rehearse and inhabit the Greek pastoral. The catachresis of his name—Del Mar is neither Greek nor "American"—

articulates or rather comes to articulate the displacement of one whose exile is instrumental to a constant recollection of the father. In other words, he is disowned by his name, which does not mean he doesn't seek it.

Jack's childhood charts an even more direct path to queerdom. His father, a well-known bull rider, refused to share his talents with his son (McMurtry and Ossana 2005, 17). His withholding thus asserts his authority in a more powerful or—shall we say—latent way. The short story is unequivocal in its description of the scene of castration. Ennis, upon climbing the stairs after Jack's death to see Jack's bedroom, recalls Jack's story about how Jack came to learn that he was "dick-clipped" and his father was not. "He had been three or four, he said, always late getting to the toilet . . . and often as not left the surroundings sprinkled down. The old man blew up about it and this one time worked into a crazy rage: Christ, he licked the stuffin' out a me, knocked me down on the bathroom floor, whipped me with his belt . . . Then he says, 'You want to know what it's like with piss all over the place? I'll learn you,' and he pulls it out and lets go all over me . . . but while he was hosing me down I seen he had some extra material I was missing" (Proulx 2005, 25). Not only does this scene predispose the one who has been disposed upon to go seeking that missing part but it also leads him to seek it in backrooms in Mexico. A metaphorical logic is in play here, making of the homosexual a type whose acts can be explained by appeal to a pathology or an overarching logic.[11] If it weren't for fathers there would be no homosexuals, but if it weren't for homosexuals, the law of the father would be unenforced, even perhaps unenforceable. If such memories for Jack are indelible, that does not confirm their accuracy. Such a form of transference virtually guarantees that that there will be gaps in the metaphorical logic of the film; the suturing, as I have tried to indicate throughout, is exposed.

Castration engenders guilt, and the guilty suffer economically as well. They have no possessions. At the very least, they do not have the economic mobility necessary to settle down. After Jack asks Ennis, as he often does, what they are going to do, Ennis replies, "I doubt there's nothing we *can* do. I'm *stuck* with what I got here. Makin' a livin's about all" (McMurtry and Ossana 2005, 49; second italics added). If all he has can even be called a living, it is surely no livelihood, and it prevents him from setting up house in the neighborhood. He is always on the move, a transient cowboy forever out of reach for Jack. The reversal or inversion here is not that class precludes their union, but rather that the impoverished one rather than the rich one is out of reach.[12]

Nowhere is Ennis's abjection and destitution more poignantly expressed than in virtually his final words to Jack, after Jack makes what has become the homophobic shibboleth of the film or the quintessential put-down of queer cowboys: "I wish I knew how to quit you." "Then why don't you," Ennis pleads, "Why don't you let me be? It's because of you, Jack, that I'm like this. I'm nothin'. I'm nowhere" (McMurtry and Ossana 2005, 83). Jack then moves toward Ennis, Ennis pushes him away, Jack comes toward him again, and Ennis does not resist. "Come here . . . it's all right. It's all right . . . damn you, Ennis." The screenplay continues, "And then . . . they hug one another, a fierce, desperate embrace—managing to torque things almost to where they had been, for what they've just said is no news: as always, nothing ended, nothing begun, nothing resolved" (2005, 83). It is at this point that the film flashes back to Brokeback Mountain 1963. Jack, despite all his border crossings, has a place for Ennis to come to. The ellipses in both his speech and the screenplay's directions suggest a spatial territorialization that is simultaneously undone by language, or rather, it is unsayable. Of course, the place is Brokeback Mountain, an irretrievable past to which all male-male homosexual relationships are assigned. Nonetheless, the moving toward Ennis who is coming toward Jack recalls the reversals of sexual positions—all the more apparent in the use of the word "torque," which is the root of "queer." Such torquing circumscribes a space for them to come together, to comfort one another. Ennis, as we recall, even sings to Jack something from a long-ago memory (2005, 84). The past, Brokeback Mountain, takes one to a more distant past, which, as the continuing sets of ellipses indicate, resists articulation. The homosexual-heterosexual continuum, so essential for the policing of desire, is interrupted. The flash of what was never begun, ended or resolved in the past opens up a space in which queers can be themselves; i.e., torque, which makes it all the more urgent that the film return to the "continuous" present and Jack and Ennis to "their separate and difficult lives" (McMurtry and Ossana 2005, 84).

Rarefied (Rearified) Scenes

The attempt to keep a look out for homosexuality by viewing it through the lens of inversion depends upon a rear view, and a rear view is always temporally and spatially obscured. What is not seen, or cannot be seen, thereby becomes possible, its potential is there precisely because it is virtual or because it might also not be, which is the same one can say of any picture postcard: It is not "here." The most instructive example of how this potentiality undoes the law of inversion is in how it frustrates castration and the enforcement of the laws governing homo- and heterosexual unions that issue from castration. Such a threat, as we know, also extends to the economic order based upon who has "it" and does not. As Leo Bersani points out, coitus-a-tergo is not specific to male homosexuals, but a compensatory possibility is. The penetrator offers his cock to the penetrated. But if making his cock disappear inside another man threatens the penetrator with castration, the stiff cock of the penetrated is a compensatory offering (Bersani, Homos 1995, 112). In *Brokeback Mountain* such an economy accords with a poststructural epistemology. In the tent Jack places Ennis's hand on his cock, which inspires Ennis to flip Jack on all fours and penetrate him. He does so with the assurance that what he will give Jack has already been returned to him. In such fashion, the castrated or dispossessed have always only had it in reserve. Potentiality can thus be stated as follows: "I will not have been not castrated." Or, "I will not have not loved." The double negative does not convert to a positive, "I will have loved," but to a potentiality that inheres in the difference between an affirmative formulation and its negated denial. Such potentiality echoes the affirmative without the affirmative ever having been iterated. It retains the character of a threshold, which is not, however, a passageway to actuality. If such semantics are too unwieldy, the shirt that Jack steals from Ennis articulates such potentiality, if only by resisting such articulation. While evincing the end of their relationship, the shirt also preserves its possibility to both be and not be; that is, not *not* be.[13] When they are in Jack's closet, which we learn retrospectively, Ennis will not *not* be. And when the shirts are moved by Ennis, with his shirt now on top, Jack will not *not* be. The movement of the shirts constitutes the construction of a paradoxically de-territorialized space in which the shirts are a trace of not *not* being, for such potentiality never attains to anything but a trace or an echo.

That impossible possibility comes to be articulated, insofar as it can be, with the intrusion of what I will call the hyper-real in the film, namely when Ennis learns from Jack's wife, Lurleen, of Jack's death. Once Ennis's postcard to Jack is returned, the mode of communication that secured the poststructural epistemology is threatened. Ennis is thus forced to communicate via telephone. The extent to which knowledge about the homosexual is undermined is immediately apparent when Ennis informs Lurleen that Brokeback Mountain was where Jack and he once herded sheep. " 'Well, he said it was his favorite place,' she responds, 'I thought he meant to get drunk'" (McMurtry and Ossana 2005, 87). Does she know now why it was his favorite place? Lurleen's "level voice" (McMurtry and Ossana 2005, 86) betrays nothing. The illegibility or epistemological uncertainty becomes explicit with the explanation of his death. Lurleen offers the official account: a tire blew up, its rim broke Jack's nose and knocked him unconscious, whereupon he drowned in his own blood. At that point, the film flashes to a "man being beaten unmercifully by three assailants, one of whom uses a tire iron" (McMurtry and Ossana 2005, 87). The screenplay and short story would have us believe that Ennis, at best, is uncertain as to what really happened, and at most, reads behind the alibi offered by Lurleen. But the flash could just as likely be a flashback whereby Ennis attempts to stitch together the truth by referring to what he claims to have remembered was the scene of the bashing of Earl that his father insisted he visit. If the flash of the bashing is in Ennis's mind, it relies on what he might have witnessed as a child but only after such memory has been routed through decades of internalized homophobia. And who is to say that his father's account after the fact is any more accurate?

Lurleen's account triggers in Ennis a memory of a memory, but both memories are suspect or unreliable. If, in fact, Jack was murdered and the flash is a more accurate account of events, what was the motive? The poststructural epistemology of the film points to a gay bashing, but when they last met, Jack offered a different possible motive: "I kinda got a thing going' with a ranch foreman's wife over in Childress. Expect to get shot by Lurleen or the husband, one or the other" (McMurtry and Ossana 2005, 80). Belated to be sure, knowledge about the homosexual requires a lot of cross-referencing and suturing. The film, unlike the story and screenplay, does not foreclose the possibility that Lurleen is imagining the true events as she tells Ennis the official party line. Based upon what Ennis last heard from Jack about an affair with another woman, she could have been in on the bashing, if there was one. Was she onto Jack? But what was she onto? His homosexuality, in which case her response to learning about the real significance for Jack of Brokeback Mountain would appear less uncertain. Or would it? Do her eyes well with tears because she now knows why Jack never stiffened for her? Or does she now realize that he never really was cheating on her with another woman, or does Ennis tip her off to a different sort of contagion his trips to Mexico might have introduced into the family? Or is she onto Jack's apparent affair with "another fella" that Jack's father sarcastically remarks was "goin' a split up with his wife and come back here?" (McMurtry and Ossana 2005, 90). And what is the source of the father's sarcasm? Is he making fun of Jack because of his outlandish dreams or because of his open secret, i.e., his homosexuality? People, partners, and places now constitute an economy of uncontainable substitutions. The ease with which the double entendres of the first parts of the film could be read—sleeping with sheep, sinning, hitting on the rodeo clown, and looking for "missin'" asses—is no longer comforting. Even before the scene or scenes of Jack's death, Ennis's final scene with Cassie indicated that the epistemological closet was under siege. After Ennis insists that he probably was no fun, Cassie replies, "Oh, Ennis . . . girls don't fall in love with fun!" (McMurtry and Ossana 2005, 86). But do he and Cassie even share the same meaning of "fun"?

Language is returning to the closet, re-concealing itself.[14] And as it does, it is perhaps necessary to take one last breath here and situate this final reading in the context of the theoretical argument worked out in the introduction. In the opening discussion of "Death in Venice" Tadzio apparently signaled to Aschenbach, gesturing toward a space beyond the reach of the camera, beyond all the controls over queer love that have plagued men and women given to same-sex desire since the early to mid-nineteenth century in the West. To recall, for a brief moment the figure of Tadzio is dappled; the sun and mist appear to make of his frame an emerging pointillist image. Is Tadzio assuming shape or disappearing? Rather than answer that question, I considered that fleeting moment as worthy of examination as a site or pregnant with potentiality or something that both is and is not. That potentiality became a means to re-think LGBTQ current politics, whose agenda, insofar as it is cleaved to military service and marriage, were outgrowths of the values that shaped the emerging nuclear family and nation state around 1800. At the same time, narratives from that period possessed untapped energies for a reparative reading (recalling again Sedgwick), for different kinds of queer coming-togethers. The opening chapters explored how the "queer" came to be a type, a necessary but reviled exile whose existence on the margins also served to secure the borders of those living inside them. But, of course, only in exile might one espy or approach the space to which Tadzio pointed. The eventual task of the project was to reanimate those repressed energies of the earlier texts, to listen for stirrings or echoes that could help articulate ever more clearly the potentialities of those last scenes in "Death in Venice." For this project, those stirrings first achieved clarity enough in Roland Barthes's reading of *The Sorrows of Young Werther* to allow for the formulation: I will not have not loved. (Queer echoes need time to traverse great spaces.). This chapter picks up on the potentialities embedded in that formulation to traces other such potentialities not in 1800 Germany but rather in the American West on Brokeback Mountain. If the introduction pieced together a counter-temporality from modern American/English queer theory and contemplations about AIDS, the readings that comprise the chapters sought literary expressions of this coming community, forever displaced in the future. Finally, the discussion of inversion in Proust, to repeat, is on dizzying display here with a new twist. And as language returns to the closet, that space is secured by an oath, unbreakable but forever unfulfilled, holding out bold alternatives to the current LGBTQ agenda.

Nothin' and Nowhere

From the beginning, there existed the threat that inversion would generate a logic or acquire a dimension that threatened to uncouple the binary of sexuality. The most obvious threat to positioning the homosexual was the unreadable positions of the homosexual couple after fucking; who was in whose arms did not provide the rear view necessary for assigning fixed roles. The placing of Jack's ashes in two places indicated how even in death there was a struggle to keep the homosexual in his place, particularly one who had ventured across the border to Mexico. And just what part of Jack Twist is in or on the shirt first in his closet and then in Ennis's? The souvenir of gay love is now plural, dispersed and disseminated. The curiosity is that it is an apparent return to the closet, but one whose depth is always undone, and not an escape from it, which threatens the biopolitical vice squad. Can we thus speak of a panoptic reversal, whereby the series of inversions now has one looking through the other end of the binoculars? Whereas earlier the double vision of binocularity served to reinforce a sexual binarism, now nothing comes into focus; the object under inspection is retreating from sight, just as language is calling something into reserve. And for good reason. Twist, the figure around whom double entendre so often pivoted and thus acquired meaning, is disseminated. His ashes will be in two places.

Worth mentioning is that in July of 1981 the *New York Times* published its now infamous article, describing the so-called gay plague. The movie professes absolute ignorance of AIDS, and there is no reason to even suspect that Jack considers himself at risk, although tens of thousands will already have been infected with the virus. The epistemological structure of knowledge about the virus is consistent with that of the film. By going to

Mexico Jack nonetheless is asking for it, even if that will only come to be known later. He solicits sex, probably even paying for it since he has the kind of mobility Ennis lacks. When he finally admits to Ennis that he has gone south of the border in search of what Ennis refused to give him, he solicits a near violent response from Ennis, thereby reinforcing the violence that underwrites but also forecloses their relationship. Moreover, his proud boast, moments before, that his latest affair was bound to get him killed indicates that he cannot resist asking for it. When he finally gets it, death, he accomplishes metonymically in death what he could never have before, an unbreakable bond with Ennis, secured by a closet. Such closet is a metonymy for the house he hoped to set up on the outskirts of his father's ranch, save that there is no room for the father here.

Crossing borders is thus linked to ever closer spaces, which through such crossings are flattened, an effect of looking through the wrong end of the binoculars and reversing the panopticon. The movie now goes from the phone booth to the Twist homestead to Jack's room, preserved as it was when he was a child, to his closet; then, to the flatness of a trailer park to the inside of a trailer to the closet within a trailer to a shirt atop another shirt. In other words, the uncontainable logic of inversion sponsors two movements that are irreducible to one another. No logical enterprise links dissemination with the closet. And so characteristically uncharacteristically, Ennis, who has been virtually homeless his entire life, offers shelter to Jack—or to Jack's shirt. To be sure, there has been no liberation from the nostalgic future anterior that reduced the homosexual relationship to a series of postcards. The blood-stained shirt preserves the memory of a relationship that was always only subjected to the self-policing violence of a panoptic regime. But the undoing of the film's metaphorical logic, whereby the inversion of inversion produces a disseminated closet or a closeted dissemination, is nothing short of remarkable in the final scene. In the tiny closet within the closet or inside a *mobile* home on the great Northern plain are Jack's and Ennis's shirt.

Closets replace sweeping landscapes and plains replace mountains. These closets, however, are mobile. Ennis took the shirts from Jack's closet, and the final scene begins as he places numbers on a new mailbox, which recalls the exchange of postcards that constituted their relationship between high-altitude fucks. Ennis, as we know, has performed one more reversal or inversion, placing his shirt on top—a metonymy for sexual repositioning and for Ennis's embrace and remembered embrace of Jack on Brokeback Mountain. If that embrace, as both looked out onto a wide, seemingly open, rolling and un-policed expanse, allowed Ennis "not to acknowledge who was in his arms," the metonymical embrace offers a form of sheltering in the tiniest of spaces in the flattest of landscapes. His fixing the button on one of the shirts substitutes as well for the embrace. The sheltering is offered by one who himself was never protected from anyone and barely offered shelter by his parents before they missed that one curve in the road. On the closet door, inside the most claustrophobic of spaces, is the postcard of Brokeback Mountain, which, in the short story, was special-ordered. The card can be seen only if the door is opened, but such opening is clearly within a neatly circumscribed space. The shirts are on a wire hanger on a nail next to the postcard. Ennis adjusts the postcard so that it forms an even line or assumes a symmetrical position with the view from the window of the "great bleakness of the vast Northern Plains" (McMurtry and Ossana 2005, 97). Inside/outside, enclosed/unenclosed, top/bottom make no sense here. Can one even speak logically of inversions here? Brokeback Mountain is inside a closet, reduced to two dimensions, and the window looks onto an outside whose horizon is as near as the window itself. The gaze does not roam as did Aguirre's. Looking in or looking out—is there a difference? All depth perception is foreshortened or flattened. Even if the panopticon can penetrate the space—and it does as far as the camera is concerned—how does it register such a visual field? If there is no depth, how does one pathologize homosexuality?

Moreover, Ennis's last words are in the form of a performative, "Jack, I swear. . . ." He apostrophizes Jack as if he were in the closet or existing in the shirt or recalled by the postcard or just somewhere out there haunting the plain. But like Bartleby's favorite reprise, "I prefer not to . . ." the swearing is open-ended; no semiotic can predict or register what is sworn. His words, "I swear," echo the swearing of his last meeting with Jack on Brokeback Mountain, "Jack fucking Twist" (McMurtry and Ossana 2005, 82), as he cursed the lover who confessed to crossing the border into Mexico and who now is everywhere and nowhere. In this instance the swearing comes with a twist, a term of endearment even if there is no fucking going on. And in one final inversion or twist, it is now Ennis who cannot quit Jack and has no desire to do so. Even that is uncertain, since in the short story his recurrent dreams produce alternate affects, i.e., tears or smiles (Proulx 28). More important, his swearing commits to nothing and excuses nothing. It opens up onto a possibility that is as foreclosed as the horizon espied through the window and as vast as the elliptical form of its utterance that bears no semiotic congruity with closets inside closets.

Ennis, never seduced by the myth of coming out, secures the closet, just as his last act is to close the closet door, but he is also "nowhere." He affirms the sheltering embedded in his vow. Little more can be said about such a space and the pure performative that issues not from outside the closet but seemingly from within it. The space is more likely a threshold, where in and out, open and closed or closeted are contiguous. As the space that allows for Ennis to take his vow, it might be just as imaginary or real as the "pretend" space Jack always sought, "where the bluebirds sing and there's a whiskey spring" (McMurtry and Ossana 2005, 88).

And it is good as such. Whatever possibilities can issue for gay love, constructed as it is according to the great American myth of coming out, must never reveal their secret even when that secret is an open one, which is to say an empty one. Or in returning it to the closet, Ennis, once the instrument and enforcer of the border patrol, is now sovereign of a threshold (just as he is the driver of the truck in the last scene).[15] Of the sea, he is mobile insofar as he is queer to all spaces. Even if he fixes the numbers on his mailbox, his abode speaks to a mobility that is certainly not economic but virtual or potential, consistent with the illogic of his name. Jack has quitted him and not quitted him, preserved and sheltered in Ennis's last words, "Jack, I swear. . . ." The vow is spoken and not spoken and responds to no command, least of all to one issued by the father and his law. What is sworn to Jack can neither be quitted or acquitted. If such a threshold, linguistic, spatial and temporal, is like Ennis, "nowhere and nothing," that nowhere is sheltered by a vow that betrays nothing.

Notes

Introduction

1. Luchino Visconti's 1971 film, which will be discussed below, makes this explicit. The protagonist in the film is a composer (à la Mahler) whose exacting standards strangle all emotion. A flashback shows the audience totally rejecting a recent performance, which delights his friend and rival and whose cruel, uproarious laughter haunts Aschenbach at times during the film.

2. In attempting to piece together fragments of an unacknowledged or unrealized past, the mixing of genres, in this case literature and film, helps to illuminate a dimension otherwise obscured. That is, the film says something about the short story that the latter is unable to say for itself, and vice versa.

3. See *Potentialities*, especially the introduction by Heller-Roazen, 14–18.

4. The visit occurred July 2015. A full transcript of his remarks can be found at: https://www.whitehouse.gov/the-press-office/2015/07/16/remarks-president-after-visit-el-reno-federal-correctional-institution.

5. See Derrida, *Spectres*, 59–65. For an understanding of the centrality of the "idea" in the work of Walter Benjamin see Khalib, 2–13.

6. My indirect reference is, of course, to Benjamin's Angel of History. See Mosès, 65–128.

7. See Pahl, "Geliebte Spricht," 220–247. " 'Geliebte, sprich!'—wenn Frauen sich haben," In *Penthesileas Versprechen: Exemplarische Studien über die literarische Referenz*, ed. Rüdiger Campe, Freiburg: Rombach Verlag, 2008.

8. The Truvada website (Truvada.com) confirms its effectiveness in reducing the risk of HIV infection "when used with safer sex practices." The oddness lies in the fact that many gay men subscribe to the regimen for the very purpose of having license to screw without a condom. Worth noting as well is that long-term use has been associated with severe kidney damage, which is why users need to have blood drawn every 3 to 6 months. The benefits of PREP must also be considered in light of the possibility that gay men are convinced to adhere to a regimen that might do significant harm to vital organs. At the very least, gay men are watched,

followed, and tracked as a means of reducing a risk that requires adherence to safer-sex practices—at least according to its website—that some gay men adhering to PREP s regimen precisely do NOT want to practice.

9. The first showing of the quilt was in 1987 on the National Mall in Washington, D.C. As of 2012 the quilt was comprised of 48,000, 3' × 6' panels weighing more than 54 tons. www.aidsquilt.org.

10. Of course, the situation for HIV infected patient in the West, particularly since 1994 has changed dramatically with the introduction of the cocktail. That doesn't diminish the Western-centric perspective of Garcia Düttmann's analysis which presumes a certain self-conscious awareness about the disease and among its carriers.

11. The contested origins of AIDS, including the false identification of Patient Zero—a flight attendant accused of purposely infecting unsuspecting partners to spread the disease—have often, as in this case, been twisted to conform to the world's understanding of gay people as sexual predators. That it is now presumed to have originated in West Central Africa resonates with the tropical or jungle-like origins of the plague in "Death in Venice."

12. Clearly, I am re-purposing Maimonides and his proof of God via negative theology. God does not not exist. *GP* 1.56–1.59.

13. Heidegger's citation of Schelling is found in his lecture course from 1936 that also links sickness and truth. Odd is that Garcia Düttmann does not contextualize historically Heidegger"s own thinking about disease and evil in these lectures, especially given the importance of the year for the Third Reich and Heidegger's own shift in thought or "The Turn" ("Die Kehre").

14. Epigenetics, which traces the genetic mutations introduced by trauma and the transmission of that mutation to future generations, offers a very real and certainly less lurid example of how such communities might unfold. Moreover, the discovery of that mutation in the child of a Holocaust survivor resonates with Bersani's and Garcia Düttmann's observations: queer communities mourn a past that never was, a death before its time. They give voice to the lingering echoes of voices never heard—a potentiality that they carry forward and pass on (www.ncbi.nlm.nih.gov/pubmed/24029109).

15. Ohi has followed up this volume with another fine mongraph, *Dead Letters Sent: Queer Literary Transmission*. What is queer about transmission is its belatedness; the voice that animated the letter previously is silenced and replaced by another or rather potentially replaced. "If not always marked explicitly as such, potentiality is a recurrent topos in queer writing, where it is a mode of sexual and political critique and where imaginings of utopian sexual possibilities take shape in reading and rewritings of precursor texts" (Ohi, Dead Letters 29).

16. The clarity of the neologism is enhanced by its shared root with "panopticon," thereby linking optimism, which carries with it no small measure of consent, to the controls of the panopticon. The panoptimistic subject complies hopefully.

17. Bersani's notion of self-obliteration has obvious resonances here, with the apparent difference that sex itself and not just desire initiates the breakdown.

18. Tony Kushner's *Angels in America*, while offering a much needed boost to lift us out of desperation and offer some form of hope, is really just that, a Gay National Anthem, whose joyous promise of "a seat at the table" conveniently brackets out the devastation wreaked and often unaddressed across the globe (particularly when the play's two parts were written).

19. While "invert" was the widely accepted or used term to describe those given to same-sex desire in the nineteenth century, the German word "verkehrt" already gives an indication of how polysemic the term is. "Traveled," "perverted," and "inverted" given an indication of how inversion opens up various paths that are not easily mapped.

20. Halperin points out that among gay audiences (who need or may not practice same-sex sex but share what he considers to be a gay sensibility or gayness before sex) explicitly themed gay shows are less appealing than those in which the gayness of the show is dispersed and not explicit (Halperin, 92–108).

21. My use of "self" is not intended to reduce the political to a band of brothers or selves, but rather to highlight Schmitt's debt to Hobbes, since both ground their thinking in a "natural" or naturalized fear of the Other.

22. See Leo Strauss's "Notes on Carl Schmitt, The Concept of the Political," in the same volume, 81–108. Page 89 cited here.

23. See *The Nation*: http://www.thenation.com/article/Andrew-sullivan-over-exposed/. The comments in particular demonstrate the delight many in the gay community took in learning of the "moral" lapses committed by the poster child of a conservative gay politic. To be fair, one can imagine scenarios where his barebacking as an HIV positive man put no one at risk except himself, which, Andrew, is pretty immature.

24. For an analysis of the political naiveté and danger of espousing a genetic basis for same-sex desire, see Brookey, 1–46. The title, which only speaks to male-male same sex desire, implies that lesbians, while certainly not excluded from recent research into the genetics of desire, have not yet been invented sufficiently to be reinvented.

25. In season three Mora discovers that health issues and age disqualify her from getting sexual reassignment surgery. At that point, her interest in woman's attire disappears.

26. Unclear is whether such a connection would qualify as ecogenetic (e.g., trauma from exposure to an environmental toxin) or epigenetic (methylated gene trauma) which lacks transmission of any specific type of memory. Future research is focused on treating the methylated gene.
http://discovermagazine.com/2013may21-grandmas-experiences-leave-epigenetic-mark-on-your-genes. Research that considers if and how such a vocabulary of the primal scene might write itself onto the methylated gene might begin

by considering Freud's *Moses and Monotheism* and his discussion of phylogenetic memory.

27. The keen analysis here is radically at odds with recent, very disturbing comments allegedly made by Puar at Vassar College, during which visit she suggested or did not deny rumors that Israelis were harvesting the organs of Palestinian children. In other words, she was, if the following account is accurate, rehearsing once again the long history of blood libel against the Jew. For a decent analysis of the event see: http://www.haaretz.com/opinion/.premium-1.705213.

28. See in particular, Rey Chow, *The Age of the World Target: Self-Referentiality in War, Theory, and Comparative Work*.

29. See, for example, http://www.theguardian.com/world/2014/jul/31/uganda-anti-gay-laws-lgbt-activists.

30. Much credit still goes to the volume edited by Alice Kuzniar, *Outing Goethe and His Age*, for the recognition that male homo-sociality around 1800, with its effusive displays of friendship, was tinged by the homoerotic. Also, see the most helpful volumes by McLeod and Engelstein.

31. The "After" in the title points to a larger contribution of the volume, namely that the history of sexuality is a moment that has been overcome or could be. That is to say, sexuality as a series of acts comes to undo any possibility of mapping a linear history. Foucault's model is thus seen to invite its own deconstruction, serving as a reliable map of how sexuality came to be pathologized and how to identify points of intervention to disrupt that history.

32. See Tobin, Brothers, 20–24.

Chapter 1

1. See Benshoff less for his critical review of the literature and more for a catalogue of how a queer element persisted throughout the Golden Age of Hollywood that was linked with the monster lurking within or about.

2. In the made-for-television film, *Frankenstein: The True Story* (screenplay by Christopher Isherwood and his longtime partner Don Bachardy) the doctor has a budding friendship with his creation, even attending the opera with him, until the devolution of the monster's appearance drives his creator and one-time buddy to reject his monstrous companion.

3. References to the different editions of the text are denoted by the year before the page number. For the most part, all citations are from the 1818 text.

4. For one, what the monster undergoes is mediated from the horrible vision that "arose in [Mary Shelley's] mind with a vividness far beyond the usual bounds of reverie. I saw—with shut eyes-but acute mental vision . . . the hideous phantasm of a man stretched out . . . frightful must it be" (ix). Beyond the translations that occur onto the page, there are the repeated revisions and, most significantly,

the framing devices used in the novel itself, about which more will be said below. Unless otherwise noted, references are to the 1831 version originally published by Colburn and Bentley. The differences between the 1818 version and this one are hardly insignificant. For example, the earlier edition grants the monster free will while in the latter version he is much more a victim of circumstance and science. That difference more than any other underwrites my decision to work as well with the 1831 version. By regarding the monster as an inevitable expression of the many-layered conflicts of the time, I find the latter version exposes the controls imposed upon its destructive force in an attempt to secure the home front.

5. An interesting read is Botting, who sees the invitation to so many critical approaches by the text as part of the weft of the narrative. Likewise, Craig's dialogic analysis helps situate the various critical discourses that emerge from such dialogic constructions.

6. For an alternative Lacanian reading, see Collings.

7. With respect to the geography itself and its political mappings, see Randel.

8. Crucial in this regard is Komisaruk: "A crisis of affect drives the tragedies in *Frankenstein*, and the worst offenders come from 'good homes.' Despite evidence that the bourgeois family breeds exclusionary attitudes at many levels, Mary Shelley's characters often regard it as an oasis of interpersonal affinities in an indifferent world—a position the critic may identify with the author herself" (409).

9. See May for a provocative reading of sibling rivalries in the text.

10. For an exploration of the complicated dynamics structuring parent/child relations in the novel, see Claridge.

11. I am not the first, of course, to characterize the monster as emblematic of a specifically modern condition. Moretti's fine essay, "The Dialetic of Fear," connects Frankenstein and Dracula to particularly modern conditions: "The fear of the bourgeois civilization is summed up in two names: Frankenstein and Dracula. . . ." "Born in the full spate of the industrial revolution," Frankenstein tells the story of the birth of the proletariat, who like the monster have neither name nor identity. Dracula embodies the erotic fear of the era (Moretti 67). My reading replaces the family as the locus of conflict, Moretti sees the two monsters as outcasts from the great Victorian "corporation" where anyone who "breaks its bonds is done for" (Moretti 84). I replace the corporation with the Swiss Family Frankenstein, which locates the erotic within the family. Still, we both see pressures in the text to marginalize a particularly modern monster.

12. Gubar and Gilbert are equally necessary here in assessing the autobiographical content of the novel. Among the many important indices for reading the text offered here is the recognition that those critics who understand the novel as a work of the female imagination fail to recognize its "literariness," a self-consciousness that accompanies the imagination, which means that the novel is an exercise in and also of Romanticism. For example, Milton is rewritten by Shelley "to clarify its meaning," which for a woman is a journey through hell (Gubar 226). Or, more

generally, the question pursued is: "What was the effect upon women writers of that complex of culture myths summarized by Woolf as Milton's bogey?" The emphasis is on artistic survival for anyone surrounded by "patriarchal poetry" (Gilbert 213).

13. Important in this regard, especially for how it understands the rupture brought about by male/male bonding is Daffron (418-25).

14. While there is no need to rehearse Shelley's stance toward her novel in the various introductions, the recasting of the introduction signals a continuously shifting of the domestic terms to be settled or at issue in the novel. This, of course, is not unexpected, given the disorder signaled by the monster and the upheavals and displacements that follow.

15. For a reading that runs counter to mine and sees the novel as a critique of Orientalism see Lew, 255-28.

16. What many have identified is sympathy, I have recast as self-pity. See Marshall for an extended discussion of the role of sympathy in the novel.

17. For as clear as possible a demonstration of Fichte's "Tathandlung" see von Molnár, 29-57. My reading draws heavily upon this remarkably concise explanation.

18. For a longer discussion of how feminism and philosophy play out in the novel see Yousef.

Chapter 2

1. Letter to Felix Mendelssohn of 8 July 1829, quoted in Werner (1963), 36–38. Mendelssohn did not completely fulfill his father's request to drop the Mendelssohn altogether and signed his card "Mendelssohn-Bartholdy." His sister remarked in a letter to him in 1831, "Bartholdy . . . this name we all dislike." (Mercer Taylor 21).

2. Important in this regard is Katz 80-103. A remarkable reading of Moses Mendlessohn's *Jerusalem* and how it actually renders Judaism unnecessarily redundant and obsolete despite its professed aims can be found in Hess 91-136. Likewise, the account of anti-Jewish sentiments that included shipping them all off to Madagascar to harvest coffee surfaces around these times. The horrors of the next century have their roots already in the public discourses surrounding Jewish emancipation. Noteworthy is that any possibility of irony in certain remarks such as the following by Fichte, becomes quite literal during National Socialism: For a Jew to become a German, "it is necessary to cut off all their heads in one night, and to set new ones on their shoulders, which should contain not a single Jewish idea" (Fichte, GA 1/1 292-93).

3. The text could be read as well to register Chamisso's own anxiety about transforming himself from a Frenchman to a German. At a time when Chamisso is thought to have feared that he was moving down in the world, the Jew is moving up (Chamisso 766-67). These shifts in mobility present numerous possibilities for

ambiguity. It might no longer be possible to differentiate between Frenchman and German, German and Jew, and even "straight" and "queer." By revising and linking notions of Jewishness and sexual errancy, the text thus serves to readjust axes of differences for arresting, among other things, class mobility and its attendant confusions. In other words, it expresses Chamisso's own attempt to secure social standing

4. This is a mere reformulation of the repressive hypothesis. See Foucault, *History of Sexuality*, vol. 1, 15–50.

5. "Apparatus" ("*dispositif* in French"), quite frequently used in Foucault's later texts, also seems to become just as nebulous with every use. Agamben offers the following broad definition in an attempt to capture its many applications in these later works: "literally anything that has in some way the capacity to capture, orient, determine, intercept, model, control, or secure the gestures, behaviors, opinions, or discourses of living beings" (Agamben, *What Is an Apparatus* 14).

6. See Schorske for how Freud's science is inextricably linked to his uncertain status as a Jew and how those anxieties inform or adulterate his readings (Schorske 189–201).

7. See Edelman, *Homographesis*, 11–25.

8. Freud's text, it must be pointed out, was intended as a defense of his theory of libido against the competing theories of Carl Jung and Alfred Adler. Melanie Klein's work, of course, is organized around object relations and the incorporation of the death drive into the construction of the super ego. Klein's placement of the mother/infant relationship, particularly as it concerns the mother's offering or withholding her breast, set her at odds with strict Freudians for whom fears of castration were primary. During the war years the British Pscyho-Analytic Society debated to what extent Klein's theories had strayed too far from Freud's and no longer could be considered psychoanalysis. Instead, they decided to teach two schools of thought: Freudianism and Kleinism. See Grosskurth 358–449.

9. "In truth Freud sees nothing and understands nothing. He has no idea what a libidinal assemblage is, with all the machineries it brings into play, and all the multiple loves" (Deleuze and Guattari, *A Thousand Plateaus* 37). Whitney Davis is essential reading for understanding how the visual dimension and actual drawing of the dreams underwrites Freud's analysis.

10. See Golman, *New York Times*: http://www.nytimes.com/1990/03/06/science/as-a-therapist-freud-fell-short-scholars-find.html?pagewanted=all

11. The apparent success of the Berlin salons in bringing Jews and Germans together has undergone several revisions since then to the point now that the halcyon, if short-lived, friendship signaled by Germans visiting the salons of Berlin's leading Jewish women appears to be mostly fiction. See Weissberg, 24–43.

12. "Just as Jews and women are without extreme good and extreme evil, so they neither show either gains or the depth of stupidity of which mankind is capable. The specific kind of intelligence for which Jews and women alike are notorious is due simply to the alertness of the exaggerated egotism; it is due, moreover, to the

boundless capacity shown by both for pursuing any object with equal zeal, because they have no intrinsic standard of value—nothing in their souls to judge of the worthiness of any particular object" (Weiniger 317).

13. See Kohler for a discussion of W. von Humboldt's 1809 program for Jewish inclusion, 63-71.

14. See Chamisso's remark at the end of the text: "Schlemihl's experience calls out to us: "Think on that which is solid!" (Chamisso 778) Also see Gray for an analysis of Schlemihl's excessive wealth in the context of Germany from 1770-1850, 244-61.

15. See Mosse 72-73, 13-14.

16. See, for example, Sadan (198-203).

17. See Wisse (126).

18. See, for example, White (224-25).

19. See Wisse for a discussion of the terms migrations, particularly p. 126.

20. https://de.wikipedia.org/wiki/Peter_Schlemihls_wundersame_Geschichteo. hj

21. Bersani's comments in *The Freudian Body* are instructive here: "Castastrophe is produced when violence stops, when the disclosures provoked by desire's mobility seek, as it were, to *take place*, to have a place" (Bersani, FB 70). For my purposes, I read that place as the space of interiority that leads to branding the queer-jew as permanently other.

Chapter 3

1. For an overview of previous interpretations, see William Ray, 521-46. Attempts to align the essay with German romantic idealism go as far back at least to Hanna Hellman, who in 1911 rediscovered the essay "Über das Marionettentheater," reprinted in *Kleist's Aufsatz 'Über das Marionettentheater": Studien und Interprationen*, ed. Helmut Sembdner, 17-31. For most of the last century, the text was read in terms consistent with Hellman's, most notably by Benno von Wiese, "Das verlorene und das wieder zu findende Paradies: Eine Studie über den Begriff der Anmut bei Goethe, Schiller und Kleist." In the 1980s attention shifted to the rhetorical structures of the text and debunking the bald assertions of the interlocutors, most notably by Paul de Man, "Aesthetic Formalization in Kleists' 'Über das Marionettentheater,'" and James Rushing, "The Limitations of the Fencing Bear." In the 1990s Gail Hart, "Anmuts Gender: The 'Marionettentheater' and Klesit's Revision of Anmut und Würde," offered a feminist critique while Brittain Smith, "Pas de Deux: Doing the Dialogic Dance in Kleist's Fictitious Conversation 'About the Puppet Theater,'" focused on what he called the "dialogic dance," that is, the performative aspect of the text, to recover an interpretive thread. Two things are apparent from this overview: (1) the history of the text's reception parallels con-

temporary theoretical trends, and (2) more recent deconstructive exercises, such as Hart's "Anmuts Gender"; Helmut Schneider's "Deconstruction of the Hermeneutic Body: Kleist and the Discourse of Classical Aesthetics," in *The Body and the Text in the Eighteenth Century*; and Smith's "Pas de Deux" all gesture toward homoerotic undercurrents in the text. All future references to Schneider's text are denoted by "Schneider" followed by the page number.

2. All references to "Über das Marionettentheater" are to Heinrich von Kleist, *Sämtliche Werke*, ed. Helmut Sembdner, 7th Edition, 4 vols. (Munich: Hanser, 1982), 3:338–45. All future references to Kleist are to this edition and are denoted as "Kleist" followed by the page number.

3. While Michael Foucault traces the modern obsession with sex and sexuality from the nineteenth century onward in volume 1—a cue followed by Sedgwick Kosofsky, among others—my interest is trying to discover currents earlier in the century that invited such an obsession. See Eve Sedgwick Kosofsky, *Epistemology of the Closet*, for a focus on the later nineteenth century. This is not strictly a genealogical approach but rather a recognition of how manifold the possibilities were to discuss same-sex desire and thus eschew any canonization, so to speak, of sexuality. The text, at one point, refers to the marionette as "Gliedermann" (Kleist, 342), literally man of members, which presumes at the very least the possibility of dismemberment and even castration, although it would be a proleptic conceit to consider the latter.

4. For the most concise formulation of how that which signifies nothing has come to signify the homosexual, see D. A. Miller, *Bringing Out Roland Barthes*, 51–55. Of course, the same can be said about Jews, as Scholem points out, who converted or assimilated during the nineteenth century of the so called Age of Emancipation. See Gershom Scholem, *On Jews and Judaism in Crisis*, 131.

5. Sedgewick's oft-noted chart that questions every assumption about sexuality—partners, gender, roles, class, and so on—is intended to disable any discussion of sexuality anchored to a binary understanding. It thus exposes how the entire idea of concealment/unconcealment, which, she claims, is the epistemological crucible of our time, conceals the very impossibility of any kind of secret linked to sexuality since the content is too disparate to possess a univocal content (Epistemology 31).

6. Janet Haley, *Split Decisions: How and Why to Take a Break from Feminism* rehearses all the rifts in feminist thought for the past twenty-five years or so to argue for taking a break from feminism. These rifts include those with other subdisciplines, such as queer studies, postcolonial studies, and African-American studies. The point, in part, is to allow the conflicts to remain unresolved as a healthy, pluralistic discourse. To take a break from queer studies would mean, as I try to argue in summary fashion in the first part of this essay, to forego queer reading as a means to foreground sexuality and to embrace queerness as a political assault on identity politics. In this respect, I am interested in how disrespecting hermeneutic protocols queer each and every text as it no longer seeks to silence

and overcome differences between the reader and the text, but rather champions such difference.

7. The elision of female (same-sex) sexuality in the literature of the time can be addressed in part by thinking of masculinity, as proposed throughout, as subjunctive.

8. Prosthetics is, of course, only one of many metaplasms that could fancifully describe the mixing of parts, sounds, and meanings that a real employment of "queer" would imply. Metathesis, for example, describes most often the inversion of contiguous sounds (foliage). A queerness, as it were, is central to the function of language or its transmission. An important example, at least for Americans, is the word "ask," which Chaucer, for example, spells as "ax." (*Oxford English Dictionary*, second edition, under "ask")

9. "In fact, Platen is a man more of the rump than of the head. The name 'man' does not fit him at all; his love has a passive, Pythagorian character. He is a Pathetikos in his poems, he is a woman, who at once defies the feminine and is also a male tribade. . . . [I]n his "Liebhaberei' I detect something untimely, namely, the timid and coy parody of the high ancients . . . In antiquity such romantic spirits were in keeping with the practices of the time and were displayed with heroic openness. But the count frequently masks himself in pious feelings and so avoids any mention of gender . . ." Heinrich Heine, "Die Bäder von Lucca," 7.1:140–41. Male tribadism is particularly apt in this context since it is coined by Heine after Kleist had penned his text, just as homosexuality is coined decades after both authors' texts. Thereby, I hope to highlight a certain absurdity, if you will, of reading sexuality back onto a text written when sexuality was a meaningless term or construct.

10. Andreas Kraß, "Der Stachel im Fleische," *Literatur für Leser* 307 (2008): 123–32. All future references to this essay are denoted by "Kraß," followed by the page number.

11. Textual narcissism, it should be clear, means finding one's own premises reflected in the text. "Das Marionettentheater" is particularly suited for such a description, given, as we will see, how invested it is in the practices of reading. In this regard, See Block, "Strings Attached: Interpretive Ruse in Kleist's 'Über das Marionettentheater,'" 42–60. Such practices extend to the interlocutor's interpretation of the examples they cite and the insistence that the other accept the proffered reading. Otherness, expressed in this instance as stubborn resistance to interpretive appropriation, is preserved by being unreadable.

12. Of course, the spiritless embody grace in Kleist's text, whereas in Platen's poetry it is pompous and suffocating. The two need to be thought of together; that is, how grace is suffocating if it preempts a fall, or what later in the essay I will denote as a second fall in which men desire men.

13. Smith is particularly convincing in this regard, noting, for example, how Herr C— snobbishly tilts his head upward when challenged by the narrator or how the latter offers his story about the ephebe after his understanding of Genesis, (i.e., his *Bildung*,) has been challenged.

14. Not long before its appearance in the *Abendblätter* the Prussian state had warned against he moral dangers of puppet theater, which were often places to hook up with prostitutes. See Wild, *Theater der Keuschkhei*, 13-64. The journal was also censored just before the appearance of "Das Marionettentheater." See Block, "Strings Attached . . . ," 58.

15. All translations are mine.

16. See David Halperin, *One Hundred Years of Homosexuality* and Jonathan Katz, *The Invention of Heterosexuality* (1-19).

17. For a discussion of how Kleist's couched references to Iffland's sexual proclivities is not supported by any vocabulary to describe such acts—if they even occurred—between two men, see Paul Derks, *Die Schande der heiligen Päderestie: Homosexualität und Öffentlichkeit in der deutschen Literatur*, 432-35. Gayle Rubin, "Thinking Sex: Notes for a Radical Theory of the Politics of Sexuality," decouples sexuality from gender and is thus relevant here. She renders "isms" in relationship to sexuality impossible, since sexual acts are now a matter of dense contingencies, and not even logically bound by a gender binary.

18. Asserting that some term or condition links the three major examples of the text's argument is hardly reliable. For example, passivity may be a common thread. The lifeless marionette is manipulated by the machinist, as he is called. The ephebe responds to the lifeless model of a Greek statue, whose aesthetic standard is already in play even before he becomes conscious of his actions. And the fencing bear impresses only insofar as he has an attacker. But such examples, even if such links were convincing, are all products of a false consciousness. If a queer reading seeks to install itself, it does so by seeing lifelessness as its form of production or its ideal, a dead text that refuses to invite reading, which, paradoxically, disables such a reading before it offers itself.

19. Derks traces how "platonic" became a term to describe behavior such as Winckelmann's in the attempt to purge it of any unseemliness (81-89). Of course, it also evacuates the term of any meaning insofar as platonic love implies no touching. The love that dare not speak its name can only misname itself since there is no term at the time to describe it.

20. Paul de Man's "Rhetoric of Temporality" remains exemplary in exploring the irony that results from such a temporal delay, 187-228.

21. There is obviously a Hegelian ring to this historical process, all the more so since entry is through the back door. This recalls Hegel's assertion that philosophy is like the owl of Minerva; it arrives, in other words, after the fact.

22. "And the advantage of such a puppet over living dancers? The advantage? First of all my good friend, a negative one: namely that it would be incapable of affectation."

23. As noted in the previous chapter, Freud distinguishes between a primary narcissism, which is not linked to homosexuality and in which a child cathects itself as a whole with a parent, and homosexual narcissism, which develops later, when the subjects' narcissism meets with "admonition of others." This in turn, awakens

a critical consciousness. Original sin and homosexual critical self-consciousness are thus linked in Kleist (88–94). See also Michael Warner, "Homo-Narcissism," 190–206.

24. Kraß's phrase, "den Zahn in den Fuß . . . schlagen" (beat tooth into the foot) indicates, with its play on the literal and figurative levels of language, how original the difference is or how rooted it is in language itself.

25. Herr C— describes the ungraceful movements of contemporary dancers as *Mißgriffe*, "Mistakes" or literally "misgrasps" (Kleist 342), which captures the dual sense here that the interlocutors always grab the wrong things or understand each other only in misunderstanding each other, "misgrasping" each other.

Chapter 4

1. Roland Barthes: *A Lover's Discourse, Fragments*. Trans. Richard Howard, New York 1978. All references are to this edition and are followed by the page number.

2. Samuel Weber: *Unwrapping Balzac*, 163–67.

3. Johann Wolfgang von Goethe: *Goethes Werke*, Vol. 6. Ed. Erich Trunz, Hamburg: Christian 1968. All references are to this edition and are followed by the page number.

4. See Reinhart, Mayer-Kalkus: "Werthers Krankheir zum Tode: Pathologie und Familie in der Empfindsamkeit," 120–44.

5. Singularity, not Hegelian generality, constitutes an absolute in its difference. See Weber: *Benjamin's–abilities*. 297–308.

6. This formulation echoes unmistakably Deleuze, whom Barthes footnotes: "All this comes from Deleuze's account of the affirmation of the affirmation" (24). See Gilles Deleuze: *Nietzsche and Philosophy*, 188–89.

7. Potentiality, which should not be confused with virtuality, distinguishes Deleuze from Benjamin. In contradistinction to Deleuze, for whom virtuality comes to be actualized as an integrated whole, Benjamin's "now" is never present but always divided. It is only potentially itself by not being itself, as an echo of itself which has always been divided. See Weber, *Benjamin's–abilities*, 51.

8. Guy Hocquenghem: *Homosexual Desire*, 79.

9. See the letter of March 15 in which Werther's presence at the soiree of Graf. C. . . . offends the upper classes. This, of course, is Werther's read on his criticism, and no doubt, the reason his person offends is tied less to his class than to his ignorance of the significance of class. With regard to class and homosexual desire, see Hucquenghem: *Homosexual Desire*, 93–112.

10. See Daniel Heller Roazen: *Echolalias. On the Forgetting of Language*, 12. I am arguing that repetitions produced by affirmation of the eternal return of the same render audible textual ghosts of an unwritten text.

11. "Exiguous" still apparently describes a space. I am suggesting two things (1) the space is tremulous because the space marks the intersection of cross purposes and thus is never stable, and (2) through repetition it is never truly a fixed space but only potentially fixed. It is exiguous because whatever fixed potential it has is very slight.

12. Leo Bersani: *Homos*, 88.

13. Hocquenghem: *Homosexual Desire*. 97-100.

14. Jane Brown argues that Goethe anticipates the language of psychoanalysis. See "Goethe, Rousseau, the Novel and the Origins of Psychoanalysis" In: *Goethe Yearbook* 12 (2004) 111-28. Freud, of course, is of the same mind. See Avital Ronell: *Dictations. On Haunted Writing*. Lincoln 1986, 11-27. I prefer to see Werther as both constituting the subject as a psychological being and contesting that constitution.

15. The editor is the conscience of the text, or in psychoanalytic terms, its super-ego.

16. The language of tears is now clearly ambiguous. Before it was a sign of immediacy, now a modality of morality.

17. That is to say, one is always only before the law; the law is that one is always before it. One could just as easily remark that the law is without content and known only by or through its effects. Echoes of Kafka are not coincidental. See Jacques Derrida: "Devant a loi," 128-49.

18. Temporality has become a central concern of queer theory. See "Theorizing Queer Temporalities: A Roundtable Discussion." In: *GLQ: A Journal of Lesbian and Gay Studies*. 13:2-3 (2007) 177-95.

19. Barthes: *Incidents*. Trans. Richard Howard, Berkeley 1992, 51-55, 59.

20. Barthes: *Incidents*, 51-52.

21. See Nietzsche: *Ecce Homo*. 6/3, 91-92.

22. Nietzsche: *Also Sprach Zarathustra*, 6/1, 163.

23. Nietzsche: *Nachgelassene Schriften. Kritische Gesamausgabe*, 8/3, 410.

24. Eve Sedgewick-Kosofsky brilliantly maps the relationship according to the paranoid and certainly "homosexual" logic of Freud's reading of Dr. Schreber. The paranoid homosexual converts "I (a man) *love him* (a man)" into 'I do not *love* him,' 'I *hate* him,' and 'I love *her*' and even 'I do not love him. *She* loves him.' *Epistemology of the Closet*, 161-62. "She," we might speculate, is Cosima Wagner. See *Ecce Homo* in edition cited above, 82, for substitution of the name Nietzsche for Wagner.

25. See David Halperin: *One Hundred Years of Homosexuality*. The timeline for the codification of homosexuality is a literal reading, of course, of Foucault's provocative thesis in the first volume of the *History of Sexuality*. That timeline can be contested but not the philological evidence that tracks the first appearance of the word "homosexual" in the OED to the end of the nineteenth century. Thomas Lacquuer (*Making Sex: Body and Gender from the Greeks to Freud*) suggests that

codification of sexuality was already taking hold a century earlier. That would place Goethe at the crossroads.

26. How such effects come to be constructed as unnatural is evident in the regressive character of Werther's desire that has him looking back to ancient Greece and nor forward; thus, his love for Homer that is replaced by a passion for the morbid and fraudulent Ossian. See Hocquenghen: *Homosexual Desire*, 107-08.

27. Taking my cue from Kuzniar's *Outing Goethe and His Age*, I read for the homoerotic overtones that are inseparable from the effusions of male/male friendship that emerged during the Enlightenment and Storm and Stress.

28. "Ja, liebe Lotte. . . ." Is the letter to Lotte or is it Werther reporting to Wilhelm what he wrote to her, will write to her? The letters before and after are clearly addressed to Wilhelm. More important, they speak of her absence. In the first, Werther cannot produce a portrait of her; in the one that follows, he vows to see her less. Writing to Wilhelm is thus how one summons Lotte (Goethe 41).

29. Ibid., 640.

30. For the manner in which same-sex desire is essential to Goethe's poetic production see Susan Gustafson: *Men Dating Men*, 92-99.

31. See Tobin: "In and Against Nature: Goethe on Homosexuality and Heterosexuality," 94-110.

32. D. A. Miller: *Bringing out Roland Barthes*, 37.

33. Since we are talking about discourse here, Jacques Derrida's use of "iteration" in *Limited Inc.* is instructive (47). The potential for that which is written to be repeated means that the "now" of writing is always different from itself. That is consistent with what I outlined as the temporal disjunction of both Barthes's and Goethe's text in the introduction.

34. See Sedgewick-Kosofsky: *Epistemology of the Closet*, 100.

35. *Die Briefe* was published in 1803. Thus, it is a retrospective ordering of Werther's desire that enables it to accord to the logic of psychoanalysis.

36. One cannot repress resonances with "auf den Strich gehen" or to become a prostitute. That renders thinking as a mode of prostituting oneself, of occupying no position except that which is responsive to an Other and is never exact or stable, irresistible in this context.

37. See Agamben, *The Time that Remains*. In his reading of Paul (and Benjamin) and messianic time, he turns to *Corinthians* to describe what he calls "vocation" and "revocation." An example of how repetition occurs with a notable difference is offered in the foundation, "those having wives be as not having wives, and those weeping as not weeping, and those rejoicing as not rejoicing" (230). The logic of either/or—one weeps or one does not weep—is replaced by something other that echoes in and through language as a potentiality that is never actualized or is actualized only in messianic time.

38. As Heller-Roazen argues, aleph cannot be pronounced because it represents no sound at all, yet in the Jewish tradition it is the "fundamental principle

of construction" (Heller-Roazen 21). Unlike aleph, the queer echo I am writing about can be pronounced, but then it loses its character as something potential or as something that both is and is not; and thus queer to itself.

Chapter 5

1. The short story is unequivocal in this respect. It begins with Ennis dreaming of Jack Twist, who is already dead (Proulx 1) and ends with a return to the moment when Jack began appearing in his dreams (Proulx 27-28).

2. See Ebert, who "can imagine someone weeping at this film, identifying with it, because he always wanted to stay in the marines, or be an artist or a cabinetmaker." Without fancying what it might mean to dream of being a life-long marine while watching two cowboys screw on the big screen, it is clear that discussions about the gayness of the film presume some things that aren't that clear: (1) this is even a love story; (2) that "gay" is suitable or not anachronistic in this context, particularly since "queer" is used instead. See Mendelsohn for an argument of why it is indeed a gay film.

3. A possible explanation of the term is that "rose" applies to the appearance of the anus and stemming to the penis that is inserted into the anus. In the short story, Aguirre sees more than he does in the movie: "They believed themselves invisible, not knowing Joe Aguirre had watched them through his 10 × 42 binoculars for ten minutes one day, waiting . . . before bringing up that message that Jack's people had sent word that his Uncle Harold was in the hospital with pneumonia and not expected to make it" (Proulx 7). Aguirre discourages Jack from visiting his uncle. That is, whatever displeasure he expresses later about the activities of the two hands on Brokeback Mountain, he seems by his discouraging Jack to leave that he wants it to continue.

4. See Braun for a precise analysis of he how the panopticon enables and is concomitant with the biopolitical regime. Agamben's *Homo Sacer* remains one of the most compelling recent study to link the biopolitical with the state of exception. Neither, however, links these control mechanisms with sexuality.

5. My use of the term is consistent with how we tend to understand *Nachträglichkeit*. Since poststructuralism has no epistemology or is devoid of content, the very manner in which the structure of inversion provides knowledge of what comes to be known as homosexual makes the ironic used of the term helpful. My definition, of course, is dependent upon Sedgwick's understanding of such knowledge as "preterited" (Sedgwick 134), a term I will adopt. My use of "open and empty secret" likewise comes from Sedgwick (Sedgwick, 164, 174-80.

6. Foucault links inversion to gender in the *The History of Sexuality, Part II* (18-20). Judith Butler renders such a distinction between gender and sexuality slippery at best. Gender expectations remake the body, just as the body engenders

those expectations. See Hekma for the impossibility of a pure distinction between gender and sexuality. Since there is no indication of gender reversal in the film, I use the term "inversion," albeit idiosyncratically, in terms of sexuality.

7. See Deleuze, "Masochism," for how the father is always the hidden point of reference and for how sadomascochim attempts to overcome the consequent abjection through "deriding" the father (3–10). S/M is not an issue, at least not an overt one here, but de-riding the father in the context of the Twists is potentially productive. Jack never learns to ride rodeo from his father, who constantly derides him. The question is then what happens to the father when the son literalizes the term and rides (mounts) and de-rides (dismounts) another man, or vice versa?

8. This is another example of how sexuality obscures race. But at least he is not queer to mountain country, which, I guess, means he is straight.

9. Randall comes onto Jack shortly thereafter, inviting him to spend some time with him at a cabin: "We ought to do down there some weekend. Drink a little whiskey, fish some. Get away, you know" (McMurtry and Ossana 2005, 76). Dancing with Lashawn is also dancing with Randall. And true to the way things come to be known in the film, Jack may have taken the bait. At the end of the film, Jack's father reports that Jack was no longer talking about setting up house with Ennis but rather with another "fella [who was] goin' a come up here with him and build a place . . . some ranch neighbor of his down in Texas. He's going to split up with his wife and come back here" (90).

10. The sign is not readable in the film.

11. See Edelman for how a metaphorical logic seeks to contain and explain heterosexuality. Equally significant is his reading of the primal scene in Freud's Wolfman, which, as even Freud acknowledges, demands that the representation and interpretation of the scene precede the actual scene; i.e, it is manipulated a posteriori. (*Homographesis* 174-91.)

12. See Hocquenghem for how psychoanalysis with it emphasis on castration determines property rights (Hoqcuenghem 72-74).

13. My formulation draws heavily upon Agamben's *The Time that Remains*, in which the formulation of Messianic time is not a double negative but an "as not" (Agamben, *Time* 22-26, 88). The short story offers the basis of my reason for using the "not . . . not." Ennis says, "I am not queer," rather than "I ain't no queer," as he does in the film. The double negative does not permit a simple affirmation of the sort "I am queer." Such terms are nevertheless senseless, given how easily Jack and Ennis fuck with women. Queer just doesn't cut it with Jack or Ennis; they are something other, which requires reading the double negative as not just a positive.

14. A formulation reminiscent of Heidegger is intentional. If the closet is the epistemological crucible of the our era, then concealment/unconcealment has something of that same structure, which one would have to work out elsewhere but clearly finds resonances in Sedgwick.

15. At some point, it would be interesting to consider Ennis in terms of the sovereign and the state of exception, insofar as he is both inside and outside the law he comes to enforce. That makes the notion of a closet all the more complex. A question I leave unanswered is whether Ennis, who now drives the truck and will soon come to occupy a space resistant to panoptic surveillance, is an example of what Agamben in *State of Exception*, after Benjamin, calls a true state of exception in contradistinction to the one which installs the biopolitical regime or that advocated by Carl Schmitt (Agamben, *State of Exception*, 1–31.)

Bibliography

Agamben, Giorgio. *Homo-Sacer. Sovereign Power and Bare Life*. Trans. Daniel Heller-Roazen. Stanford, CA: Stanford UP, 1998.
———. *Potentialities: Collected Essays in Philosophy*. Trans. Daniel Heller-Roazen. Stanford, CA: Stanford UP, 1999.
———. *State of Exception*. Trans. Kevin Attell. Chicago and London: UP of Chicago, 2005.
———. *The Time that Remains: A Commentary on the Letter to the Romans*. Trans. Patricia Dailey. Stanford, CA: Stanford UP, 2005.
———. *What Is an Apparatus and Other Esssays*. Trans. David Kishik and Stefan Pedatella. Stanford: Stanford UP, 2009.
American Heritage Dictionary of the English Language, 3rd ed. Boston: Houghton Mifflin, 1992.
Arendt, Hannah. *The Portable Hannah Arendt*. Ed. Peter Baehr. New York: Penguin, 2000.
Barthes, Roland. *A Lover's Discourse, Fragments*. Trans. Richard Howard. New York: Hill and Wang, 1978.
———. *Incidents*. Trans. Richard Howard. Berkeley: U of California P, 1992.
Beachy, Robert. *Gay Berlin: Birthplace of a Modern Identity*. New York: Vintage, 2015.
Benshoff, Harry. *Monsters in the Closet: Homosexuality and the Horror Film*. Manchester, UK: Manchester UP, 1997.
Botting, Fred. "Reflections of Excess: *Frankenstein*, the French Revolution, and Monstrosity," in *Reflections on Revolution: Images of Romanticism*. Eds. Alison Yarrington and Kelvin Everest. London: Routledge, 1993, 26–38.
Berlant, Lauren, and Lee Edelman. *Sex of the Unbearable*. Durham, NC: Duke UP, 2014.
Bernstein, Susan. "Memory Text: Philippe Lacoue-Labarthe (1940–2007)." *October* 122 (2007): 121–27.
Bersani, Leo. *Homos*. Cambridge: Harvard UP, 1995.
———, and Adam Phillips. *Intimacies*. Chicago: UP Chicago, 2008.
Block, Howard. *Medieval Misogyny and the Inventon of Western Romantic Love*. Chicago: UP Chicago, 1991.

Block, Richard. "Queering the Jew Who Would Be German." *Seminar* 40, no. 2 (2004): 93–110.

———. "Strings Attached: Interpretive Ruse in Kleist's 'Uber das Marionettentheater.'" *New German Review* 3 (1995): 42–60.

Braun, Katrin. "Biopolitics and Temporality in Arendt and Foucault." *Time & Society* 17, no. 1 (2007): 5–23.

Bredbeck, Gregory. *Sodomy and Interpretation: Marlowe to Milton*. Ithaca, NY: Cornell UP, 1991.

Brookey, Robert Alan. *Reinventing the Male Homosexual: The Rhetoric and Power of the Gay Gene*. Bloomington: Indiana UP, 2002.

Brooks, Peter. "What Is a Monster (According to *Frankenstein*)." In *Body Work: Objects of Desire in Modern Narrative*. Cambridge: Harvard UP, 1993, 199–220.

Bronfen, Elizabeth. "Rewriting the Family: Mary Shelley's *Frankenstein* in its Biographical, Textual Context." In *Frankenstein: Creation and Monstrosity*. Ed. Stephen Bann. London: Reaktion, 1994, 16–38.

Brown, Jane. *Goethe's Allegories of Identity*. Philadelphia: UP Pennsylvania, 2014.

———. "Goethe, Rousseau, the Novel and the Origins of Psychoanalysis." *Goethe Yearbook* 12 (2004): 111–28.

Brown, Marshall. "*Frankenstein*: A Child's Tale." *Novel: A Forum on Fiction* 36, no. 2 (2003): 145–75.

Butler, Judith. *Gender Trouble: Feminism and the Subversion of Identity*. New York: Routledge, 1990.

———. *Undoing Gender*. New York: Routledge, 2004.

Calhoon, Kenneth. *Affecting Grace: Theater, Subject, and the Shakespearian Paradox in German Literature from Lessing to Kleist*. Toronto: UP of Toronto, 2013.

———. "Educating the Human Race: Lessing, Freud and the Savage Mind." *The German Quarterly* 64, no. 2 (1991): 178–89.

Chamisso, Adelbert von. *Sämtliche Werke in zwei Bänden. Nach dem Text der Ausgaben letzter Hand*, vol. 1. Ed. Jost Perfahl. Darmstadt: Wissenschaftliche Buchgesellschaft, 1975.

Cixous, Hélène. "Fiction and Its Phantoms: A Reading of Freud's 'Das Unheimliche.'" In *New Literary History* 7, no. 3 (1976): 525–49.

Claride, Laura. "Parent-Child Tensions in *Frankenstein*: The Search for Communion." *Studies in the Novel* 17 (1985): 14–26.

Chow, Rey. *The Age of the World Target: Self-Referentiality in War, Theory, and Comparative Work*. Durham, NC: Duke UP, 2006.

Cohn, Dorritt. *The Distinction of Fiction*. Baltimore: Johns Hopkins UP, 1999.

Collings, David. "The Monster and the Imaginary Other: A Lacanian Reading of Frankenstein." In *Frankenstein*. Ed. Johann Smith. Boston: St. Martin's, 1992, 245–58.

Condon, Bill. *Gods and Monsters*. Film. Dir. Bill Condon. 1998. Hollywood: Lions Gate, 2004.

Craig, Siobhan. "Monstrous Dialogues: Erotic Discourses and the Dialogic Constitution of the Subject in *Frankenstein*." In *A Dialogue of Voices: Feminist Literary Theory and Bakhtin*. Eds. Karen Hohne and Helen Wussow. Minneapolis: UP Minnesota, 1994, 83-96.
Crimp, Douglas. "Mourning and Militancy." *October* 51 (1989): 3-18.
Daffron, Eric. "Male Bonding: Sympathy and Shelley's *Frankenstein*." *Nineteenth-Century Contexts* 21 (1999): 415-35.
Delaney, Samuel R. *Times Square Red, Times Square Blue*. New York: New York UP, 1999.
Deleuze, Gilles. *Cinema I: The Movement Image*. Trans. Hugh Tomlinson. Minneapolis: UP Minnesota, 1983.
———. *Masochism: An Interpretation of Coldness and Cruelty and the Entire Text of Venus in Furs*. New York: Braziller, 1991.
———. *Nietzsche and Philosophy*. Trans. Hugh Tomlinson. Albany, NY: SUNY, 1983.
Deleuze, Gilles, and Guattari, Felix. *A Thousand Plateaus*. Trans. Brian Massumi. Minneapolis: UP of Minnesota, 1987.
De Man, Paul. "Aesthetic Formalization in Kleist's Über das Marrionettentheater.'" In *The Rhetoric of Romanticism*. New York: Columbia University Press, 1984, 263-90.
———. "The Rhetoric of Temporality." In *Blindness and Insight: Essays in the Rhetoric of Contemporary Criticism*. Minneapolis, UP of Minnesota, 1983, 187-228.
Derks, Paul. *Die Schande der heiligen Päderestie: Homosexualität und Öffentlichkeit in der deutschen Literatur, 1750-1850*. Berlin: Rosa Winkel, 1990.
Derrida, Jacque. "Devant a loi."In *Kafka and the Contemporary Critical Performance: Centenary Readings*. Trans. Avital Ronell. Bloomington: Indiana UP, 1987.
———. *Limited Inc*. Evanston, IL: Northwestern UP, 1988
———. *Spectors of Marx*. Trans. Peggy Kamuf. London: Routledge, 2004.
Dinshaw, Carolyn, et al. "Theorizing Queer Temporalities: A Roundtable Discussion." *Journal of Lesbian and Gay Studies* 13, no. 2-3 (2007): 177-95.
———. *Sexualities and Communities, Pre- and Postmodern*. Durham, NC: Duke UP, 1999.
Dohm, Christian Wilhelm von. *Über die bürgerliche Verbesserung der Juden*, vol. 1. Berlin: Nilolai, 1781-83.
Duyfhuizen, Bernard. "Periphrastic Naming in Mary Shelley's *Frankenstein*." *Studies in the Novel* 27, no. 4 (1995): 477-92.
Edelman, Lee. *Homographesis: Essay in Gay Literary and Cultural Theory*. London: Routledge, 1994.
———. *No Future: Queer Theory and the Death Drive*. Durham, NC: Duke UP, 2004.
Ellis, Havelock. *Studies in the Psychology of Sex, Vol. 2: Sexual Inversion*. New York: Filiquarian Publishing, 1923.
Engelstein, Stefani. *Anxious Anatomy: The Conception of the Human Form in Literary and Naturalist Discourse*. Albany, NY: SUNY, 2009.

Fenves, Peter. *The Messianic Reduction: Walter Benjamin and the Shape of Time.* Stanford, CA: Stanford UP, 2014.
Fichte, Johann Gottlieb. *Gesamtausgabe der Werke.* Eds. Reinhard Lout, et al. Stuttgart: Fromann-Holzberg, 1962–2012.
Fone, Byrne. *Homophobia: A History.* New York: Picador, 2000.
Foucault, Michel. *The History of Sexuality: An Introduction*, vol. 1. Trans. Robert Hurley. New York: Vintage, 1978.
———. *The History of Sexuality, Vol. 2, The Use of Pleasure.* New York: Vintage, 1985.
———. *The History of Sexuality, Vol. 3, The Care of the Self.* New York: Vintage, 1986.
Freccero, Carla. *Queer/Early/Modern.* Durham: Duke UP, 2006.
Friedel, John. *Briefe über die Gallantereien von Berlin auf einer Reise von einem österreichischen Offizier.* 1782. Ed. Sonja Schnitzler. Berlin: Eulenspiegel, 1987.
Freud, Sigmund. "On Narcissism." In *The Standard Edition of the Complete Psychological Works of Sigmund Freud*, vol. 14. Ed. James Strachey. London: Hogarth, 1953–74, 69–102.
———. *Three Case Histories.* New York: Macmillan, 1963.
Freund, Ismar. *Die Emanzipation der Juden in Preussen unter besonderer Rücksichtigung des Gesetzes vom 11. März 1812.* Berlin: Popelauer, 1912.
Garcia Düttmann, Alexander. *At Odds with AIDS.* Trans. Peter Gilgen and C. S. Curtis. Stanford, CA: Stanford UP, 1996.
Genet, Jean. *Querelle of Brest.* Trans. Gregory Streatham. New York: Faber, 1966.
Gilbert, Sandra M., and Susan Gubar. *The Madwoman in the Attic: The Woman Writer and the Nineteenth-Century Literary Imagination.* New Haven, CT: Yale UP, 1979.
Gilman, Sander. *Jewish Self-Hatred: Anti-Semitism and the Hidden Language of the Jews.* Baltimore: Johns Hopkins UP, 1986.
Glazova, Anna, and Paul North, eds. *Messianic Thought Outside Theology.* New York: Fordham UP, 2014.
Goethe, Johann Wolfgang von. *Goethes Werke*, vol. 6. Ed. Erich Trunz. Hamburg: Christian Wegner, 1968.
———. *Briefe aus der Schweiz.* https://archive.org/details/briefeausderschw02402gut.
Goleman, Daniel. http://www.nytimes.com/1990/03/06/science/as-a-therapist-freud-fell-short-scholars-find.html?pagewanted=all.
Gölz, Sabine. "How Ethnic Am I," in *PMLA* 113, no. 1 (1998): 46–51.
———. *The Split Scene of Reading: Nietzsche/Derrida/Kafka/Bachmann.* Atlantic Highlands, NJ: Humanities Press, 1998.
Grattenauer, Karl Wilhelm Friedrich. *Wider der Juden. Ein Wort der Warnung an alle unsere christlichen Mitbürger.* Berlin: Schöne, 1803.
Gray, Richard. *Money Matters: Economies and the German Cultural Imagination 1170–1850.* Seattle: UP of Washington, 2008.
Grosskurth, Phyllis. *Melanie Klein: Her World and Her Work.* New York: Random House, 1986.

Gustafson, Susan. *Men Dating Men: The Poetry of Same-Sex Identity and Desire in German Classicism*. Detroit: Wayne State UP, 2002.

Halberstan, Judith. "Forgetting Family: Queer Alternatives to Oedipal Relations." In *A Companion to Lesbian, Gay, Bisexual, Transgender and Gay Studies*. New York: Blackwell, 315-24.

Halperin, David. *How to Be Gay*. Cambridge: Harvard UP, 2014.

———. *One Hundred Years of Homosexuality and Other Essays on Greek Love*. New York: Routledge, 1990.

Hart, Gail. "Anmut's Gender: The 'Marrionettentheater' and Kleist's Revision of Anmut und Würde." *Women in German Yearbook* 10 (1995): 83-95.

Heidegger, Martin. "The Word of Nietzsche: God Is Dead." In *The Question Concerning Technology and Other Essays*. Trans. William Lovitt. New York: Harper and Row, 1977, 53-112.

Heine, Heinrich. "Die Bäder von Lucca." In *Historisch-kritische Ausgabe der Werke*, vol. 7.1. Ed. Manfred Windfuhr. Hamburg: Hoffman und Campe, 1973-77, 81–152.

———. "Hebräisches Melodien." In *Historisch-kritische Gesamtausgabe der Werke*, vol. 3/1, 123-72.

Hekma, Gert. "A Female Soul in a Male Body: Sexual Inversion as Gender Inversion in Nineteenth Century Sexology." In *Third Sex; Third Gender: Beyond Sexual Dimorphism in Culture and History*. Ed. Gilbert Herdst. New York: Zone Books, 1994, 213-40.

Heller-Rozen, Daniel. *Echohalias: On the Forgetting of Language*. New York: Zone, 2005.

Helfer, Martha. "'Confessions of an Improper Man': Friedrich Schlegel's *Lucinde*." In *Outing Goethe and His Age*. Ed. Alice Kuzniar. Stanford, CA: Stanford UP 1996.

Hellman, Hanna. "Uber das Marionettentheater." In *Kleists Ausfsatz "Uber das Marionettentheater": Studien und interpretationen*. Ed. Helmut Sembdner. Berlin: Erich Schmidt, 1967, 17–31

Hess, Jonathan. *Germans, Jews and the Claims of Modernity*. New Haven, CT: Yale UP, 2002.

Hirschfeld, Magnus. *Die Homosexualität Des Mannes Und Des Weibes*. Berlin: L. Marcus, 1914

Hocquenghem, Guy. *Homosexual Desire*. Trans. Daniella Dangoor. Durham, NC: Duke UP, 1979.

Hoffman, E. T. A. *Gesammelte Werke*, vol. 1. Ed. Nino Erné. Hamburg: Standard Verlag, 1964.

Huet, Marie-Hélène. *Monstrous Imagination*. Cambridge: Harvard UP, 1993.

Hull, Isabel. *Sexuality, State and Civil Society in Germany 1700-1815*. Ithaca, NY: Cornell UP, 1991.

Isherwood, Christopher, and Don Bachardy. *Frankenstein: The True Story*. Film. Dir. Jack Smight. Universal City, CA: Universal Studios, 2006.

Jagosse, Annamarie. *Queer Theory: An Introduction*. New York: New York UP, 1996.
Johnson, Barbara. "My Monster/My Self." *Diacritics* 12, no. 2 (1982): 2–10.
Kim, Richard. "Andrew Sullivan Overexposed." *The Nation*, June 5, 2001. http://www.thenation.com/article/andrew-sullivan-overexposed/.
Katz, Jacob. *Out of the Ghetto: The Social Background of Jewish Emancipation 1770–1870*. Cambridge: Harvard UP, 1973.Katz, Jonathan. *The Invention of Homosexuality*. Chicago: U of Chicago P, 2007.
Kilian, Eveline. "Alternative Temporalities: Queer Time." In Proust, Marcel. *A la receherche du temps perdu*, Dorothy Richardson, Dorothy. *Pilgramage. Modernist Cultures* 10, no. 3 (2015): 336–56.
Kleist, Heinrich von. *Samtliche Werke*, 7th ed., vol. 3. Ed. Helmut Sembdner. Munich: Hanser, 1982.
Kohler, Max. *Jewish Rights at the Congress of Vienna*. New York: The American Jewish Committee, 1918, 63–71.
Komisaruk, Adam. " 'So Guided by a Silken Cord': Frankenstein's Family Values." *Studies in Romanticism* 38 (1999): 365–85.
Krafft-Ebing, Richard von. *Psychopathia Sexualis: eine Klinisch-Forensische Studie*. Stuttgart: Enke, 1894.
Kraß, Andreas. "Der Stachel im Fleische." *Literatur für Leser* 307 (2008): 123–32.
Kristeva, Julia. *Powers of Horror: An Essay on Abjection*. Trans. Leon Roudiez. New York: Columbia UP, 1982.
Kushner, Tony. *Angels in America: A Gay Fantasia on National Themes*. Play. New York: Theater Communications Group, 2013.
Kuzniar, Alice A., ed. *Outing Goethe and His Age*. Stanford, CA: Stanford UP, 1996.
———. *The Queer German Cinema*. Stanford, CA: Stanford UP, 2000.
Lacquer, Thomas. *Making Sex: Body and Gender from the Greeks to Freud*. Cambridge: Harvard University Press, 1990.
Lautmann, Rüdiger. "Das Verbrechen der widernatürlichen Unzucht. Seine Grundlegung in der preußischen Gesetzrevision des 19. Jahrhunderts." *Kritische Justiz* 25, no. 30 (1992): 294–314.
Lee, Ang, director. *Brokeback Mountain*, River Road Entertainment, 2005.
Levine, Michael. *Weak Messianic Powers: Figures of Time to Come in Benjamin, Derrida, and Celan*. New York: Fordham UP, 2013.
Levinson, Brett. *Market and Thought: Meditations on the Political and the Biopolitcal*. New York: Fordham UP, 2004.
Lew, Joseph. "The Deceptive Other: Mary Shelley's Critique of Orientalism." *Frankenstein: Studies in Romanticism* 30 (1991): 255–83.
Librett, Jeffrey. *The Rhetoric of Cultural Dialogue: Jews and Germans from Moses Mendelssohn to Richard Wagner and Beyond*. Stanford, CA: Stanford UP, 2000.
Lucey, Michael. *Never Say I: Sexuality and the First Person in Colette, Gide, and Proust*. Durham, NC: Duke UP, 2006.

Mancini, Elena. *Magnus Hirschfeld and the Quest for Sexual Freedom: A History of the First International Sexual Freedom Movement.* New York: Palgrave Macmillan, 2010

Matt, Peter von. *Verkommene Söhne, Missratene Töchter: Familiendisaster in der Literatur.* Munich: Hanser, 1995.

Milner, Jean-Claude. *Constat.* Paris: Seuill, 1992.

Maimonides, Moses. *Guide for the Perplexed.* Trans. M. Friedländer. New York: Barnes and Noble, 2004.

Mann, Thomas. "Death in Venice" *and Seven Other Stories.* Trans. H. T. Lowe Porter. New York: Vintage, 1963.

Marshall, David. *The Surprising Effects of Sympathy: Marivaux, Diderot, Rousseau, and Mary Shelley.* Chicago: UP Chicago, 1988.

Marx, P. A., P. G. Alcabes, and E. Drucker. "Serial human passage of simian immunodeficiency virus by unsterile injections and the emergence of epidemic human immunodeficiency in Africa." *Philosophical Transactions of the Royal Society of London Series B-Biological Sciences* 356, no. 1410 (2001): 911–920.

May, Leila Silvana. "Sibling Rivalry in Mary Shelley's *Frankenstein*." *Studies in English Literature, 1500-1900* 35 (1995): 669-85.

Mayer-Kalkus, Reinhart. "Werthers Krankheit zum Tode: Pathololologie und Familie in der Empfindamkeit." In *Urszenen. Literatur Wissenschaft als Diskursanalyse.* Eds. Friedrich Kittler and Horst Turk. Frankfurt am Main: Suhrkamp, 1977.

Mendelsohn, Daniel. "An Affair to Remember." *New York Review of Books* 23 (2006): 12.

McMurtry, Larry, Diana Ossana, and Annie Proulx. *Brokeback Mountain: Story to Screenplay.* New York: Scribner, 2006.

Miller, D. A. *Bringing Out Roland Barthes.* Berkeley: U of California P, 1992.

———. *Place for Us: Essays on the Broadway Musical.* Cambridge: Harvard UP, 1998.

Mosse, George. *German Jews Beyond Judaism.* Bloomington: Indiana UP, 1985.

Mosse, Werner. "From 'Schutzjuden' to 'Deutsche Staatsbürger Jüdischen Glaubens': The Long and Bumpy Road of Jewish Emancipation in Germany." In *Paths of Emancipation.* Eds. Pierre Birnbaum and Ira Katznelson. Princeton, NJ: Princeton UP, 1995, 59-93.

Molnár, Géza von. *Romantic Vision, Ethical Context: Novalis and Artistic Autonomy.* Minneapolis: UP Minnesota, 1987

Moretti, Franco. "Dialectic of Fear." *Signs Taken for Wonders.* Trans. Susan Fischer, David Forgacs, and David Miller. London: Verson, 1983, 83-108.

Mosès, Stéphane. *The Angel of History: Rosenzweig, Benjamin, Scholem.* Trans. Barbara Harshav. Stanford, CA: Stanford UP, 2009.

Muñoz, José Esteban. *Cruising Utopia. The Time and There of Queer Futurity.* New York: New York UP, 2009.

Nancy, Jean Luc. *Un pensée finie.* Paris: Galilee, 1999.

Nietzsche, Friedrich. *On the Genealogy of Morals and Ecce Homo*. Trans. Walter Kaufmann and R. J. Hollingdale. New York: Vintage, 1989.

———. *Also Sprach Zarathustra: Kritische Ausgabe*. Eds. Giorgio Colli and Mazzino Montinari. Berlin: DeGruyter, 1968.

———. *Ecce Homo: Kritische Ausgabe*. Eds. Giorgio Colli and Mazzino Montinari. Berlin: DeGruyter, 1968.

Obama, Barack. "Remarks After Visit to the El Reno Federal Correctional Institution." July 7, 2015. https://www.whitehouse.gov/the-press-office/2015/07/16remarks-president after-visit-el-reno-federal-correctional-institution.

Ohi, Kevin. *Dead Letters Sent: Queer Literary Transmission*. Minneapolis: UP Minnesota, 2005.

———. *Henry James and the Queerness of Style*. Minneapolis: UP Minnesota, 2009.

Pavlyshyn, Marko. "Gold, Guilt and Scholarship: Adalbert Chamisso's *Peter Schlemihl*." *German Quarterly* 55, no. 1 (1982): 49–63.

Peppis, Paul. *Sciences of Modernism: Ethnography, Sexlogy, and Psychology*. Cambridge: Cambridge UP, 1991.

Pfeiffer, Joachim. "Friendship and Nature: The Aesthetic Construction of Subjectivity in Kleist." In *Outing Goethe and His Age*. Ed. Alice Kuzniar. Stanford, CA: Stanford UP, 1996, 215–27.

Puar, Jasbir K. *Terrorist Assemblages: Homonationalism in Queer Times*. Durham, NC: Duke UP, 2007.

Randel, Fred. "The Political Geography of Horror in Mary Shelley's *Frankenstein*." *ELH* 70 (2003): 465-91.

Ray, William. "Suspended in the Mirror: Language and Self in Kleist's 'Über das Marionettentheater.'" *Studies of Romanticism* 18, no. 4 (1979): 521-46.

Ronell, Avital. *Dictations: On Haunted Writing*. Lincoln: UP of Nebraska, 1986.

Rubin, Gayle. "Thinking Sex: Notes for a Radical Theory of the Politics of Sexuality." In *Pleasure and Danger: Exploring Female Sexuality*. Ed. Carol Vance. Boston: Routledge & Kegan, 1984, 267–319.

Rushing, James. "The Limitations of the Fencing Bear." *German Quarterly* 61, no. 4 (1988): 528-39.

Rürup, Reinhard. "The Torturous and Thorny Path to Legal Equality: 'Jew Laws' and Emancipation in Germany from the Late Eighteenth Century." In *Leo Baeck Institute Yearbook* 31 (1986): 5–32.

Ruskin, Cindy, et al. *HIV/AIDS and the NAMES Project*. New York: Pocket Books, 1988.

Sadan, Dov. "Lesugia: shlumiel." *Orologin* 1 (1950): 198-203.

Schmitt, Carl. *The Concept of the Political*. Trans. George Schwab. Chicago: UP of Chicago, 1996.

———. *Political Theology: Four Chapters on the Concept of Sovereignty*. Trans George Schwab. Chicago: UP of Chicago, 2005.

Schneider, Helmut. "Deconstruction of the Hermeneutic Body: Kleist and the Discourse of Classical Aesthetics." In *Body and the Text in the Eighteenth Century*.

Eds. Veronika Kelly and Dorothea von Mücke. Stanford, CA: Stanford UP, 1994, 209–28.

Scholem, Gershom. "Jew and Germans." In *On Jews and Judaism in Crisis: Selected Essays. Gershom Scholem*. Ed. Werner Dannhauser. Trans. Werner Dannhauser. New York: Schocken, 1976, 71-92.

———. *The Messianic Idea in Judaism*. New York: Schocken, 1995.

Schorske, Carl. *Fin-de-Siècle Vienna: Politics and Cultures*. New York: Vintage, 1981.

Sedgwick, Eve Kosofsy. *Epistemology of the Closet*. Berkeley: UP California, 1990.

———. "Paranoid Reading and Reparative Reading: Or, You're So Paranoid, You Probably Think This Essay Is About You." *Touching Feeling: Affect, Pedagogy, Performativity*. Durham, NC: Duke UP, 2003, 123-44.

Sedgwick, Eve Kosofsky, and Frank Adam. *Touching, Feeling: Affect, Pedagogy, Perfromativity*. Durham, NC: Duke UP, 1998.

Shelley, Mary. *Frankenstein*. New York: Dover, [1831] 1994.

———. *Selected Letters*. Ed. Betty T. Bennett. Baltimore: Johns Hopkins UP, 1995.

Sherwin, Paul. "Creation as Catastrophe: *Frankenstein*." *PMLA* 95, no. 5 (1981) 883-903.

Smith, Brittain. "Pas de Deux: Doing the Dialogic Dance in Kleist's Fictitious Conversation 'About the Puppet Theater.'" In *Compendious Conversations: the Method of Dialogue in the Early Enlightenment*. Eds. Rüdiger Ahrens, et al. Frankfurt am Main: Peter Lang, 1992, 368-82.

Spector, Scott; Helmut Puff, and Dagmar Herson, eds. *After the History of Sexuality: German Genealogies with and beyond Foucault*. New York: Berghahn, 2012.

Steakley, James. "Sodomy in Enlightenment Prussia." In *The Pursuit of Sodomy": Male Homosexuality in Renaissance and Enlightenment Europe*. Eds. Kent Gerard and Gert Hekma. New York: Harrington Park, 1989, 163-75.

Strauss, Leo. "Notes on Carl Schmitt." In *The Concept of the Political*. Trans. J. Harvey Lomax. Chicago: U of Chicago P, 1996.

Taylor, Peter Mercer. *The Life of Mendelssohn*. Cambridge: Cambridge UP, 2000.

Tobias, Rochelle. *The Discourse of Nature in the Poetry of Paul Celan: The Unnatural World*. Baltimore: Johns Hopkins UP, 2006.

Tobin, Robert. "In and Against Nature: Goethe on Homosexuality and Heterosexuality." In *Outing Goethe and His Age*, 1996, 94-110.

———. *Peripheral Desires: The German Discovery of Sex*. Philadelphia: UP of Pennsylvania, 2015

———. *Warm Brothers: Queer Theory and the Age of Goethe*. Philadelphia: UP of Pennsylvania, 2000.

Toury, Jacob. "Der Eintitt der Juden ins deutsche Bürgertum" in *Das Judentum in der deutchen Umwelt*. Eds. Hans Liebeschütz and Arnold Paucket. Tübingen: Mohr, 1977.

Ulrichs, Karl Heinrich. *The Riddle of Man-Manly Love*. Trans. Michael Lombardi-Nash, 1994. http://www.oac.cdlib.org/findaid/ark:/13030/kt2000304d/entire_text/.

Vedeer, William. *Mary Shelley and Frankenstein: The Fate of Androgyny.* Chicago: UP Chicago, 1986.
Visconti, Luchino, director. *Mora a Venezia.* Warner Brothers, 1971.
Warner, Michael. "Homo-narcissism; or, Heterosexuality." In *Engendering Men: The Question of Male Feminist Criticism.* Eds. Joseph Boone and Michale Cadden. New York: Routledge, 1990, 190–206.
———. "Introduction." In *Fear of a Queer Planet.* Minneapolis: U of Minnesota P, 1993.
———. *The Trouble with Normal: Sex, Politics, and the Ethics of Queer Life.* Cambridge: Harvard, 1999, vii–xxxi.
Weber, Samuel. *Benjamin's -abilities.* Cambridge and London: Harvard UP, 2008.
———. *Unwrapping Balzac: A Reading of the La Peau de Chagrin.* Toronto: UP Toronto, 1979.
Weeks, Jeffrey. *Against Nature: Essays on History Sexuality, and Identity.* London: Rivers Oram: 1991.
Weil, Jiri. *Mendelssohn Is on the Roof.* Trans. Marie Winn. New York: Farrar, Straus and Giroux, 1991.
Weininger, Otto. *Sex and Character.* New York: Howard Fertig, 2003.
Weissberg, Liliane. "Literary Culture and Jewish Space around 1800: The Berlin Salons Revisited." In *Modern Jewish Literatures: Intersections and Boundaries.* Philadelphia: UP of Pennsylvania, 2011, 24–43.
Werner, Richard. *Mendelssohn: A New Image of the Composer.* Cambridge: Cambridge UP, 1963.
White, Ann, and John White. "The Devil's Devices in Chamisso's *Peter Schlemihl*: An Article in Seven-League Boots." *German Life and Letters* 45, no. 3 (1952): 220–25.
Wiese, Benno von. "Das verlorene und das wieder zu findende Paradies: eine Studie über den Begriff der Anmut bei Goethe, Schiller und Kleist." In *Kleists Aufsatz Über das Marionettentheater: Studien und Interpretationen.* Ed. Helmut Sembdner. Berlin: Erich Schmidt, 1967, 196–220.
Wild, Christopher. *Theater der Keuschheit–Keuscheit des Theaters: Zu einer Geschichte der Anti-theatralität von Gryphius bis Kleist.* Freiburg: Rombach, 2003.
Wisse, Ruth. *The Schlemiel as Modern Hero.* Chicago: UP Chicago, 1971.
Yerushalmi, Yosef Hayim. *Zakhor: Jewish History and Meaning.* Seattle: UP Washington, 1982.
Yoshino, Kenjii. *Covering: The Hidden Assault on Our Civil Rights.* New York: Random House, 2006.
Yousef, Nancy. "The Monster in a Dark Room: *Frankenstein*, Feminism, and Philosophy." *Modern Language Quarterly* 63 (2002): 197–226.

Index

Agamben, Giorgio, xxii, xxiii, xxv
Agape, 15–17
AIDS, xxxi–xxxvi, xliii, xliv, lxvi, 24, 27, 103, 120
America, xvi, xlvii, l, li, lii, lvi, 76, 103, 104, 109, 114, 120, 123
Androgyny, 13
Arendt, Hannah, 38, 51–52
Aristotle, 22, 24, 27

Balzac, Honorè de, 77
Barebacking, xvii, xlvii
Barthes, Roland, 101, 119, lvi; *A Lover's Discourse*, lvi, 56–77, 119
Bashing, 51, 114, 118
Beachey, Robert, lii
Belatedness, xxxviii, 18
Benjamin, Walter, vii
Berlant, Lauren, xxxviii
Bersani, Leo, xxvi, xxviii, xxix, xxxvii–xliii, 14, 107, 117
Bildung, 7, 41, 95
Biopolitical, xxvii, 74, 102, 108, 114, 120
Bloch, Ernst, xiii
Broadway, xxxv–xxxvi, xxxviii, xli
Bredbeck, Gregory, 47, 108
Brokeback Mountain, lvl, 75, 101, 103, 104, 107, 110, 113–114, 116–118, 120–122

Briefe über die Glalanterie, 46
Brooks, Peter, 4–5
Brown, Jane, 20, 22
Bug chasers, xxxii, xxvii, xxviii

Cartesian cogito, xxxiii, xxxvi.
Castration, 33, 83, 90, 96
Chamisso, Adalbert, lv, 31, 32, 35, 37, 43, 46; *Peter Schlemihl,* 29–54
Chow, Rey, li
Cixous, Hélène, 33–34
Closet, 87, 101, 119–121, 123
Cohn, Dorritt, xvi, xviii, xxvi
Congress of Vienna, 42
Coitus-a-tegro, 105, 117
Coming-out, 70, 103, 104, 107, 123
Condon, Bill, 126
Counter-temporality, 78, 120; -rhythm, 102
Crimp, Douglas, xxxiii, xxvii

Dappled, xix, xxiv, xlii, 2, 119
Death drive, xxiii, xxvii, li, 6, 16, 20, 27, 104
Delaney, Samuel, xxxviii, xlv, xlviii
Deleuze, Gilles, xix, 81; and Guattari, Félix, xxxiv
de Man, Paul, 67, 72
Derks, Paul, 64
Derrida, Jacques, xxiv, xxxi, xxxiv

Desire, xiv, xv, xxi, xxv, xxv, xxxvii, xl, xli, xlvii, xlix, l, lii, liii, liv, 2, 5, 11, 15–17, 20, 22–25, 30–34, 39, 44–45, 47–53, 56, 62, 69, 79–80, 82, 83, 85, 87–97, 104–106, 108–112, 116, 122
Diderot, Denis, 24
Dinshaw, Carolyn, xxi, xii
Dohm, Christian Wilhelm, 41
Duyfhuizen, Bernhard, 8, 10

Edelman, Lee, xxi, xxii, xxv, xxxviii, 131, 140
El Reno Federal Corrections Institution, xiii
Enlightenment, 29, 41, 44, 46, 48, 53
Eros, xiv, xv, xvii, xl, xli, xlv, xlviii, lii, 12, 15, 16, 18, 22–23, 34, 95, 97, 102–104, 106

Family Values, xx, 23, 24, 101
First Amendment Defense Act, 19
Foucault, Michel, lii, 26, 30, 55; *Discipline and Punishment*, liii; *History of Sexuality*, liii, 45
Freccero, Carla, xxi, 69–79, 81, 83
French Revolution, 18, 21, 57
Freud, Sigmund, xvii, liii, 32; "The Uncanny," 33; *Three Case Studies*, 34–35; "On Narcissism," 48, 49, 56
Future perfect, xxiv, 98, 99, 121; anterior, 98–99, 121

Garcia Düttmann, Alexander, xxx–xvi, xliii
Gay outlaw, xxii, xvii, xxxviii, xxxix, xl, xliii, xliv, xlvii, liv, 31, 51, 92
Gide, André, xxxix, xl, 85
Gift giver, xxvii
Godzilla, 20, 23, 24
Good Morning America, xlv

Goethe, Johann, xx, lv, lvi, 20–22, 24; *Briefe aus der Schweiz*, 94–97, *The Sorrows of Young Werther*, xxxvi, liv, lv, lvi, 75–100, 102, 119
Grace, 23, 58, 61–73
Grattenauer, Karl Wilhelm Friedrich, 39

Hadley, Wayne, xxx
Haller, Albrecht von, 48
Halley, Janet, xlviii, 56
Halperin, Daniel, xxxiv–xxxvi, xxxviii, xxxxix
Hamlet, xxv
Halberstam, Judith, xxi
Heine, Heinrich, xlv, 45–46, 51, 57–59, 63–64
Hekma, Gerd, 44
Hep Hep Riots, 46
Hermeneutic, xxiii, 57–58, 65–67, 70–71
Heteronormative, xii, xxxvi, li, 25, 110, 114
Hirschfeld, Magnus, xlix, lii
Hocquenghem, Guy, 83, 104
Hoffmann, E. T. A., 32; *The Sandman*, 33–35; *Adventures of New Year's Eve*, 35–37, 39, 54
Homo sacer, xxvii, xliv
Homonormative, xxii, xxxiv, li
Hull, Isabel, 44, 45
Humboldt, Wilhelm von, 41, 48, 53
Hyperreal, 117–118

India, 24
Interiority, xxxv, xxxvi, xliii, 19–20, 22–23, 25, 32, 36, 56, 68, 84, 87, 102
Inversion, xli, 31, 39, 40, 44, 47 67, 69 70, 84, 93, 102–104, 106, 111–113, 115–117, 120–122

Jagosse, Annamarie, xxiv
Jew, liv, lv, 29–32, 36, 38–40, 48, 50–53, 56, 101; Jew hatred, 49–52
Johnson, Barbara, 13–15

Klein, Melanie, 33
Kleist, Heinrich von, lvl; "On the Puppet Theater," lvi, 56–77, 119
Klopstock, Friedrich Gottlieb, 79, 89, 91, 92, 95
Klossowski, Pierre, 96
Knigge, Adolf Franz Friedrich Ludwig Freiherr von, 38
Krafft-Ebing, Richard, liii
Kraß, Adreas, 57–58, 62–73, 75
Kristeva, Julia, 17, 26, 27–28

Lacan, Jacques, xxvii
Law of the father, xlii, 17, 18, 22, 106, 115
Linnæus, 48, 53

Magnus Hirschfeld Institute, xlix, lii
Mahler, Gustav, xviii
Male tribadism, lv, 55, 57–58, 60, 62–65, 66, 67, 69, 71, 74
Mann, Thomas; "Death in Venice," xiii, xiv, xvii, xx, xvi, xlii, 58, 89, 119; Tadzio, xiii, xiv, xvi, xviii, xiv, xxvi, xxxiv, xl, l, 119
Marlboro man, 113
Marriage, xx, xxv, xxxix, xlv, xlviii, lvi, 15, 16, 103, 119
Masochism, xviii
Matricide, 12–17, 23, 27
McMurtry, Larry, 105, 107, 109–116, 118–119, 122
Melville, Herman; "Bartleby the Scrivener," 122
Mendelssohn Bartheldy, Felix, 29–30

Messianic, xiii, xviii, xx, xxi, xiv, xxvi, xlvi, xlvii, liii, lvii, 30, 32, 34–36, 54, 74–75, 77, 98, 101–102, 104, 110
Metoplasm, 52
Miller, D. A., xxv–xxxvi, 23, 96, 97
Milner, Jean Claude, xxxii
Milton, John, 2, 5
Mirror image, 35, 36, 66
Monster, 25–27, 30–31, 35, 40, 53, 78, 84
Mooney, James, xxviii
Morris, Paul; *Plantin' Seed*, xxvi
Muñoz, José Esteban, xxiii, xxxiv, xxv

Nachträglichkeit, 33, 96
NAMES Project, xviii, xix–xxx, 27
Nancy, Jean-Luc, xxxiv, xliv
National Socialism, xlii, xlix
Nealon, Christopher, xxi
New York Times, 120
Nietzsche, Friedrich, lvi, 82–83; Eternal return of the same, 79–81, 94; Nietzschean ass, 80–83, 88

Obama, Barrack, xxiii
Oedipus, 34; Oedipal, 5, 7, 16, 17, 19
Ohi, Kevin, xxxvii–xxxviii
Oral sex, 106
Orlando, FL, 1
Ossana, Diana. *See* McMurtry, Larry

Pahl, Katrin, xxv
Panopticon, xx, xl, xliv, liv, 26, 31, 104, 121, 122
Pentecost, 105, 112–113
Performative, 55, 58, 61, 67, 77, 122, 123
Pfuhl, Ernst von, 62
Platen, Carl Gustav von, 57–58, 64
Plato, xiv, 79, 87

Polymorphous, 96, 104
Polyopton, 11, 40
Post-structural epistemology, 106–110
Potentiality, xxii–xiv, xxvi, xxx, xxxvii–xxxviii, lii, lv, lvi, 20, 26, 78, 83, 93, 96, 99, 102, 117, 119
PREP, xxviii
Primal scene, ix, 13, 33–34, 92
Prosopopoeia, xlix, 3–4
Prosthetic, lv, 55–57, 59, 63, 65, 69, 71, 74
Protease inhibitors, 43
Proulx, Annie, 104, 107, 115, 122
Proust, Marcel, xl, xlii
Psychoanalysis, lii, 16, 17, 19, 20, 22, 23, 25, 32, 33, 49, 53, 77, 89
PTA, xxxix, li
Puar, Jasbir, li–lii

Queer, xiii, xiii, xiv xii, xx, xxi, xxv, xvi, xviii, xxx, xxxiii, xxiv, xxxv, xxxvii, xxxviii, xxxlv, xlvi, xlvii, xlviii, l, li, lii, lii, liv, lv, lvi, lviii, lx, lxii, 19, 20, 22, 47, 48, 50, 54–56, 66–76, 78, 82, 90–91, 93–94, 97, 99, 102–105, 107, 108–109, 114, 116, 118, 119–120, 122

Rainbow flag, xxxix, xliii
Religious freedom, xxxix, xlvii
Repression, 22, 34
Robinson, Clarence, Jr., xxx–xxxi
Rousseau, Jean Jacques, 22
Rüling, Anna, liii

Schelling, Friedrich, xxxiii
Schiller, Friedrich, 67
Schlemiel, 30, 44, 46, 47, 51, 96
Schneider, Helmut, 58, 65, 66–69, 71–72
Scholem, Gershom, xxv, xxxvi, 41

Schwerpunkt, 63–67, 69
SCOTUS, xxi, xxvi, xli, xliv
Sedgwick Kosofsky, Eve, xlii, xliii, 45
Sentimental, xxxvi, 78, 91, 93, 96, 97
Sexology, lii, 2, 20, 24
Sexuality, xv, lii, liii, lv, 17, 31, 37, 55, 56, 57–60, 62–63, 96, 97, 101, 103, 104, 120; heterosexuality, xl, xlviii; homosexuality, xxxiii, xxxix, xl, xlvii, xlviii, lv, 31, 33, 34, 44, 46, 48, 49, 62, 68, 103, 106, 108, 111–112, 114, 116, 118, 119, 122
Shadow, xxx, xliii, 30, 34, 35, 36, 38, 41–45, 47–52, 110; *Eigenschatten*, 35–36; *Schlagschatten*, 35–37, 47, 54
Sheep, 103, 105, 108–109, 112, 114, 117, 119
Shelley, Mary, liv, 2, 3, 7, 11–12, 17–18; *Frankenstein*, liii–lvi, 1–31, 35–37, 40, 53, 77–78, 84, 120
Sherwin, Paul, 19
Silken cord, 5, 10, 15
Spector, Scott, liii
Stonewall, xxxv, xxxvi, lvi, 23, 75, 103
Sullivan, Andrew, xlvi–xlvii

Talmud, xxvi
Taxonomy, 53
Taylor, Elizabeth, xxviii
Terrorist, xliii, l, li, lii, 101
Thanatos, 16
Times Square, xxxviii, xliv–xlv, 48
Tobin, Robert, 46, 95
Trump, Donald, xxi
Transparent, xlix–l

Uganda, lii
Ulrichs, Karl Heinrich, lii

Varnhagen, Rahel, 51–52
Vedeer, William, 11–13, 19, 22–23

Virgil, xliii
Visconti, Luchino; *Death in Venice* (film), xviii, xx, 2
Volk, 29, 42, 44, 45, 54, 60

Wagner, Richard 29, 93
Wandering Jew, 43
Warm brothers, 40, 46, lv

Warner, Michael, xlvi, xlvii, 53
"Water Walkin' Jesus," 105
Weber, Samuel, 77
Weil, Jiri, 29–30
Weininger, Otto, 4
Whale, James, 1–2, 26
White House, xxxix, xliii
Wretch, 7–10, 12–14, 21, 39–40, 84

www.ingramcontent.com/pod-product-compliance
Lightning Source LLC
Chambersburg PA
CBHW020732240426
43665CB00052B/452